The Value Path

Embedding Innovation in
Everyday Business
When the Customer Makes the Rules

Peter Keen and Ronald Williams

ISBN-10: 1475209622
ISBN-13: 978-1475209624
Library of Congress Control Number (LCCN): 2012907016

DEDICATION

For Grae

and

for Sherry

We've run out of words to express our love and appreciation
(You may well say "At last!")

Contents

Acknowledgments

This book is just a megabyte of data, a mere 80,000 words and less than a week of twitter, chat, and gentle, informed political wisdom for many inhabitants of the Web. Creating the book, of course, goes well beyond just writing the words and behind our names on the cover is a community of friends, colleagues, students, clients and most of all family that added so much to both the process and the result.

We jointly want to thank them. Many of our early ideas were shaped and tested in our consulting and teaching, in particular in Cisco, where Bill McCarthy and Lucy Chaddra were stalwart in opening up a global platform to us, in the University of North Carolina's executive and global MBA programs, and in a wide variety of company and academic settings.

We were helped in the move from draft to published book by feedback from Craigg Ballance, C.L. Kendall, Professor Emeritus at the Kenan-Flagler Business School, and Ronald Reising from Duke Energy. Sara Keen came to our help at an opportune time and heroically won the battle to tame our endnotes and references. CreateSpace provided first-rate design and copy editing.

Some personal thanks from Peter:
Testing ideas and learning from feedback have been vital in shaping our work. I have benefitted so much from colleagues and students at The EGADE Business School, in Monterrey Mexico, where I am a Visiting Professor and my fellow researchers at American University. Professor Martha Corrales at EGADE has been has been a constant support and generous collaborator. I am immensely grateful to her for all her creative contributions and tenacity.

On the family front, my wife Sherry remains my most cherished support even after enduring my writing over a dozen books in the past eighteen years. It's a cliché that writing is a nonstop preoccupation and that it takes time and attention away from just about everything else but what is not at all cliché is just how immense a difference a warm and caring environment makes. Our cats are great helpers of course and Callie has never met a paragraph that she can't improve by walking across the keyboard.

Some personal thanks from Ron:
Like Peter, I would have been lost without having a platform to develop and test ideas. For that I most want to thank Al Segars who took me onto the faculty at the Kenan-Flagler Business School

after I retired from IBM and said go teach your own ideas, you will learn what works and doesn't work. Hugh O'Neill, Associate Dean of the Executive MBA program at Kenan-Flagler, took an early draft of our book and suggested that we might want to head in a different direction, which we did. Garland (Chip) Kincheloe and my son and former student, Morgan Williams, helped a lot by simply letting us know that they thought the book was good.

On the home front, my wife, Grae, endured a lot and provided a great deal of support, particularly considering that I never started out to be an author. While neither my wife nor I really understood the time and effort required when Peter and I launched the effort, she bore the brunt of my continuous work and often myopic focus. I really thank her for understanding that writing this book was important to me. To maintain a sense of humor she frequently asked me if I was going up to my office to quilt today, implying that this was a never ending task. Well the quilt is complete and hopefully you like it.

1 The New Mantra: Innovate or (and?) Die

Ultrasuccesses and Ultrafades

"Innovate or Die" is the mantra of our times; no firm can expect to succeed in a world of turbulence and competitive challenge just by doing better tomorrow what it does today. Any discussion of innovation is implicitly a conversation about value, since value generation is obviously the core driver of business. Given that companies are betting their future on innovation, maybe it's time for them to first take a fresh look at "value."

Value may not be what they assume it is. Value is changing everywhere because it is determined entirely by the choice space for customers, providers, partners, and investors. It is not fixed or stable. Open up the choices, and the very nature of value shifts.

That's the lesson from the fortunes of *ultrasuccesses*: companies that through their innovation surged to such dominance, they transformed the dynamics of competition. They became, literally, textbook exemplars and reshaped many elements of management practice. They include Wal-Mart, Southwest Airlines, Amazon, Apple, FedEx, and Starbucks in the United States and Toyota, Tesco, Bharti Airtel, Li & Fung, and Zara abroad.

But there are many former ultrasuccesses that were once just as dominant as these and as apparently invincible in their innovation and yet lost their way, relatively quickly and unobtrusively. Instances are Barnes & Noble, Blockbuster, Kodak, RIM, Toys "R" Us, Nokia, Gap, Sears, Kmart, Dell, Nortel, and such largely forgotten names as Wang, Tandem, Digital Equipment, Pan Am, and A&P. Some disappeared into bankruptcy, while others slumped to being just marginal performers, struggled to survive as independent companies, or were acquired on the cheap by a private equity fund or competitor.

These are examples of "Innovate *and* Die." Such companies often try to ramp up what made them ultrasuccesses, investing in new products and technology or making mergers and acquisitions in an effort to innovate their way out of erosion. Too often, this doesn't work. The products are excellent and the acquisitions bring new resources, but the companies are stuck on a path that just isn't creating new dimensions of value. So they try even harder to find ways back to growth, but within the value assumptions that brought them earlier success.

This is especially commonplace in firms known for their product innovations. They largely look to R&D, technology, and features to reenergize their value creation. Nokia and RIM are examples. Both companies are trying to recover the market share and profitability that they continue to lose to Apple and Android-based competitors. They have launched major all-or-nothing commitments to new operating systems and feature-packed products.

Few commentators are optimistic about their likely success. RIM's obituaries are being edited by the month. Nokia is revamping its entire strategy, organization, and marketing. They were both once the first in their field—Nokia in just about every area of mobile handsets, including smart phones, and RIM in creating its addictive BlackBerry, the e-mail-on-the-go device suitably nicknamed Crackberry. Both keep aiming for a new first that will restore them to best in the customer's mind.

Sony is in the same situation and is emblematic of "firsts" that don't increase company value. Its history of product leadership ranges from the transistor radio to the Walkman to the PlayStation 3. It describes itself as "the Leader in Product Innovation."[1] But for the past seven years, the most common headline has been "Profits Down." It reported a 2011 loss of $2.9 billion, a slight improvement over 2010. Product-innovation brand doesn't equate to value-creation brand.

A press release commented that Sony's gaming division experienced "higher marketing costs to promote network service platforms and lower sales of its PlayStation 3 hardware, due to a strategic price reduction."[2] Translated, that means: Our premium gaming device is becoming a commodity, and we are facing a price war and losing margins. We're trying to make the product part of a broader set of services and spending a bundle on promotions. Oh, and by the way, we are getting killed in TV manufacturing.

These examples highlight the topic of *The Value Path*—the link between innovation and value shifts, and vice versa—and its recommendations for managers and planners responsible for some aspect of innovation in their organization. We look at the general lessons from firms that turn invention—the commitment to developing new products, services, or processes—into value and then sustain their value creation in a context of almost constant change.

How do some firms manage to smoothly extend their growth into entirely new areas of competition even though their innovations could not have been anticipated from their earlier strategies and history? Amazon is one instance here: moving from discount book retailing to leadership in the entirely different domain of cloud computing; transformation of book publishing, starting with making e-books the core of book industry growth; and challenging Apple's dominance of the tablet market through its Kindle Fire. These are all revolutionary, but achieved by moving along an evolutionary path rather than making bold leaps across a chasm.

Our analysis is best described as sense making. It reviews what's been going on across the business terrain and aims at teasing out the common patterns that underlie firms that have stood out as true innovators that shook up management practice. There's not much to learn from companies that fail to innovate and fall behind the competitive pack beyond "Don't be so dumb."

The main lessons for the future come from the ultrasuccesses that have become *superextenders*. These are the companies that put it all together and keep on doing so. They are the archetypes of the firm that makes innovation part of its everyday business life and provide the main examples and recommendations in *The Value Path*.

But there's also plenty to learn from ultrasuccesses that out-imagined, out-planned, and out-executed the best of established competitors, but then lost their way. They didn't suddenly become dumb on their slide back down the value path. These *ultrafades*, to provide a contrasting term, don't make obvious blunders, and there's often no apparent cause of decline. It's worth teasing out what they stuck with for too long. or what they missed, that left them falling behind the forces of change when they had previously so superbly moved ahead of them.

Dell is an instance of an ultrafade; for ten years, it was rare for a business book on innovation not to cite Dell as one of the major ultrasuccesses of its era. It transformed supply chain management to the same degree that Toyota reshaped basic thinking about manufacturing and quality. It was a pacesetter in exploiting the Internet in selling. Financially, it outperformed every player, forcing several to drop out of the market. It operated with half the overhead of its main competitors and generated stratospheric financial returns on invested capital because it used so little of it.

Then the pieces stopped working smoothly in concert. Dell wasn't quite early enough, fast enough, or radical enough to adapt its innovative strengths to a time of accelerating new choices. What happened to cause the slide from dominance to also-ran? In many ways, not much: it was uneventful, and that was the problem. Dell continued to move along a path that had so far created immense value for customers, company, partners, and investors.

It built on its assets but at the expense of investing in adaptability. It was increasingly left adrift as players such as HP and Acer offered new choices in the now-commoditized PC and server markets. Customers sought out mobile devices and went to stores like Staples and Best Buy to browse the goods and corporate buyers looked for services, not just volume sales of hardware.

When Dell put its remaining factories up for sale in 2008, there were no buyers. In 2003, it had been lauded for its "brilliant" manufacturing operations.[3] Five years later, this erstwhile "killer advantage" was now just real estate. Meanwhile, Apple's very lack of manufacturing and wealth of sourcing relationships was helping it kill off an awful lot of competitors.

With few changes, the Dell story could be retold as that of Gap, Nokia, Yahoo, or Kmart: a rapid growth surge as customers saw new value in their offers, confident expansion, widening admiration and imitation, and then a quiet erosion. The fading away is often an unnoticed trickle, rather than a visible crisis. At the very time hindsight reveals that such superperformers have lost their way, they are still being used as an exemplary business school case study and moral fable in the management literature.

Such a firm builds on its heritage, which comes to look like a permanent foundation for success. It reaches iconic status when its "Way" becomes embodied in books that offer a guide to competitive superiority: *The Machine that Changed the World, The IBM Way: Lessons from the World's Greatest Marketing Organization, How Dell Does It, Jack Welch and the GE Way,* and *Built for Success: The Starbucks Story.* It can take years before the unraveling becomes apparent; then the firm is pushed to defensive reaction rather than adaptive proaction.

Toyota redefined manufacturing and was unbeatable in the car market for over three decades. It's only over the past few years that key elements of its systems and culture have been revealed as impediments to sustaining its ultrasuccess. Even Wal-Mart slipped in its sales per store and is taking action to correct its miscalculation of what its customers really value.[4] It had failed in its efforts to nudge them upmarket to higher margin opportunities, such as branded apparel. Customers have plenty of other places to find what they want, and they made their moves, often to Amazon.

Most executives would be delighted for their firm to have Toyota's or Wal-Mart's more than thirty-year window of success and would not worry too much now about what might happen thereafter. Increasingly, though, time is not on the side of any firm, and the gap between surge and ebb is narrowing rapidly.

Newspapers and book publishers are as aware of this today as they were largely dismissive of the impending buffeting of their entire commercial foundations less than a decade ago. In smart phones, product cycles used to average two years. Now the window is just months. There may be more value opportunity for customers, providers, and partners in those months than in the preceding biennial shelf life, but obviously turning opportunity into impact requires a very different set of capabilities based on speed, adaptability, and flexibility, rather than scale, efficiency, and stability.

Nokia's new leaders highlight all these capability gaps as the genesis of its problems. It remains—just—the global leader in total sales units, but every cycle of innovation has left it slipping. It is a company built for scale at the cost of speed. It is struggling in customer and company choice spaces where speed is vital and more and more of its competitors have made this the very core of their strategy and operations. Its capabilities have been defined by its asset base and are now constrained by it, rather than leveraged by a rich range of relationships.

Nokia is racing to shift gears and change course. Its innovation agenda is now focused on partnering—mainly with Microsoft in the drive for both companies to recover their lost position in smart phones. A senior Nokia executive stated in late 2010, "We are no longer trying to make everything or buy everything. We are looking at partnering as a serious strategy."[5] The word "serious" is intriguing. Why wasn't it serious before, and what changed in Nokia's environment to make it so important now?

Nokia is an example of the sense-making base for *The Value Path*'s analysis and recommendations. The messages are not that Nokia really messed things up after decades of brilliance, but that the shifts in choice space, the dynamics of competition, and the very contrasting new value paths of firms such as Apple, Google, and HTC may point to a general pattern among ultrasuccesses and ultrafades.

This pattern is hinted at in the Nokia executive's follow-on comments: "Our new CEO has been really shaking us up and challenging us in a positive way to think from the outside in rather than from the inside out. This will result in opening up to outside innovation much more."

These comments can be restated as: "We haven't been customer-led—'outside-in'—in our thinking, and we have been narrow in our range of innovations. We need to open up our boundaries and connect to partners if we are to compete effectively." He might have added that Nokia doesn't have much time to make its moves. As time becomes more and more of a nonrenewable, soon-consumed management resource, waiting out weather changes is not a strategy. No, you can't buy time, but you can co-opt partners to help you now rather than build in-house for later.

That said, at what stage is it too late for a firm to recover its position? Even if it increases its own speed, the new leaders aren't slowing down. They are moving on, too. Nokia's global market share fell from 31 percent in early 2010 to 23 percent by the end of 2011, according to research firm Gartner.[6] This drop of almost a third in under two years occurred despite its having excellent products.

The Nokia example highlights a general challenge of resource management. Google and Amazon illustrate effective responses. Their ability to scale comes from their flexibility, not their fixed assets. Their expansion is paced by tightly coordinated relationships. They create their ultrasuccess by offering compelling new dimensions of value in a shifting choice space, and their resource management enables them to target their innovation to combine being better in relation to competing offers in terms of existing dimensions, such as service or price.

At the same time, they are positioned to be different by adding new dimensions. Innovation applies to both better and different. Google continues to be better in search than its competitors, adding new features and improving ease of use and personalization. Amazon similarly innovates all the time in being better in its prices, products, service, and customer-relationship building. They maintain their advantage in the competitive game.

But they are positioned to innovate in ways that change the rules of the game. Android is an operating system for mobile devices that is different from those used by Apple and Nokia. Google leveraged it to open up a flood of new products offered by relationship partners, and Android has become a brand in and of itself. The Kindle similarly made Amazon's offers different in terms of the dimensions of customer value: book buying and delivery; self-publishing; a variety of publications, from short "Singles" to magazines to standard books; and a wealth of customer reviews.

"Better" amounts to being able to take a lead in a competitive game. "Different" changes the rules of the game. Again and again, ultrafades live too long on "better" and are constrained in terms of adding "different." They run out of time. It's a cliché that time is the new currency of innovation. Carrie Fisher's wry epigram in her novel *Postcards from the Edge* captures the customer ethos of our time: "Instant gratification takes too long." Time to gratification translates to time to market. Companies don't have to just get the product right, but get it right at the right time. Miss one of the "rights" and the other doesn't compensate. Customers are on the move.

The firm that has planned its resource base so it has the capabilities to combine flexibility and time is obviously in a far better position to deal with uncertainty and volatility than ones that factor value into their planning and operations as a constant rather than a variable and as a financial metric that is the outcome of the firm's operations.

So, for example, well-focused R&D is assumed to create new products that produce value, as measured by revenue growth. Assets provide the engines of production, distribution, and sales that generate efficiency and productivity, with much of the value coming from cost advantages. Mergers and acquisitions add the resources needed to either extend the firm's reach to new markets and customers or strengthen its existing position.

This all seems commonsensical, but what jumps out in the sense-making review of ultrasuccesses and ultrafades is that the conventional management practice rests on a few, largely untested assumptions. The first is that value is an attribute of the product or service, and the second is that it is fairly stable in its dimensions. The experiences of ultrasuccesses and ultrafades just do not correspond to that perspective. Value is determined by the choice space open to customers and companies.

As that space changes, so does value. New consumer choices such as Costco, the Dollar Store, Target, Amazon, and Kohl's have shifted Wal-Mart's customer value just as much as Wal-Mart had earlier affected Kmart's. Amazon has eroded Best Buy's customer value by matching its existing value dimensions of price, products, and service and adding new choices of convenience, variety, and information.

Best Buy didn't do anything "wrong," and Amazon did not attack it directly. Customers switched their choice of provider for the very same products and services in very much the same price range. Customers are increasingly picking the Amazon experience over the Best Buy deal. There's little Best Buy can do in response, since it lacks distinctive alternative dimensions of value to build on.

A striking example of the impact of customer choice on what "value" means is Microsoft's Kinect. This is a gaming device, originally marketed as an add-on to the Xbox console. The target buyer is pretty clear—kids of any age, including their dads—and the dimensions of value highlight fun, excitement, play, and experiences in virtual reality. But much of the most striking and potentially profitable value creation was unplanned and indeed unpredictable.

When Nissan planned to unveil its new Pathfinder at a car show, it had no vehicle to display, only the fiberglass shell. It used a new Kinect version that worked with Windows to create a virtual tour of the car. This showed attendees what they would see if they were in the car, tracking their head movements, recognizing objects they were looking at, and zooming in on them. The head of marketing for Nissan in North America said this "truly is a game-changer" and that they would use it in prelaunch demos in dealerships.[7]

In 2012 about 350 companies were developing Kinect for such virtual tours, including plane makers and home-improvement firms. Its use is growing in hospital applications, such as surgeons being able to make gestures to swipe through CT scans without risk of touching the germs on a keyboard or screen. There are many emerging applications for employee training, and Kinect-based ads are in the works. An article published over two years after the gaming console hit its market is headlined: "Upcoming Kinect Development Kit Could Change In-Store Shopping"; it "opens the door for businesses."[8]

The article doesn't indicate what it opens up for them to do. They'll find out only when they step through the doorway. It offers them a new space for exploration. The choices they can now make will fuel the innovation, which will be opportunistic. Or they can leave the door shut; it's their choice. After all, why should a car maker or hospital start messing around with video games?

In practice, this new choice space offers the chance to create new dimensions of value: a different, rather than better, something. The value is potentially immense. But it is for a customer base for which the Kinect was not designed—businesses, engineers, hospitals, marketers—and provides a value dimension that doesn't even have a label beyond "virtual" something. The value never existed until businesses and software entrepreneurs wandered into the consumer gaming space of choices—devices on sale in a range of outlets—and in effect invented themselves as an entirely new class of customer.

Historically, Microsoft would have closed down that space very quickly. Much of the innovation involves tinkering with the Kinect software and hardware. Microsoft loses many millions of dollars from fraud and copying of its software and protects its rights aggressively. It typically moves in with lawsuits, thought police, detection tools, and a few billion dollars of anticybercrime counters.

With Kinect, Microsoft has blessed the outlaws and added the tools and even a developer's boot camp to open up this space of mutual opportunity. Had it closed it down in the old way, then everything would have shifted—including "value."

Even discounting the hype, it seems fair to agree with an analyst at Forrester Research: "This is a turnaround chance for Microsoft...it isn't about video gaming, it isn't about Windows, it's about the future of everything."[9] But all the traditional measures of value as fixed and stable outputs of innovation are inapplicable; when the gaming device was launched, there was no "value proposition," no "user need" to fill, no market to have a market share of, no market forecast, and no customer. The Kinect was not a business market innovation; the new customers made it so.

Many commentators expect Nintendo's upcoming Wii U to be superior to the Xbox 360, especially for "frame-obsessed game-fighting fans" because of its superior image latency. So which of these inventive products will turn out to be the most innovative in terms of value creation? The customer will let us know. But which customer?

Value Realities

Figure 1.1 lists the four Value Realities that summarize the messages that emerge from making sense of what has been happening across the kaleidoscopic business landscape for decades, but at an accelerating pace and with expanding impact. They are shown with an implicit suffix that captures the key point they reflect: "This is just the way it is." It is not the way some companies would like it to be or assume it is. In particular, value is not a financial output under their direct control. It is not stable. It is multidimensional. And the forces that open up opportunities for ultrasuccesses also can close them down; the very same strategies that they employed to create value can fail to cope with the shifts and turn them into ultrafades.

Our list of Value Realities emerged from working backward from companies that are anomalies. Rather than describe, say, why Amazon, Wal-Mart, or Tesco so decisively undermined the market dominance of Barnes & Noble, Kmart, and the UK supermarkets, it seems more useful to ask if there were any consistent and common patterns that point to how they gained their edge and then test if those patterns also explained firms that could and should have been able to exploit the same opportunities but didn't.

The Value Realities point to how companies are now playing the game, the game being the competitive battle in a market that is already open and likely to open up more and not close down. (This is not a tidy or linear process; regulation and trade protection have long been historical blockers, with Japan, India and China all noted for frequent and selective blocking of access to their markets. And just try to make sense of all the US trade barriers and sugar import, export, and re-export complexities that keep prices over 40 percent above world averages.)

If your company wants to be a player, then it had better recognize that these are the rules that the winners accept and exploit and the losers ignore or try to block. The more the choice space opens up, the more direct and immediate the impact. And, no, even the Industry Bully can't announce that "it's my ball, and I'm taking it

Reality 1: The buyer determines value	Given choices, the buyer, not the seller, determines which dimensions of value matter and how offers compare.
Reality 2: Value is always relative and shifting	Value is always relative and shifting, because it is a function of an expanding choice space, driven by a consistent set of historical forces that disturb the business terrain
Reality 3:Companies leverage ecocomplexes	Companies increasingly exploit the choice space to leverage adaptive ecocomplexes of relationships rather than go it alone.
Reality 4: Entrepreneurs will offer new dimensions of value	The distinctive characteristic of the entrepreneur is to leverage the forces of disturbance to offer new dimensions of value or find new ways to enhance existing ones.

Figure 1.1: The New Realities of Value
(That's just the way it is)

and going home." There's always another ball to choose. And <u>another game being created.</u>

Reality 1: The buyer determines value

Any provider obviously must focus its offers in the market to ensure value to itself as well as the customer; no firm is going to survive by selling commodity products below marginal cost or offering unlimited free service, for instance. As Peter Drucker pithily commented, profit is the cost of staying in business. The natural tendency for any firm is thus to leverage its existing assets and core competencies to determine the essential nature and range of its innovations; it has a preferred set of products, preferred distribution base, and preferred terms of business.

It also has a range of productive resources that it would like to continue to produce financial value for the firm. Those resources were built and evolved on the basis of the company's supply attracting demand, not the other way around. Factories were built to reach the market and stores to draw in customers. Airlines needed to fill their planes and juggle the use of their jumbos, wide and narrow bodies, and regional jets accordingly.

So the natural business logic is to leverage and improve the payoff to the firm from its supply. It drives demand from that base: more marketing, new products, and better prices. It invests in its sales force and adds distribution outlets. It reaches out into its market and builds the resources that help it literally and figuratively move its goods.

But unless it is in a position to limit customer options—for instance, through regulatory protection, industry barriers to new entrants, or market dominance—the priority today has increasingly shifted to how to dynamically transform many elements of supply. Buyers are able to fill their demand by moving away from established behaviors and established sources of fixed supply. Demand locates supply, and when new providers and outlets offer compelling new dimensions of value, the choice shift can entirely change the value equation. Reality rules.

The dimensions of value are its bylaws. Value dimensions are essentially the set of headings for a list of your priorities and relative ratings of your options for some purchase. Take the example of large-screen TVs. Standard value dimensions include price, features (screen size, LCD/LED, audio quality, USB ports, and many other elements within the dimension), service and warranty, and manufacturer reputation. There are also more subjective ones, such as appearance and styling ("how will it look in our living room?"), ease of use and controls, and trust in the seller.

Value reflects your personal assessment of the dimensions that are most important to you and the comparisons between options within those dimensions. Why did you choose the car you now drive? Forget the idea that the purchase criterion is just price and features or some metric of "marginal utility" explored in academic economics journals, and cut out all the stuff about how rationally you evaluated options, technical specs, and financial trade-offs. You may be one of the admirable people who do this, but there are many more whose honest answer is "because I like it and can afford it."

These dimensions establish the Value Realities. Once in a while, an innovation establishes a compelling new dimension—the something different, not just someway better. "Compelling" here means it captures attention and creates responses such as "I should really take a look at this" and "Now, this is interesting and could be worth trying." Kinect is an example, as is Amazon's Prime subscription, which provides unlimited free shipping and access to more than ten thousand free movies and e-book lending library.

Over time, compelling new dimensions become standard ones and often commoditize. American Airlines redefined the business travel market through its AAdvantage frequent-flyer program, which has since become a necessary, though commodity, dimension for all carriers. For most, it is a cost, not a value creator, but Value Realities still demand it.

When Dell offered customized configuration and online ordering of PCs and fast delivery, that was a compelling "something different" that Compaq, HP, IBM, and others just could not match. Now it's standard; but for many years it altered Value Realities across the PC market for customers, Dell, and its competitors.

Reality has certainly ruled the newspaper' space. In many ways, the collapse of the print industry was not caused by any drop-off in quality, accuracy, or scope of coverage. Customers decided that they wanted news but didn't need newspapers. A wide range of firms outside the established newspaper industry had new choices in how they sourced news, distributed it, and packaged it. The new dimensions of value they created for customers were compelling: access, timeliness, buzz, video, and personalization, for instance.

The *Huffington Post* or *Yahoo News!* isn't a "better" newspaper than the *Washington Post* or *Chicago Tribune* in terms of being a reliable, in-depth source of coverage of important items. But from the customer's perspective, they offer many people more value, *given the now available choices.* Just about any online service, search firm, portal, or social network offers customers choice after choice in this regard.

Newspapers now compete with other new sources through the customer experience, rather than the product. The *New York Times*, for instance, launched a service on March 17, 2011, that combines limited free access with a "paywall" for nonsubscribers, under the marketing banner of "Experience the *Times*. Any way you want it." This effort to remonetize its own product so far has not looked likely to be a big success. The paper is still burdened by its heritage.

Politico is a highly influential printed newspaper that has been able to exploit, rather than be immobilized by, elements of its print heritage. *Politico* has a puny circulation of thirty-two thousand, but five million daily website visitors. It was set up by a small group of journalists and launched in a few months. It now has a staff of about a hundred journalists. It's become the political insiders' "real-time download of power data"[10] that is credited with cutting the news cycle from one to two days to fifteen to twenty minutes. That's compelling—for some people, at least.

Here the new choice space for suppliers in how they turn news into value has intersected with the choice space for buyers in what value dimensions they respond to. That creates something new, where the determinants of customer value appeal to an audience that has been called "obsessive-compulsive," with the political Washington media scene referred to as "Hollywood for the ugly."[11] They are certainly not the average reader, nor *Politico* a typical newspaper. Its customer value dimensions are nowhere near what the old average reader of the typical newspaper looked for; for those readers, *Politico*'s style and focus are a turnoff, not a turn-on.

Firms that treat value as fixed and largely determined by product characteristics, technology, processes, or financial metrics such as revenue, price, cost, or return on investment are leading candidates for Innovate and Die. If value is a known and stable target, then "invention" is likely to be equated with "innovation": launching something new or better will create value.

That's the logic of R&D budgets that many policy commentators and executives see as the key to national innovation. But plenty of evidence over many decades shows no correlation between R&D expenditures and payoffs. The *Financial Times* reported on a survey of the world's top one thousand corporate R&D spenders, conducted by Booz Allen in 2005. It found "no discernible statistical relationship between R&D spending levels and nearly all measures of business success including sales growth, gross profit, operating profit, enterprise profit, market capitalisation or total shareholder return."[12] Invention doesn't create value. Compelling choices do.

Politico is just one instance; as a product—paper or website—it's nothing special. To turn invention into innovation demands thinking in terms of choices across the business terrain, not just products in "the" market, and sensing why customers make the choices they do. No firm should assume that historical company value dimensions can drive or determine future customer value.

Reality 2: Value is always relative and shifting.

Value can appear stable and absolute when choices are constrained (within a monopoly, for instance) or where every player offers variants on the same products and services (as in a regulated oligopoly such as health-care insurance or a mature industry like construction supplies). But three main historical forces continue to disturb the business terrain in ways that expand the choice space and open up opportunities for entrepreneurs and forward-thinking companies to offer entirely new dimensions of value and for customers to seek them out.

The three forces of disturbance are (1) deregulation and trade liberalization, (2) technology, and (3) interconnectability of parts and processes through standardized interfaces. They are shown in figure 1.2.

Just one instance of the forces' impact on value is air travel, where deregulation opened up the market to low-cost carriers and removed price restraints. Technology created an opportunity space that Expedia, Orbitz, and Priceline quickly filled and in many ways exploited to take away the airlines' own branding power—you pick an Expedia flight rather than look for Air Whatsit.

Standardized interfaces enabled and even encouraged these companies to interconnect their own and airlines' online reservation systems and then add links to hotels, Facebook, theater and concert ticket sellers, and vacation-deal providers. Everyday examples of interfaces are the 1-800 numbers that connect to services that vary immensely in location, nature, complexity; you don't need to know or care how they work—just connect. Expedia/Facebook "mash-ups" are a cottage mini-industry for building software apps on the same basic principles.

Modularity and standardized interfaces open up opportunities to source a flow of partner and supplier improvements. Niche providers can work independently on what is inside the "black box" of a component or process. A simple example is a computer

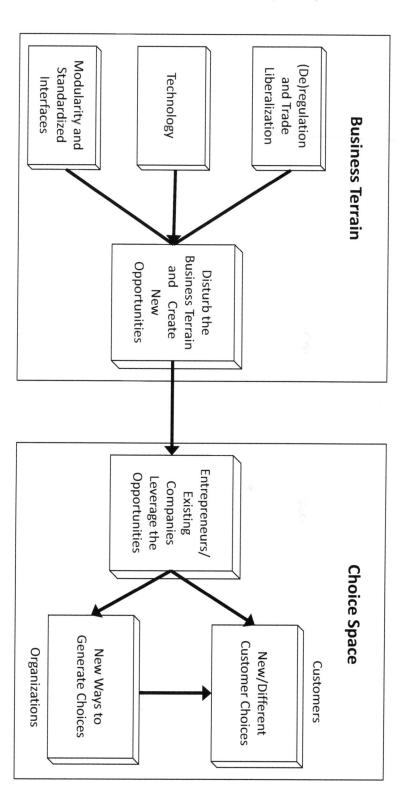

Figure 1.2: Historical Forces of Disturbance

motherboard. It uses a plug-in design with slots and sockets for a wide range of peripherals. Whenever suppliers improve the cost or performance of, say, a graphics card, the firm branding the computer can quickly switch providers. The motherboard in effect creates an open market for suppliers and inventors.

These three forces are historical in the sense that they have continued to drive in the same overall direction for a century or more. There are frequent blocks, slowdowns, and occasional reversals, but these drivers of external change are noncyclical, and there is no plausible scenario except a collapse-of-everything-as-we-know-it disaster that points to less trade liberalization, less technological development, and less modularity and interconnection of components in manufacturing, processes, media, and services.

The disturbances that the forces make to the status quo are increasingly tectonic; but it's the aftershocks, rather than any single tremor, that fissure the landscape and lead to a Twitter, Facebook, Bangalore software industry, and Skype.

For example, the aftershocks led to *customers* destroying the travel agent structure that had controlled airline "distribution." They effected this by doing nothing direct; they simply moved to where they saw new value, with Priceline's name-your-own-deal offer being an early subversive force. Deregulation opened up choices, technology created opportunities for new dimensions of value beyond the flight, and modularity enabled coordination and interconnection of separate services, information, and providers. Customers explored and exploited their opportunities, and new players wooed them imaginatively.

The most radical impacts of the forces of disturbance come from entrepreneurs who offer a compelling new "something." Priceline is just one example. Even ultrasuccesses often become ultrafades when the forces of disturbance intersect with such innovators grabbing the customer by offering something really different and really special, quickly and with low capital investment. Expedia and Orbitz did not have to build a fleet of planes nor make the same massive investments in airline reservation systems as the major carriers. They exploited the airline business by not being an airline.

Reality 3: Companies leverage ecocomplexes.

It's commonplace to talk about business ecosystems. We choose the term *complex,* rather than system, to highlight the fluid nature of the agreements, interdependencies, truces, roles, and financial interests that comprise, say Apple's or Netflix's relationships, which permeate every aspect of their value architecture—the combination of the narratives that describe how the firm plans to generate value, the value engines that deliver it profitably, and the opportunity platform that enables the company to expand and adapt.

Both Apple's and Netflix's ecocomplex includes "frenemies": friends that are enemies. These are ecocomplex partners that are at the same time competitors. Apple is Samsung's largest customer, and Apple is dependent on it for the high performance components in its iPads. But Samsung's Galaxy tablet competes directly with the iPad. Both companies are suing to get each other's products banned in country after country, filing individual and very expensive patent infringement suits in Australia, Korea, Germany, the Netherlands, the United States, and elsewhere, which must be piling up millions of frequent-flyer miles for the battalions of legal troops.

Netflix similarly has often-volatile relationships with many content providers of movies and TV programs. If you make a list of the firms positioning to be leading digital media players and check off if they are a Netflix partner of today, an ex-partner, a competitor now, or ready to become one, many will fall into the "all of these" category. Examples are Time Warner, Apple TV, Paramount, Comcast (in late 2011, seen as a "fren-" but increasingly very much an "-emy" in the frenemy equation), MGM, and Dreamworks.

In both companies, relationships have become, in effect, a core part of their asset base. Apple does not have factories and R&D units for it to make what Samsung and others bring to it. Netflix depends on "its" studios, channels, and program libraries, just as its partners depend on Netflix bringing customers to them.

Innovation in general comes more and more from relationships rather than in-house resources, and a choice space is defined by the competing ecocomplexes. You can experience this in your own living room asking your companion, "Do you want to watch a movie?" In the now long-gone, far-distant old days—five years ago, maybe—you chose a cinema, ordered a pay-per-view movie on your TV, went to Blockbuster, or bought a DVD. Now you switch on an ecocomplex.

In many instances, a new ecocomplex-enabled player finds its way to the customer's attention. Metaphorically, it looks to switch you on, using relationship assets to help it bypass the incumbent's occupancy of the choice space.

The old realities of value creation are embodied in the term Big Business. The era of giant multinationals, even more gigantic nationalized agencies, and advantages of scale in production and distribution favored a reliance on building and owning just about all resources. Megaplayers benefited from access to financial capital that kept potential new entrants out of the game. US Steel, once the most dominant firm on earth, owned mines, ships, mills, and railroads, as well as its manufacturing plants. Vertical integration was the norm in many industries, and mergers and acquisitions one of its main tools.

That has been shifting for several decades, and the new norm is to coordinate relationships, rather than own assets. Even small players lacking an established base can erode or bypass the advantages that successful incumbents had when choices were limited and destabilization of the business status quo largely intermittent and incremental. The forces of disturbance enable these small players to target new markets or intrude on ones previously closed by regulatory or trade barriers, at lower costs, with less capital, and with the flexibility of a "green field" entrant.

These players can move to market quickly by coordinating the customer demand chain and company supply chain through Internet-based technology. They develop alternatives to establishing their own manufacturing, marketing, or IT infrastructures. Many of these firms will fail, but they may still change the rules of competition by pointing to a new opening in a previously closed area of choice on the landscape.

Airline deregulation in any country was immediately followed by dozens of start-ups buying used planes and targeting a few routes with special deals for tourists. Very few survived, but their mere presence changed the game, and the small number of new ultrasuccesses, such as Jet Blue, Ryanair, and EasyJet, hold better cards than most major carriers.

In particular, where existing players have moved with and within their industry, players looking to break up the club will find ways to entice the customer away from the industry choice space and into their own sphere of offers. They shift from outsourcing tasks to cosourcing capabilities and resources. They are increasingly defined less by their organizational structure than by their networks of relationships.

Apple is an obvious instance. The telecommunications, music, and media industries "owned" their products, customer base, and distribution, in the sense that any new entrants were outsiders that had to discover some new way of finding a place on the industry landscape. The incumbents expected to be able to exploit these advantages to set the terms for Apple's guest presence in *their* territory. It hasn't quite worked that way. They depend heavily on their Apple relationship, and Apple drives the terms.

That dependence has spread across the arena. Sprint now needs Apple for it to stay viable in its own business space. It has committed to buying around $15 billion worth of iPhones, an investment that will not be profitable for the company until 2015.[13] Instead of Apple paying to be on Sprint's network, Sprint has risked just about all of its future to be part of Apple's ecocomplex. The music industry long ago surrendered control of its own product to Apple. The price of music downloads is its decision, not the providers' option.

This all leads to Reality 4, the one that seems to most differentiate ultrasuccesses and ultrafades and answers the question, "Whatever happened to XYZ—is it still around?"

Reality 4: Entrepreneurs offer compelling new dimensions.

Providing something new has always been the role of the entrepreneur, but the forces of disturbance have increasingly enabled a rapidly expanding company choice space within which to reshape the customer choice space. Amazon initially leveraged technology to offer lower prices and convenience, based on not needing to own and operate physical stores. Google made branded online search relevant to a mass market for the first time and then tied advertising to it.

Dell sold direct, bypassing distributors and customizing PC configurations at lower prices than competitors' out-of-the-package products by creating a low-cost supply chain. Wal-Mart did much the same with its supply chain to offer everyday low prices, and Starbucks transformed a commodity product by preparing it to suit individual taste in an inviting setting. It's still just a coffee product; its premium value was created by the experience.

Incumbents generally assume that such entrepreneurs with their targeted different dimensions of value will not be able to compete with the incumbents' more established value drivers. All too often they are self-deceiving and blocking reality. Yes, maybe 98 percent of the intruders will fail, but it's the other 2 percent that customers may raise to success. Establishment players dismiss the start-ups with their new offers; for them, "compelling" often means "gimmick," with the underlying implication that if they don't already offer it, then it can't be that important.

Then, when customers show that it is important to *them*, the firms assume they can add those new dimensions as needed. Later, as the competition begins to really bite, they race to add them but can never fully incorporate them into their branded experience.

Meanwhile, if the start-ups become successful, they expand their own dimensions of value. Barnes & Noble and Borders belatedly built online, full-service bookstores but could never match Amazon's vast product selections beyond books, its reviews, and shipping offers. Neither could Wal-Mart, which is by far the biggest seller of books in the world but is stuck in a shrinking, discount-dominated sector. (Book sales have dropped at least 1 percent a year for well over two decades. This trend has increased in the core trade-book segment that has been the stronghold of stores and libraries; revenues dropped 34 percent in 2011.)

At some point, the game so changes that the earlier leaders are not even laggards. They are ultrafades.

Branding the Customer Experience

Here's the game-breaker question: what is your firm branding today, and what will it brand in the new choice space? Add to this: who are the customers of tomorrow, and what do you know about them? In this time of uncertainty and change, can your company's branded experience withstand targeted attacks by entrepreneurs on the value dimensions you offer—such as price, speed of delivery, or product features?

How adaptable is your firm? Can it not only just grow within its value dimensions but also sustain its identity, add new value dimensions, and morph its capabilities? It had better do so, since some entrepreneur or existing ultrasuccess with an adaptive resource base is already moving ahead of you; it is branding its innovativeness, not just its specific innovations. An Apple product signals innovation, Amazon's corporate name does the same, and FedEx, Google, and Twitter have all become verbs that add up to an innovation brand.

Brands reflect identity, customer trust, differentiation, and a promise of value. Product brands are increasingly being eroded because they contribute less and less to all these aspects of the customer–provider relationship, especially since the forces make it so routine to source products globally.

A simple illustration of the difference between branding the product and the experience is, once more, Amazon. Have you personally bought a book from Amazon in, say, the past six months? If so, what was the publisher's name? It's about 90 percent likely that your answer is "dunno" and 99.9 percent likely that if you were told, you'd not care; Amazon or the author is the brand, not Simon and Schuster, HarperCollins, or Hachette. (This is a point that more and more authors are finding of interest—and opportunity.)

Of course, most book buyers have never known or cared who the publisher is, though authors, bookstores, advertisers, reviewers, and agents did. But as the dimensions of customer value have changed so dramatically, so too have the ecocomplex opportunities for these parties. For authors, the publisher imprint matters less and less, and many find that Amazon offers a far more collaborative, productive, timely, flexible and profitable experience in bringing their work to market.

Bookstores and agents may wish the publishers were able to maintain their old brand advantages, especially in pricing, distribution, and marketing. They can't. The essence of a publishing house used to be its product brand, and media conglomerates traded them for their backlists, contracts with best-selling authors, and lead editors. It's unlikely that Amazon will buy a publishing company on the same basis. The established names don't add to the dimensions of value in the customer experience. Amazon does that.

Publishers are belatedly moving to recover their value in writer-to-reader ecocomplexes. Their initial position was defensive and amounted to: "It's our product, you sell it on our terms." A group of the largest publishing firms refused to permit Amazon to sell their books in digital form at a low price and imposed an increase, typically from Amazon's $9.99 to $12.99. In the spring of 2012, the Justice Department launched legal suits that were pretty much open and shut; three of the five publishing firms that led the egregious collusive and restraint of trade started packing for a rapid retreat somewhere remote and sunny, perhaps carrying a Kindle. Apple will fight the case.[14]

It's an interesting view of value. Publishers are in a market that has been shrinking for decades, with the e-book the only force of rejuvenation and growth. So raise the price; don't exploit the low-price distribution channels Amazon has opened up. Customer value? "The value," they might say, "is the privilege of buying a book we produce and brand. It's our value that matters; we have all those inefficiencies, inventory wastage (around 40 percent of all books shipped to stores get shipped back), delays, and lunches to pay for."

This is unreal. Reality is, first, that the buyer determines value. Second, value is always relative and shifting, Third, companies leverage ecocomplexes, and fourth, entrepreneurs offer new dimensions of value. In that context, does the agenda for the MacMillan 2012 Publishing Innovation Conference really address innovation as value creation? The two panel discussions are: "Amateur versus Professional" ("How do we define quality content?" with "we" left undefined and presumably not meaning the customer) and "The Impacts of Self-Publishing on the Industry." Which industry?[15]

Summary: Reality Rules

These four Realities are the basis for a fresh view of value that shapes not just the firm's innovation agenda, but its value architecture: how it organizes its resources to ensure it combines both effectiveness today in relation to each Value Reality and adaptive response for tomorrow. The historical forces, particularly the intersection of technology and modularity, have made it so easy to start a business that intrusion on any firm's most fecund territory is a matter of when, not if.

In the Dark Ages, Vikings raided wealthy monasteries looking for gold and to take over rich farmlands; they did not invade deserts to rob tents. They traveled light. The new barbarians (the complacent incumbent's view) or entrepreneurs (the Viking horde's PR release) do the same. Via interfaces, someone—increasingly anyone, anywhere, anytime—will provide a back office, website, technology from a cloud, modular products, and processes as the business intruder needs them.

Manufacturing capacity will be sourced somewhere across the globe, and logistics capabilities contracted for. This means the new player won't need many people or much capital initially. The modular nature of such software delivery models as SaaS (software as a service), cloud computing, and Web services mean that any firm can have a world class IT capability without an IT organization. BPO (business process outsourcing) provides best-practices accounting, HR administration, and logistics on an as-needed, variable-cost basis. The start-up can focus on leveraging its unique value drivers and over time—often a very short time—create additional dimensions of value.

As an incumbent, your best offense and defense rest on the breadth and quality of the value dimensions you offer, the branded experience associated with those value dimensions, and your flexibility to change and expand them. The broader those dimensions, the less effective a targeted invader's thrust will be. A company that offers high-quality products and superb service is less vulnerable to a price onslaught than one offering a small range of goods in a commodity market or making service expensive.

Increasingly, the most successful superextenders build a multidimensional experience as their brand. Disney is associated with family fun, not just movies or Disney World. It positions its offers of theme parks, cruises, cable channels, and stores under the high-quality family fun umbrella.

Amazon is all about the shopping experience. The Kindle was never sold as just a digital book reader, but was tied to all the dimensions of book buying: the reviews it offers; the ease of locating, sampling, and downloading a digital book; self-publishing; and a growing variety of formats, deals, and samples, such as the Kindle Singles. The Amazon ecocomplex enables innovation from many sources. The neophyte author John Locke sold a million copies of his ninety-nine-cent book series in just five months, bypassing agents and publishers. This was impossible in the old book industry.

Apple is a design and style brand; its competitors have so far been unable to challenge its supremacy in smart phones or tablets through a product brand. The Apple customer experience can be captured by memories of first seeing the iPhone. You want to stroke it, and then you want to steal it. It's very much the same hunk of electronic innards as a range of equally functional, feature-packed, and neat alternatives. But they lack that special dimension of customer value.

If your company's brand is associated with limited dimensions, such as product features and price, you are decidedly vulnerable to Vikings—sorry, we should say "entrepreneurs"—picking you out as their target. If what your company can brand in the future is preconstrained by its current resource base, organizational capabilities, or industry structure, then it will be at risk in whatever the new game turns out to be. Many ultrafades fall into this last category.

Some lose their momentum by underinvesting in the capabilities that provide for adaptation. Gap is an example. It kept on track, opening more stores to exploit its customer base and mall presence; it's now closing stores. This is a commonplace instance of a firm doing so well and generating so much company and customer value that it sees little need to plan its value architecture for value extension since, of course, it has been able to treat value is a stable target—its very success proves that. The "of course" is the assumption that joins such famous reliance on the obvious as General John Sedgwick saying, "I am ashamed of you. They couldn't hit an elephant at this distance," a few seconds after which he fell dead from a sniper shot from a thousand yards away.

The best approach to winning today is to make sure you are positioning to win tomorrow. Today favors better. Tomorrow demands different. The new competition has to offer different. You won't have much of a tomorrow unless you see these four Value Realities as setting the stage for how the game will next be played. Focus your innovation on extending your dimensions of value; know how your customers see your brand, and, if necessary, rebrand yourself; and develop a value architecture that will enable you to transform as part of everyday business as usual. Then innovation moves from being special and occasional to continuous and integral to the management routine.

2 Value Architecture: Narrative, Engine, Platform

Does Innovation Mean Better or Different?

The shifting nature of Value Realities adds up to a single key question for every business's innovation agenda: *What do you know*? For instance, what can your firm be really sure about with regard to who its major competitors will be five to seven years from now? What will be the impacts of removal of investment and trade barriers in the European Union and Asia on its primary markets, manufacturing, and distribution? Which of the many new technology developments in energy, telecommunications, and manufacturing will really take off? How will credit markets shape up domestically and internationally? Most of all, what are you taking as a given about what the customer of *tomorrow* will value?

What emerges from our sense-making review of ultrasuccesses, ultrafades, and superextenders is that there are three distinct areas where companies have to build their organizational resources for them to create, sustain, and extend value. These correspond to three logical questions to which they had better have clear answers:

- *How are we going to make money*? This is our value narrative, the articulated message about how and where we plan to create value for our customers, company, partners, and shareholders and how we will measure our results and progress.
- *How are we going to deliver results*? This is our value engine of operational capabilities that drives everyday performance and how well we run our business.
- *How are we going to continue to grow in this time of unpredictable change*? This is our opportunity platform, the organizational practices for identifying new paths to value and investing in our resource base so we can take charge of change, rather than just react to it.

How well a company fits these three components together constitutes the blueprints for innovation: its value architecture. Below are some quick stereotypes to illustrate how the broad answers to the questions constrain or open up the future. In helping managers take a fresh view of value, the questions matter as much as, or in many instances more than, the answers. Throughout *The Value Path*, you will come across well over a hundred sentences that end with a question mark. That is not intended as a rhetorical flourish, but reflects our strong belief that managers are generally pretty skilled at handling the answers—if they've thought about the question.

Take an open-ended one such as, "Are we in danger of being caught in the Asset Trap?" or a more sharply focused one such as, "Do our procurement processes—and the people who execute them— encourage or block real partnerships?" Here is the range of broad replies, starting from the unresponsive: "Not my job and not your business to ask." "That's irrelevant." "I take that as a criticism." More positive: "Good question. We haven't really thought about that." "Useful question. We do talk about this and think we're on track." And finally: "That's a big topic of discussion. We need ideas—tell us what other companies are doing that may help us here." *The Value Path* is aimed at producing the last response.

But if you don't ask the question, then you don't know if it even needs an answer. Here is an existential query from the old myth, dating from ancient Rome, of the ostrich burying its head in the sand. Why on earth would it choose to do that? It can't be fun and isn't exactly comfortable. Nor does it solve the problem that the head-burying is supposed to address: hiding from a predator.

In Douglas Adams's *Hitchhiker's Guide to the Galaxy*, a discussion of the origin of the Ravenous Bugblatter Beast of Traal describes it as "so mind-bogglingly stupid that it assumes that if you can't see it, then it can't see you." Change "it" to new competition, customer of tomorrow, ecocomplex, or opportunity, and the two example questions may take on new implications: "Are we in danger of being caught in the Asset Trap?" "Do our procurement processes encourage or block real partnerships?" It may also raise another question: "Are we overlooking non-traditional, non-industry players that are starting to build a critical mass of customers and profits?"

Returning from literary whimsy to hard-headed business, let's look at value architecture answers to the questions of how to deal with the forces of disturbance. These answers come from three firms in the energy utilities industry, two of which are fictional composites of typical actual players and one a real company. This is a mature sector, still tightly bounded by regulation and historically stable in products and comparative customer dimensions of value—mainly price, reliability, and availability. Deregulation is moving in a piecemeal fashion. About fourteen states have deregulated areas of both the gas and electrical utilities; eighteen states are yet to open up the market at all; and the rest are in between.

The capital cost of a medium to large coal-fired plant is in the region of $5 billion, with many factors affecting the exact S. Over the plant's fifty-year lifetime, the operating costs are likely to be in the $50 billion range. Nuclear start-up costs would be $18 billion or so, solar $30 billion (maybe), wind $22 billion and up, and geothermal in the "who knows?" guesswork category. All these figures are just rough indicators; building a coal plant might cost $5 billion in one instance and maybe $12 billion in another for the same capacity. The numbers indicate the scale and hint at the investment risks.

Cleanup costs, retrofitting existing plants, and meeting environmental requirements add to the costs and uncertainties. Then there are all the spreadsheet issues of costs of capital, financial rates of return, prices, taxation, and benefits to consumer and commercial users versus to the provider versus to investors versus to political and social advocates.

There are many areas of development in technology, with information technology coming into the foreground for the first time through the evolving smart grid. This is like an Internet for electrical currents instead of bits. It enables dynamic pricing via making meters equivalent to PCs, integration of multiple providers and types of energy in real-time, reduced energy losses, online problem tracking, and many other potential innovations. It's also assumed to be a primary target for elite hackers, especially Russian, Turkish, and Chinese.

So far, the primary initial market offer of smart meters for monitoring energy use and being able to offer smart pricing and incentives has been a relative bust. Why? See Value Reality 1; customers aren't choosing it. Reality 2: there is as yet no compelling new dimension of value that attracts them to shift their preferences, and the choice space is still very limited because of effective monopolization. Then factor in Reality 3: the new ecocomplexes are only just forming. Reality 4: entrepreneurs haven't as yet built mass and found their opportunity, which feeds back to Reality 1.

In most areas of the utility business, change is glacially slow, and operational considerations dominate forward-looking strategic thinking, while in others, there's a headline a day. Many ideas for a new value narrative for, say, solar are compelling and upbeat, but the needed value engines are decidedly down to earth: the 12 percent replacement rate for mirrors, the huge vats of molten salt compound that flows in troughs to convert water to steam, finding a river flow of usable water with plenty of sunshine all day and every day, and so on.

For the long term and in good times, there's a general positive view of investing in alternative energy sources, addressing climate change and environmental damage, and ending dependence on fossil fuels. All that talk disappears when the annual Blizzard of the Century hits town. Innovation? The future? Going green? Forget all that stuff, and just get the lights back on! Now!

This is obviously only a broad sketch of the context of an industry where for many decades business innovation was not on the agenda.

Our first hypothetical company is very much a traditional utility and prides itself on stability and a long record of solid operations. For it, the answers to the three questions about value generation are couched in operational terms.

How are we going to make money? Negotiate rates of return with regulators on prices and capital investment terms. Offer customers reliable service, exploit advantages of scale, and maximize revenue-generating opportunities. *How are we going to deliver results?* Build for the long-term, invest in fixed assets that provide economies of scale, control costs (including aggressive bargaining in supplier contracts), and hire and retain the best people. *How are we going to continue to grow in this time of unpredictable change?* Basically, the same way that we always have. Why spoil a good deal?

Obviously, this traditional utility will have to respond to the signals from the forces of disturbance. Deregulation is coming and will put pressures on cost efficiency and make it important to improve service. The smart grid will happen, but the impact on both the customer and the utility is still unknown. Natural gas and carbon capture and storage are opportunities for the firm over the medium-but not short-term.

Overall, it seems sensible for the company to echo St. Augustine's famous plea, "Grant me chastity and continence, only not yet." For this firm, the prayer might be, "Make us innovative and customer-centric, but would you mind letting us hold on just a bit longer, please."

The second hypothetical utility isn't quite so sure that the current business deal is still on and sees deregulation coming fast, customers generally not pleased with prices and service, and a lot of discussion about the smart grid, alternative energy, retail access, and ABMs (agents, brokers, and marketers).

So, making money? Well, customers will be shopping around a lot more, so we had better start adding a slew of new options for them: services, financing, and home energy management via the Internet, maybe in partnership with a software company, equipment maker, or retailer that is targeting this as a major part of its own innovation agenda.

There are plenty of opportunities here and a flood of new and established players. To pick out just a few: Motorola's acquisition of 4Home, Best Buy's plans to sell consumer devices, Comcast Xfinity's cloud computing service, and GE's Brillion service, which includes its smart plug that turns any 120-volt device into a sensor and Internet address. The only limit to the partnerships we can enter into is our own culture; it will be a big shift, and we will need to get rid of the NIH tradition—not invented here.

Delivering results? We had better exploit what we are really good at, which is operations. Somehow, we are going to have to deal with the problem of coal-fired plants that are inefficient, increasingly unacceptable environmentally, and very expensive to phase out and replace. And we are also going to have to develop some new capabilities.

It's obviously time for us to take a hard look at opportunities to build strategic alliances. There's that Tesco grocery chain in the United Kingdom where they deregulated twenty years ago; it's one of the leaders in signing up its customers online for energy deals. Maybe we had better start thinking about sales and marketing in a different way and begin using partners.

We will have to upgrade our technology know-how, especially in the area of the smart grid. We need to talk with Cisco, IBM, Google, the smart appliance manufacturers, and maybe some of the microgrid start-ups; it's not clear which of them are going to be competitors and which will be partners—or both?

Growing in the future? We just don't know. We obviously need to look at every area of our business and start asking what won't change and what is up for grabs—for competitors as much as for ourselves. We have to make sure we can be more flexible in our options for customers, open up the culture to be more receptive to partnering, totally rethink our capital expenditure plans. We have got to stop seeing ourselves as an electric utility; we have to move to becoming the customer's preferred energy service provider.

So, customers, assets, partners, technology infrastructure, and connections to customers and partners, culture, capital structures, and operational capabilities...do we have the flexibility in all these areas to be able to plan when we can no longer predict? The key underlying question here is to what extent do we target our innovation in terms of being better in our current dimensions of value creation, versus offering some really different dimensions?

For this responsive utility, better would include reducing time to respond to customer outages, offering new payment plans, or upgrading load-balancing tools. Different might extend services to, say, special discount deals on energy-efficient home appliances in partnership with a retailer or manufacturer; equipment and maintenance management services for a commercial customer's office-complex energy needs; or joint planning, testing, and financing relationships with suppliers of alternative energy, such as solar and wind.

THE VALUE PATH

This second utility contrasts with the first example of a traditional player in this regard. It looks to be different in its innovation, to extend, not just sustain, its value creation. Its value narrative adds consideration of new dimensions in the nature and breadth of services and the need to respond to new competitors with nonutility offers. Delivering results moves from what it can do with its internal resources to where relationships can add capabilities as the need becomes apparent. Finally, the challenge of growth for the unknown future moves away from the immediate concerns of business models for today to what we term the opportunity platform for navigating tomorrow.

Very roughly, the traditional firm—a utility in this example, but the comparisons and patterns are general across businesses—is mainly focused on its value chain: how it manages its operational capabilities to generate value now and then evolves them over time. The value-chain perspective was a very effective framework for thinking about corporate strategy in an era where the choice space was relatively predictable in terms of boundaries and pace and nature of change and competitors. Its most noted proponent, Michael Porter, explicitly viewed business in terms of industry *structure* driving competition and profitability. The industry framed the business model. The second utility is looking beyond the industry for a new value narrative that will better position it to address the emergent shifts in the competitive environment and choice spaces.

There's a third type of firm that sees change as a constant and an opportunity, not a contingent threat. In many regards, it loosens its value chain so it can adapt more widely and quickly. It doesn't want to be tightly locked into any value narrative, with the risk that it moves from ultrasuccess to ultrafade. It adopts a fairly consistent perspective on making sure it has a platform for extending innovation in the context of "We just don't know."

This has been the value architecture driver and thus the base for the innovation agenda for a well-known power utility in California. It's not at all hypothetical, but a very real and growing player licensed to offer energy services across California's growing open market. It has opted aggressively for different, not just better. Here is its viewpoint.

Making money? We see consumer energy management as an extension of our core services. Customers will want it, and the starting point is home energy monitoring and smart meters. It will take time and effort to break through the current lack of consumer interest and low adoption. But our entire way of thinking about value is built on making things easy, accessible, and convenient.

We can add many dimensions of value through our existing customer relationships. We know how to exploit anything online, especially via smart phones, and we give our consumer services away for free and make our money from partners paying to piggyback on the exposure and revenue opportunities they gain from interfacing with our user base.

Delivering results? We're investing across the board. We've added solar energy through our Brightstar deal and bought into Potter Drilling to add geothermal technology. The solar power projects we're involved in have been successfully demonstrated, and we have a $168 million chunk of the world's biggest heliostat solar tower that goes online in 2013 and a patent application for a heliostat control system.[16]

Growing? We've had our failures but innovation inevitably means taking risks, starting with the very fact that we are looking to create something new and different. We discontinued our RE<C initiative (making renewable energy cheaper than coal), but shared our engineering work with a range of other companies that are better positioned to move it to the next stages. Meanwhile, we are building a lot of new capabilities in this area that we can apply to other innovation thrusts. We want to be there when demand takes off.

On-campus energy complexes, data centers, our $6 billion investment in a 350-mile underwater cable for a "backbone" network of wind energy providers...we're pretty well positioned. How will we grow? Dunno, but there's plenty of opportunity out there, and we are a company built on technology; a flow of new—and free—offers to customers; ecocomplexes of relationships; and interconnectability of processes, products, and technology.

We consciously design our resource management blueprints to maximize adaptation, flexibility, and interconnection with our partners. That ranges from how we plan our human capital, our financial structures, management of relationships, physical and intellectual asset base, technology infrastructures, and the brand identity we are building in the eyes of our customers.

Energy is an obvious opportunity for us. After all, we *are* Google.

The same "industry" but three very different responses to the forces of change, three very different assumptions about customers, industry, and resource needs. Three different value architectures. But Google as a *utility*? No, Google as an opportunity-platform player that is positioned to make innovation in the energy arena just a natural evolution of its everyday business. Every day.

Value Architecture as a Balancing Act

Figure 2.1 summarizes the general structure of a value architecture. It is not a prescriptive invention but the road map that explains the directions that companies have taken on their value path, what happened along their way to the future, and how they were able to navigate shifts in the business terrain or instead got stuck or sidetracked along the trail.

The architecture is a complex balancing act, a point that seems generally neglected in management thought and practice that focus on just one element of management or organization. For instance, while corporate strategy can open up powerful new narratives and help firms rethink their business models, the business model is in itself not the architecture.

The value narrative has to be balanced with the value engine. Most dot-coms failed abysmally in this regard. They were classically all strategy and no delivery; great value story, though. Similarly, a business model that does not include the opportunity platform to adapt to shifts in the choice space may produce ever more value for customers while killing company value.

Customers absolutely love the wonderful display of large-screen TVs in the store, all bigger, cheaper, sharper, and more advanced than on their last visit to the store. Their makers are less enthusiastic, since the commoditization kills prices, margins, market share, and balance-sheet strengths. A value architecture adds to the business model the perspective and resource blueprints that may shift the model itself, not reify it.

What follows is a summary of the three elements of the architecture.

Value narrative

- This is how we will produce value for customers, the company, partners, and investors. It's where we see opportunities to create value for the customer of tomorrow as well as today as choice spaces shift.
- It is our statement of what we offer and how we will continue to do it better. It provides a convincing story—for customers, our own people, potential and existing partners, and investors—about how and where we will offer something different and special, now *and* in the future.
- This is a narrative in the sense that we must be able to convince all these parties of the business logic, realism, and clarity of our claim if we are to capture their attention, belief

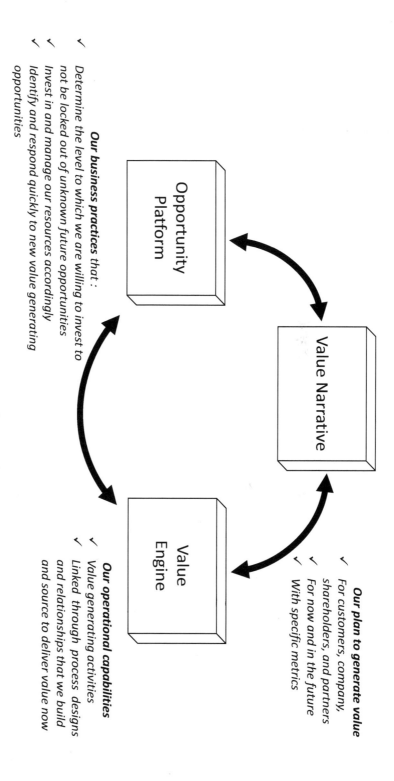

Figure 2.1: Value Architecture

Our plan to generate value
- ✓ For customers, company, shareholders, and partners
- ✓ For now and in the future
- ✓ With specific metrics

Our operational capabilities
- ✓ Value generating activities
- ✓ Linked through process designs and relationships that we build and source to deliver value now

Our business practices that :
- ✓ Determine the level to which we are willing to invest to not be locked out of unknown future opportunities
- ✓ Invest in and manage our resources accordingly
- ✓ Identify and respond quickly to new value generating opportunities

and commitment. Customers don't care about our "business model," so we must constantly be thinking in terms of their buying model: how they go about their everyday shopping and special purchases, what they look for and where, and how they see their choices.

- Does all this fit in with our branding and identity? Do we have the capabilities, can we make the shifts? Are we on a value-building path or one that is going to slow down or get blocked by commoditization, inflexible resources, unanticipated competition, or financial constraints? Do our employees understand and buy into our narrative?
- Will investors value our shares for more than just our predictable cash flows and returns on capital? Will they fund our future?
- What are the metrics of performance in terms of value capture? Are we on a revenue track where growth will kill margins as prices erode? Does capital efficiency matter more than operating profits? Do we track value creation in terms of the economics of products, relationships, market share, new lines of business, customer satisfaction/retention, or some other compass setting that directly orients us on our innovation landscape?

Value engine
- The value narrative is our guide here. Do we have the operational capabilities to deliver value now? Can we continue to improve across the board in terms of doing better in our service, customer relationships, distribution, coproduction, outsourcing, and quality measures?
- Are we able to exploit new technologies and partnering options? Can we move effectively and efficiently into new geographies? Does our efficiency rest on what we can get out of our existing resources, or will we upgrade, replace, or even do without some of them entirely (e.g., through outsourcing)?

Opportunity platform:
- How flexible and adaptive are we in terms of our resource base? Can we produce value today and use our capabilities to produce value tomorrow in an expanding choice space? Are we a company that must worry about uncertainty as a likely threat, or must we embrace it as the very basis for our sustaining growth?
- Given the shifts in the business terrain, what are our next best opportunities? Say we have to throw out a large part of our

value narrative—is that a positive or a disaster? And do we have a solid, yet flexible, resource base on which to exploit new opportunities?

The case examples we present in *The Value Path* capture the answers that are apparent in the experiences and impacts of ultrasuccesses, superextenders, and ultrafades.

There are plenty of companies that didn't ask the questions or that took the answers as implicit in standard industry practice and didn't become successes, typically faded, and missed out on just about every opportunity. They are part of the Blissful Ignorance School of Business, which drifts along behind the waves of change. At best, they float with the current and more typically are washed way offshore.

Every firm that swims rather than drifts has some blueprint for each of the three elements and how they interact, but we can use our three utilities to show how different value architectures can be.

Our first company is assuming that the future will look pretty much like the present. Since its value narrative will remain relatively constant, so too can its value engine—it sees little need to be different. Innovation will continue to be focused on service and process improvements. Since the business leaders already know that their resource investments will be made to improve the existing value engine, there is little reason for a separate opportunity platform; just leave it as part of the value engine. The key question remains, however: how many companies will survive under that scenario over the next few years?

Our second company is thinking about a new business model. The term *business model* came into vogue during the dot-com surge of the late 1990s. Note that the concept is one of building something, just as the value "chain" meant tightening linkages. An obvious question is what is a business model a model of? It tends to be equated with a baseline plan: this is the new type of firm we want to *be*.

Airlines responded to the commoditization of the industry and all its financial pressures, plus threats from discount carriers, such as Southwest Airlines. They moved almost as a herd to adopt a low-cost business model. The dot-coms used clicks-versus-bricks business models. Some adopted an e-commerce model, others a portal model, and still others became business-to-business (B-to-B) exchanges. In the end, what they really had most in common was that they burned through a lot of cash and then went out of business.

In the question about which business model we espouse, the "be" implies something fixed. When we get there, we will be fine. But how do we navigate to there, and what happens if we have to adopt another business model to do so? Do we just admit we're stuck and restructure, which is another way of saying we made a lot of investments in assets that turned out to be liabilities and invested a lot in skilled people we no longer need? Let's write off the assets and let the people go.

A business model defines what a firm plans to be without laying out where it will be able to go if—when—the Value Realities shift. In digital media, a business model today has the life expectancy of a sandcastle. Where would Amazon be now if its value architecture had not enabled it to shift its business model again and again? Where might Blockbuster be if it had had a value architecture perspective instead of just a frozen business model?

The second utility in our example needs a navigation path forward from today's model. It must be able to spot new opportunities, modify its value narratives, create *different* operational capabilities, and then do it all over again when the forces disrupt the business terrain—again. It aims at extending its current value generation, not in the sense of making this the very essence of its innovation, as Google does, but by adapting and leveraging the historical forces of disturbance to create new opportunities.

For that it needs a value architecture, not a new business model. It must shape an opportunity platform, separate from its value engine, to identify openings on the horizon and manage its resources (the building blocks for capabilities) to build and source different operational capabilities. It's all about *different*, not just *better*.

Better just isn't good enough. There will always be tradeoffs between investing for the present and investing for the future. If the operational people control the resources, you can bet how they will be allocated. The business model will dominate decision priorities. There will be less management attention paid to how to navigate from the business model of today to the innovation opportunities of tomorrow.

Our third company, Google, is already in tomorrow's energy industry today. That was never part of its original business model, just as Amazon did not in any way anticipate being the leading tablet contender to the iPad. Google and Amazon are superextenders. They don't just have platforms; they are platform companies. They thrive on the change that the forces bring.

While few companies will ever become such shape changers that they morph from dinosaur to bird, caterpillar to butterfly, and industry defined to platform enabled, there is much that the average company can learn from them as it travels its own path to sustainability and then to expansion.

Value Architecture: Narrative, Engine, Platform

For instance, superextenders' value engines exploit asset blending. They retain ownership of resources that are and will remain the foundation of their cost, quality, and time to market, as Amazon has done with technology and fulfillment centers and Google with its data centers. They source other capabilities via modular interfaces. Amazon's base business now includes shipping, third-party stores, and the manufacturing of the Kindle, all enabled through innovation by interface and none of them part of the profile of an online "book retailer."

The opportunity platform designs of the new superextender exemplars of innovation are industry-independent and built for flexibility. They are often very striking in their innovation for today, but what stands out is how they position for the next innovation and the ones after that. They use their adaptability to enter new markets at low cost, with little capital and low risk, redeploy and re-source capabilities, and extend business models. This has enabled Amazon, for example, to use its platform to take over book publishing, become a leader in cloud computing, and challenge any innovator in any emerging sector of digital media.

Tesco started out as a discount player in the UK grocery business and is now labeled as Wal-Mart's worst nightmare, one of the three largest global retailers, a leading financial services company, one of the most successful mobile phone firms, and by far the most profitable player in online grocery sales. Oh, and it is the largest seller of "branded" gas to car drivers and is the national price leader.

Tesco's loyalty card is a second currency for the entire UK economy. Its value architecture was designed with the aim of earning the customer's lifetime loyalty, not just selling groceries, which it is superb at. In many ways, Tesco is an opportunity platform readied for the next expansion and looking for the one after that. We will explore Google, Amazon, Tesco, and many others in more detail in individual chapters of *The Value Path*.

The players that do not evolve a mind-set that increasingly formalizes the opportunity platform via corporate leadership consistently run the risk of becoming caught in a value trap created by their past *success* in innovation. The three most widespread instances of these value traps are the Asset Trap, Commodity Trap, and Invention Trap.

3 Value Traps: Asset, Commodity, Invention

It is ironic that for many companies the main blockage to future innovation is their own past innovation, which can set up these three common value traps: Asset Trap, Commodity Trap, and Invention Trap.

The Asset Trap reflects a company being locked into the base of facilities, infrastructures, and resources that got it to where it is. In some instances, that foundation continues to be a launching pad for growth, but in more and more cases, the manufacturing plants, physical offices, stores, distribution centers, and other fixed investments become a burden, as old and new competitors are able to use relationships with partners and suppliers to improve costs, reduce risk, and add speed.

The Commodity Trap is often the direct outcome of waves of innovation in technology and productivity improvements in manufacturing, distribution, and supply chains. Competitors are able to use the same technology, processes, partners, and licensing to match the leaders, and very quickly everyone has the same product features and quality. Overcapacity results and new players flood in, often starting price wars or exploiting low-cost distribution channels.

The extremes of such commoditization are the technology-driven fields of smart phones, personal computers, and HDTV. Innovation is rapid, sustained, creative, and inexorable; it just can't keep ahead of the commoditization. The Japanese electronics giants are slowly going broke—and innovating and innovating and innovating in their products.

The Invention Trap is an overreliance on R&D and new-product development, where the assumption is that new and more advanced equals better value. It ignores the realities of customer choices determining the value of an invention, not the invention driving the choice because of its assumed new value. The Invention Trap is an enticing one, particularly in technology-paced markets, and it can easily sound Luddite or reactionary to suggest that in many instances invention ends up being a solution in search of a problem or a gadget in search of a need.

It is noteworthy that Google, Apple, and Microsoft, three companies that have stood out in value creation, have all bombed in an area where logically they could expect to sweep to success: Internet-smart TVs. They have not as yet offered value dimensions that are more compelling to most customers than the familiarity, ease of use, and responsiveness of large-screen TVs, with their elegant feature of a single click on the remote and *mirabile dictu*

(Latin for real neat), a picture appears, and you can immediately start watching a program. In an article titled "Is Google TV Doomed?" the remote controller for Google TV was described as "like something James Bond would use to remote control a helicopter. In the 1970s. It's ugly and complicated."[17]

In general, invention succeeds in creating value when the focus of buyer evaluation and comparison is the product. It is less likely to win out when some aspect of the customer experience is the primary differentiator. A comparison of the functionality and features of Google TV and a Vizio HDTV favors the Google product. If your own value ranking is the experience, then installing and learning to use the gizmos (assuming you daisy-chained the cables right and are really, really good at thumb typing) doesn't match the easy gesture of switching on the set and relaxing while you watch your program. Value comes from and is revealed in the actuality of choosing, not the logic of why you ought to choose something.

The Asset Trap

With the Asset Trap, the firm's value architecture rests on the logic that made large multinationals successful over past decades: invest in a fixed asset base that provides advantages of scale, technology, reach, and efficiency. Fine-tune this through cost management, productivity improvements, and investment in human-capital skills and experience, and label them "core competences." The firm's offers in the market—products and services—are driven by this asset base and capacity.

The trap snaps tightly on a firm's innovation when those offers are company-driven, not customer-led, in terms of value creation and in that they tie up financial capital. If new players are able to create new offers through capabilities that do not require owning that asset base or make it obsolete, all the elements of value creation shift.

Core competences become employee redundancies as part of "reconstruction" costs. For example, newspapers' talent pools have been almost entirely thrown out as "mojos" (mobile journalists) are brought in to make sure that "content" is modular, deployable in many online contexts, and made a fungible resource across digital media ecocomplexes. In the technical fields of engineering, pharmaceutical research, a whole generation of loyal employees has been demoralized, discarded, or displaced by outsourcing.

That is a waste of human capital for everyone: loyal employees previously promoted on the basis of their experience increasing their value, the company gaining from their commitment and expertise, and the long-term stock investors seeing, for instance, Pfizer's $6 billion in write-offs in 2009–10 as part of its "transformation initiatives" that abandon its core asset-intensive reliance on R&D, where it has cut the budget by $1.5 billion. A headline in mid-2011—"Pfizer's Dolsten [its R&D chief]: Less R&D Spending Is Better"[18]—would have been silly in 2001.

The most active area of industry disruption and reconfiguration in terms of the Asset Trap is telecommunications. Providers such as AT&T, Verizon, Telefonica, BT, and Telekom have had to invest billions of dollars annually to build new networks based on new technology, especially for mobile services. These "dumb pipes" have become increasingly commoditized, and prices have fallen rapidly. Ironically, they provide the base for companies such as Netflix, Apple, Amazon, and Google to launch profitable new offers in the market without having to make the same heavy investments.

The average return on assets of the major telecommunications services providers globally has been a meager 5 percent. One firm, Bharti Airtel, has historically generated ROA of around 20 percent. Why? Relationships, not assets. It did not build its network, but designed long-term win-win agreements with such companies as Siemens and IBM that have kept Airtel at the leading edge of technology without the infamous bleeding-edge risks and associated capital investment. It has leveraged India's world-leading BPO industry to provide it with best-of-breed back office and administrative services.

Assets are built for the long term and assume stability in the dynamics of value as the base for recovering the upfront capital expenditure. They are not termed *fixed* assets by accident. When choices are unfixed, asset-constrained innovation won't last for long. Companies then increasingly become part of a frozen ecocomplex, as industry leaders, suppliers, distribution channels, and product lines become interdependent and kept in stasis rather than mutually adapting.

One of the central themes of *The Value Path* is that rather than attribute the decline of an ultrasuccess to incompetence, look first to its success as the explanation. This parallels Clayton Christiansen's influential concept of the innovator's dilemma, where a firm has to disrupt its own ecocomplexes (Christiansen uses the term "value network") to innovate. The more it exploits new technology and is responsive to customers, the more its asset strengths contribute to its dilemma—one that new entrants do not face.

The music industry is conventionally ridiculed for ignoring the impacts of the Internet and the MP3 format, which enabled music to be delivered in digital form and resulted in services such as Napster becoming popular new choices. In fact, the music companies responded quickly, including launching clever technical tweaks of their own to exploit the MP3 standardized interface.

Rolling Stone magazine reported in mid-2007 that as early as 2000, the top music industry executives met with Napster's CEO. They understood that Napster was something their own customers wanted and proposed that they permit its 38 million users to continue to download music, which listeners were doing illegally but unstoppably. They would charge a subscription fee of $10 a month that would get split between Napster and the record companies.

Then they backed off. A *Rolling Stone* article discussed how that happened. "The record companies needed to jump off a cliff, and they couldn't bring themselves to jump," said the CEO of the Recording Industry Association of America. She commented that the music labels were being called "dinosaurs and idiots," but this underestimates the challenges they faced. "They had retailers telling them, 'You better not sell anything online cheaper than in a store,' and they had artists saying, 'Don't screw up my Wal-Mart sales.'" The manager of several leading singers and groups added that innovation demanded that the labels cannibalize their own core business.[19]

This is an instance of a growing commonplace determinant of the practical direction and nature of innovation; the asset base and ecocomplex become either the opportunity platform or opportunity boundary. The main escape from the Asset Trap is to interface your way to an asset-blending strategy of in-house resources and relationships. That's become the base for pharmaceutical firms trying to reinvigorate their product development and for telecommunications companies needing to add "value-added services" to their value-draining network base.

The Commodity Trap

Across the consumer electronics field, in just about every segment and country, the surge of new choices for customers and providers is commoditizing the entire sector in terms of price, loss of sustainable product differentiation, standardization of components, and rapid time to market and catch-up through licensing of technology. The smart phone or large-screen TV hot product of July is the Christmas season bargain item.

In mobile phones, the market leaders of just a few years ago, including Nokia and RIM, are increasingly the market losers, even though they maintain and even increase their product innovation.

Japanese service providers have led the world in technology and features for decades, but their prices and margins keep falling. In mid-2011, HP gave up on mobile devices and dumped its $500 Touchpad in a "fire sale" at $99, less than two months after its launch.[20]

This flood of product and technology innovation is creating a Commodity Trap for most players; the more advanced the product, the sooner it is matched, the faster the price falls, and the shorter the life cycle. Customers have more and more choices of what they buy, where, from whom, under which brand, and how much they pay.

Companies have choices of how they source manufacturing and assembly, exploit manufacturing, and leverage their relationships with contract designers. They can incorporate technology developments in products through licensing and make deals with network service providers. They can build integrated, "seamless" capabilities through interfacing with third-party logistics firms such as UPS and FedEx to manage supply chain processes.

Most consequentially of all, players have new choices in the software operating system that is the very core of a smart phone. RIM, Nokia, Apple, Microsoft, and the leading Asian players built their success on a proprietary OS, and new entrants, such as HTC, Huawei, HP, and China's Alibaba, either had to develop their own or adopt one of these. Apple had an effective monopoly since it did not license its OS. The bounds of the choice space were broken open by Google offering its free, "open-source" Android for any company to adopt and adapt.

While Apple remains the leader in product market share, Android has become a brand in and of itself, with around 50 percent market share. It's by far the most effective counter that Apple has faced. Motorola, once the leader with over a third of the handset market and then in continued decline, is back in the game as an Android player (and its Mobility division was acquired by Google as a direct result). Amazon has begun the commoditization of the tablet market with its challenge to Apple's iPad, the Kindle Fire, which is built on Android.

Choices have become more and more unbounded for partners, fueling commoditization. Firms build their new ecocomplexes to fill a wide range of roles. Foxconn's name appears on no branded phones, but it accounts for over half the manufacturing of all consumer electronic products sold in the United States and generates $80 billion in revenues. "Apps," small modular software components, have become a new opportunity for thousands of individuals and many firms to whose products they interface. The developer typically gets around 70–80 percent of the revenue, and Apple, RIM, Nokia, and so on, get 20–30 percent.

Apps have grown to be a far-reaching competitive factor, entrepreneurial whirlpool, and fountainhead of value generation in just two to four years. But there is no formal app industry; the major software giants, such as Oracle and SAP, were late in taking the opportunity, and there is as yet no single company that brands the apps it develops.

This entire market is an outcome of opportunities opened up by technology and modularity. Until these forces came together, there was no open choice space for software producers, device makers such as Apple, or consumers. Now, there is an app "industry" that is a set of dynamic ecocomplexes rather than a well-defined and bounded new offshoot of the established software sector. The main beneficiaries have been independent developers, many of them young, working from home or in groups of students. Customers gain because for many of them the apps are becoming more of a dimension of value differentiation than the device they run on.

All this ferment stirred up by waves of disturbance across the terrain and their reverberating aftershocks enabled new value paths for some, blocks to progress for others, and false trails for many. Value no longer rests on product innovation and R&D; these are certainly opportunities, but if, and only if, they are complemented, enhanced, and leveraged by a wider platform-centered value generator that is not eroded by the inevitability of commoditization. For Apple, this is design; for Amazon, the customer experience; and for Google, the market for search and advertising that commoditization of smart phones expands.

It may seem ironic that innovation should so erode customer value in terms of prices and differentiation by so increasing customer value. Just about every industry that is being disturbed by the reverberations of deregulation/liberalization, technology, and modularity is being pulled into the Commodity Trap. That's the way it is, and it's likely to increasingly become the norm. It makes the opportunity platform essential for sustained innovation.

The Invention Trap

Many managers see technology as the key to the new products and services that drive growth. R&D has become the very emblem of innovation; a typical CEO statement is, "The lifeblood of our business is that R&D spend," and an equally typical policy rallying cry is, "The US is simply not doing enough in R&D, and we are falling into an innovation gap."[21] The assumption here is that value is an intrinsic element of the product and service. A better product will create more value, and a successful new product will generate new value. This is a linear perspective: draw a straight line from invention to value.

The invention-to-value path ended in a roadblock for pharmaceuticals, where for a century the established route was through highly focused product development. As the forces of disturbance accelerated, other companies entered the pharmaceutical terrain, expanding the choice space and shifting value from product to relationship in customer preferences and from core competences to collaboration in product development.

The industry had been dominated by Big Pharma, the term used for the giants that had a very clear target: the next blockbuster, the billion-dollar-a-year drug. They relied on R&D, advantages of scale built through megamergers, patent protection, aggressive marketing to physicians, and "take it leave it" pricing. They earned among the highest rates of return on investment of any industry for many decades.

That's all over. The linear link between R&D and value has been snapped, and the direction reversed. The old signpost to the value path pointed to finding the right product target—drugs for diabetes, depression, melanoma, and so on—getting through the high-risk and complex design, development, clinical trial, and regulatory approval process; and then unleashing the ads and calls on physicians.

Now, instead of this company-led invention generating value in a limited customer choice space, customer value is driving company opportunity in an ever-expanding open space. Patients and insurers can insist that physicians authorize generics, which growing global powerhouse players such as India's Dr. Reddy, Israel's Teva, and Mexico's Farmacias Similares readily provide.

The pricing power of Big Pharma has also been eroded by the buying power of health-care agencies, insurers, pharmacy benefit management services, (legitimate) online discounters, and in many instances a bus ticket across the US–Canada border.

The R&D pipeline has similarly been fractured. Despite budget increases of about 15 percent a year, the flow of blockbusters is now a trickle. In 2007, Big Pharma produced nineteen new patented medications, the fewest since 1983[22] on ten times the expenditures.[23] This "Innovation Drought" (the term used by the CEO of Eli Lilly) couldn't be ended by once again ramping up the R&D budget. Lilly's head of strategic planning summarized in 2010 why his company has broken up the entire "drug development template": "Trying to do everything yourself won't work. The odds of owning everything and being at the right place at the right time are not high."[24]

Eli Lilly is a leader in the shift from Big Pharma looking very much like multinational manufacturers to becoming more of a Dell, Wal-Mart, or Amazon in integrating the end-to-end supply chain. Its management language is a new one of collaboration and flexibility: FIPNet (Fully Integrated Pharmaceutical Network); InnovCenter, a web hub that links to thousands of collaborators for solving problem-solving "challenges"; and a commitment to "open source" innovation.

The Invention Trap is to rely on new products, services, and technology in isolation from the wider context of choice. Here is an expansion of the comment quoted earlier, which was made by the CEO of Microsoft: "The lifeblood of our business is that R&D spend...We have to continuously create new innovation that lets people do something they didn't think they could do the day before."

On another occasion he is quoted as saying, "But unless we're in touch with our customers, our model of the world can diverge from reality. There's no substitute for innovation, of course, *but innovation is no substitute for being in touch either*." (Our emphasis added.)

Together, the statements are a little curious. They seem to detach the invention element of new offers in the market from the value determinant. The customer is at the end of the link from idea to impact in new-product development. This is a recognition that for a company like Microsoft, Google, or Apple, meeting existing customer needs is secondary to creating new ones. As has often been noted, customers weren't clamoring for the PC or waiting for the iPhone. It's a strategy of invention in search of value and, for many companies, R&D budgets in search of projects.

Microsoft's record of success in turning its inventions into innovations has been at best spotty, and after a decade in which it was viewed as Apple is today, it is often dismissed as a reactionary force with a lot of cash and a bad reputation. Its Vista operating system was intended to be an epochal breakthrough; it turned out to be a massive bust that few other firms could have recovered from.

One of the latest disappointments is its search engine, Bing, which was launched with the intent of challenging Google. It was well received by industry analysts and offers many distinctive features. It has so far been a relative disappointment, though, with its losses in 2011 estimated as equivalent to its revenues.

In 2010, Microsoft scored what is probably a record not for time *to* market but time *in* market. It spent an estimated billion dollars to develop its Kin mobile phone, which drew raves from the techno-sage community. Maybe the Kin was a truly great product. The world will never know. Its total time on the market from launch to retirement was about two months and sales an estimated five hundred units.[25] Customers just didn't see it as a good choice. It now has more value as a collectible auctioned on eBay.

By contrast, Microsoft's Kinect motion-sense game box shows invention at its best. It became the fastest selling consumer device in history within its first year on the market.[26] It has created a new ecocomplex of innovators who are going well beyond the gaming for which Kinect is intended, including artists who tinker with its software to create new 3D media, hospitals that have adapted it for medical diagnosis through tracking patients' limb movements, a Russian retail system that "dresses" people in clothes and shows them in a mirror, and a French scientist training Kinect to read and speak back sign language.

In chapter 1, we cited the emergence of a new value path that opened up for Microsoft through entrepreneurs adopting it as a business tool. Maybe Microsoft will be able to loosen the hold of its product invention history of the past decade and embed Kinect in a new value architecture: narrative, engine, and opportunity platform.

These examples don't point to new technology and products either as the way to go or as a false lead. Microsoft can be viewed as an object lesson in terms of both of these. It's just that the connection between invention and value is not a bold, straight, and fixed line: invention–new products–value.

You cannot tell from the invention anything about its value. The more inventions that are dreamed up; sourced; enabled by technology, global sourcing, and licensing; and brought to market to more types of buyer in more demographic markets via more distribution options, the greater the gap between invention and value unless the firm avoids the traps.

Bypass the Asset Trap by using technology and globalization to source and coordinate capabilities, rather than own them all. Avoid the Commodity Trap through branding the customer experience and extending offers that expand choices. And escape the temptations of the Invention Trap by tightly meshing every element of the value engine to combine customer, company, and partner value, while being customer led in all these regards. Still, it is not enough to be "in touch" with customers or just customer focused. The customer must be the starting point and cannot in the longer term be served at the expense of company and partner value.

The Nokia CEO brought in to stem the flow of its fade eloquently captures the state of the innovation art in an early 2011 memo to employees that presaged major shifts in every area of its strategy. As you read through the following verbatim extracts from this "Burning Platform" alarm call, please keep in mind that Nokia has been a marvelous performer for longer than Apple or Google, that it is full of very capable managers and researchers, and that if you go into any mobile-phone store across the globe, you will (for now) see more Nokia devices at more price levels than those of any other phone maker.

I have learned that we are standing on a burning platform...

There is intense heat coming from our competitors, more rapidly than we ever expected. Apple disrupted the market by redefining the smart phone and attracting developers to a closed, but very powerful ecosystem...

In about two years, Android created a platform that attracts application developers, service providers, and hardware manufacturers. Android came in at the high-end, they are now winning the mid-range, and quickly they are going downstream to phones under €100. Google has become a gravitational force, drawing much of the industry's innovation to its core...

In 2008, MediaTek supplied complete reference designs for phone chipsets, which enabled manufacturers in the Shenzhen region of China to produce phones at an unbelievable pace. By some accounts, this ecosystem now produces more than one third of the phones sold globally—taking share from us in emerging markets...

We fell behind, we missed big trends, and we lost time. At that time, we thought we were making the right decisions; but, with the benefit of hindsight, we now find ourselves years behind...

At the lower-end price range, Chinese OEMs are cranking out a device much faster than, as one Nokia employee said only partially in jest, "the time that it takes us to polish a PowerPoint presentation." They are fast, they are cheap, and they are challenging us...

The battle of devices has now become a war of ecosystems, where ecosystems include not only the hardware and software of the device, but developers, applications, ecommerce, advertising, search, social applications, location-based services, unified communications, and many other things. Our competitors aren't taking our market share with devices; they are taking our market share with an entire ecosystem. This means we're going to have to decide how we either build, catalyse or join an ecosystem...

We poured gasoline on our own burning platform. I believe we have lacked accountability and leadership to align and direct the company through these disruptive times. We had a series of misses. We haven't been delivering innovation fast enough. We're not collaborating internally.[27]

The old question about why bad things happen to good people can be recast as why do bad things happen to good companies? Because...hopefully, your own firm will not be issuing a statement containing any of the paragraphs above during the coming years.

Addendum: Customer Led Is Not Customer Nice

A core theme throughout *The Value Path* is that effective value architectures must be customer led. "Customer led" does not necessarily mean "customer nice": the often fuzzy lyricism in your bank's TV ads about "you have a friend at XYZ" or "we care" (bring up music) or tricks to ensure customer "delight" through eye contact, smiles, and attitude. Obviously, customers respond to good service, helpfulness, knowledge, and expertise. Equally obviously, anything that contributes to customer satisfaction adds a dimension of value to the product or service being offered.

That said, the issue runs much deeper. It's vital as part of truly fresh thinking to ask, "What is it that our customers really, really value in our offers, and what new choices can we create for them that they will really, really, *really* value over and above those from competitors that can't match the difference?"

Below is a short vignette that illustrates the point. On the surface, it seems unlikely that the company described can be even a marginal success; its service is intentionally abominable. In actuality, it dominates Europe's airlines in terms of company value, investor value—and value for customers, as expressed by their decision to pick the airline in growing numbers.

Ryanair is Europe's largest carrier, with 750 routes across Europe. Its average fare in 2011 was $56, with frequent bargains of under $10 for travel between two countries. It has no presence in the major hubs, such as Heathrow and Frankfurt. A competitor dismissed its use of obscure airports remote from large cities as "from nowhere to nowhere."

Yet it was one of the very few profitable airlines worldwide in 2008, despite a 13 percent reduction in prices. Its 2009 passenger growth was about 11 percent, versus a total decline for the industry of 9 percent. In 2011, it reported $800 million in profits in a year when fuel costs were at a peak. Its operating margins are 22 percent; those for Southwest Airlines, consistently the most profitable and cost-efficient US carrier, are 8 percent. The stated Ryanair approach is "to subcontract everything."

Many of Ryanair's operational capabilities were modeled on Southwest, especially its reliance on a single type of aircraft, the Boeing 737, to minimize maintenance and inventory and standardize airport and cabin processes. One aspect of Southwest that Ryanair definitely did not adopt is customer friendliness. *The Economist* magazine described it in mid-2009 as "a byword for appalling customer service, misleading advertising claims, and jeering rudeness toward anyone or anything that gets in its way."

It gained attention in the United States when it announced that it planned to charge for use of the toilet on flights. Its CEO personally imposed a fifty-cent "levy" on disabled passengers in wheelchairs after the airline lost a court case for charging an extra $30 for a traveler with cerebral palsy.

Ryanair charges almost as much for a checked bag as for the plane ticket, and imposes an on-the-spot $50 fine on anyone trying to bring "too much stuff" on in their cabin bag. It plans to have passengers carry their own bags to the plane. Horror stories are commonplace, such as the fifty-one people trapped in a French airport when their Ryanair flight was cancelled. The next one was not for ten days, and they were left entirely on their own. They had to hire a bus to travel the six hundred miles home;.the cost was $150 each. Many of the tickets for the flight itself had cost just $7.

Ryanair treats staff along the same lines, banning employees from recharging their mobile phones at work, since this is theft of company electricity (the annual savings added up to an estimated $26.80), and requiring pilots and crew to buy their own uniforms and pay for their own meals and even for their training on new planes. Pilot job applicants pay $80 upfront for an interview and $350 for a test in a flight simulator.

Ryanair's chief executive, Michael O'Leary, has made his personality the company's public image. Like Herb Kelleher, founder of Southwest, O'Leary dresses up for publicity, appearing as the pope to promote a new route between Dublin and Rome. (His mother wouldn't speak to him for months.) He plays up his raunchy, abusive, and aggressive persona, which is not at all a front; this is how Ryanair operates. Here are extracts from interviews (the printable parts, anyway):

"Will we give you a refund on a nonrefundable ticket because your granny dies unexpectedly? No! Go away. We're not interested in your sob stories. What part of 'no refund' do you not understand? You're not getting a refund so f--- off."[28]

"A plane is nothing more than a bus with wings on."[29]

"Our customer service is unlike every other airline, which has this image of, 'We want to fall down at your feet and you can walk all over us and the customer is always right' and all that nonsense."

"You could have airplanes with no seats, in ten years' time. Why do you have to sit down?"[30]

European Union commissioners are "morons," airport operators "overcharging rapists," and travel agents "f----rs" who "should be taken out and shot."[31] As for environmentalists: "can't add 2+2"; airline executives: "cloud bunnies," "aerosexuals," and "platoons of goons"; the then British Prime Minister: "a twit" and "a Scottish miser"; British Airways: "rubbish."

The *New York Times* summarized O'Leary's thinking as "an implacable belief that short-haul airline passengers will endure nearly every imaginable indignity, as long as the tickets are cheap and the planes are on time."[32] He clearly revels in the media coverage of his latest outrage and the many blogs that provide story after story of customer abuse.

His comments on his proposal to charge "discretionary toilet users" $1.50 include the hope that this will discourage use entirely so he can reduce the number of bathrooms to one per plane and add more seats. Asked how the airline would handle a passenger needing to get to the toilet because of an emergency such as food poisoning, he commented that Ryanair doesn't serve enough food for this to happen.

A reporter defined Ryanair's airport service: "Nobody helps you—it's as simple as that." O'Leary wants to charge fat people more for their ticket, but says it would take too long to weigh them at the airport. In late 2009, Ryanair removed all check-in at airport desks; passengers must get their boarding pass online. In 2011, it took an Italian judge to block it from charging a child traveling alone $40 because he did not bring his printed boarding pass. The court described this as "abusive behavior."

Yet this is by far the most successful and largest airline in Europe, and it is continuing to grow in an industry that has always been on the verge of financial disaster and/or heavily subsidized and protected by national governments. It has ordered three hundred new airplanes since the terrorist attacks of 9/11. This will bring its fleet capacity up to six hundred. (Southwest Airline has around five hundred.) Ryanair's CFO commented, "We really love a recession because it clears out a lot of the dead wood and it focuses consumers on price."

THE VALUE PATH

Can this really be a viable *value* architecture? It is actually a clever one and looks more and more robust as major carriers struggle and fail to steer away from bankruptcy. They have largely lost their identity. O'Leary argues that the forces of deregulation are driving the industry into a commoditization that is not at all cyclical; most other carriers are taking the opposite viewpoint and trying to hold on until good times return. He views deregulation as now the norm and states that the cost structures of airlines cannot in the future support high prices or expensive services.

By pushing his own costs down, O'Leary is aggressively aiming to make things worse for competitors until most of them are no longer financially viable. Many of his most outrageous comments seem aimed at making Ryanair's identity absolutely clear and clarifying expectations. He offers customers three dimensions of value: the lowest fares, fewest flight cancellations, and fewest lost bags. That's it: the value identity and the branded customer experience.

When British Airways ended its serving of canapés (a euphemism for nibbles that come in the same taste but different colors) with business-class lunch, cut out meals on flights under two hours, and started charging for transporting golf bags and skis, it got bad press and unhappy passengers. Ryanair never offered these in the first place. BA has been caught in a blurred identity that is service-ish, low-price-ish, high-price-ish, upmarket-ish, and tourist-ish.

At its peak in the early 1990s, BA was one of the dominant world players and positioned to be among the four to six "megacarriers" expected to survive industry shakeout and consolidation. It had the best global hub-and-spoke route structure, a strong brand for its corporate Club Europe and Club World "front cabin" business class, effective control of Heathrow airport, the major international hub for long-haul traffic, and industry-leading technology systems. Its premium business- and first-class seats funded the marginally profitable "back of the bus" economy fares and for a while helped BA keep, if not close to, then at least from not falling further behind the low-price carriers in revenue growth, though not in profits.

Once full-fare business-class bookings declined, this artificial subsidy became a liability. In late 2010, Ryanair's average fare was less than BA's fuel surcharge added to each ticket. BA is out of the game now with no narrative for value creation, a costly value engine, and no opportunity platform.

It is always entertaining to read the lyrical excoriations of Ryanair on one of the many websites devoted to it (Ihateryanair and Ryanairsucks, for instance) with such stories as the passenger allegedly arrested for refusing to pay for a sandwich. There are many of us who would endure two hours of forced listening to, say, Celine Dion ululating that song from Titanic at full foghorn level, rather than travel with "that bunch of filthy thieving bastards." That last comment led Ryanair to successfully sue to close down the Ihateryanair site as "highly disparaging."[33]

But in July 2011, the airline carried eight million passengers, breaking its own record for any international carrier. It is the airline of *choice*. No other airline has come close to matching the price dimension of customer value or so superbly managed its costs—on behalf of the customer. It is always ahead of the pack, and for all its notoriety is customer led in its expansion: a better price, a broader route structure, and newer planes.

Reality rules: customers define value through their choices.

4 Anomalies and Archetypes: Your Best Alerts

Anomalies: Something's Happening

The evolution of management thought has always been driven by anomalies. These are firms that are out of step with some commonsense "of course" assumptions about business. Many are also out in the clichéd "left field" and destined for merited oblivion. But occasionally an anomaly introduces some far-reaching innovation that creates a new value path for itself and shapes what other companies come to recognize as a general base for the next standard best practice. These are the alerts that help provide an innovation edge by shifting perspectives on the next "obvious."

Examples include General Motors' invention of the divisional organizational structure and SBUs (strategic business units), the base for the modern multinational and diversified business; Delta's creation of the hub-and-spoke airline system that was extended by FedEx to become the foundation of modern logistics; Toyota's pioneering of just-in-time inventory and total quality management that drove US and European manufacturing to make a sustained refocusing of just about every element of process management; Wal-Mart's store replenishment that redefined cost and service coordination; and Dell's global supply chain integration that drove a new level of capital efficiency and overhead reduction in manufacturing and logistics that has eliminated about 40 percent of working capital tied up in inventory management in US GDP.

There really is a before Toyota and after Toyota watershed, and the value architecture principles of Wal-Mart replaced those of Sears and Kmart as the shaper of modern discount retailing, irreversibly and expansively. For well over ten years, many airlines' business-model shifts might well have been titled, "Southwest sideswiped us so we have to go the discount route, too." To that might be added, *sotto voce* (meaning: don't admit this anywhere in the annual report), "We really should have seen this coming much earlier than we did."

It's fair to counter that there had been plenty of other almost literally fly-by-night discount airlines that did not survive. The most famous was Laker Airways, which broke open the transatlantic flight oligopoly in the 1980s. Laker created a value narrative that generated rapid success, but it could not build an effective architecture to provide scale of operations and global extension of routes. It lacked the opportunity platform to go beyond price discounting. Bankruptcy followed fast. Laker turned out to be just an exotic, headline-grabbing nose thumbing at the airline establishment business culture.

This chapter aims to help managers sort out the Southwests from the Lakers, the Amazons from the dot-com boom and busts, and the one-season phenoms from the Hall of Famers. The logic is simple. The four Value Realities mean that the external forces of change will lead to disturbances that open up new choice spaces. Some firm, sometime, somewhere, is going to spot an opportunity here. As the forces accelerate, which they clearly have been doing in the past few years, there will be a flurry of new players, most of which are unlikely to get off the ground.

A few will become ultrasuccesses; there will be alerts here about value shifts (Reality 1) and new choice spaces (Reality 2). The anomalies that sustain value will show distinctive trends in their resourcing of capabilities, creating new forms of ecocomplex and asset deployment (Reality 3). Some will get stuck and fade, but a few will add compelling new dimensions of value to their offers or enhance how they deliver existing ones (Reality 4). This is happening across the business landscape. That makes today's anomalies the seed for tomorrow's best practices and thus for your own innovation agenda.

Which of today's ultrasuccesses are alerts to distinctly new principles for *any* firm's value architecture design, as contrasted to evolutionary extensions—and why? It's useful here to distinguish archetypes from anomalies. Anomalies are news. Archetypes are guides and potential models.

An archetype is defined in a range of fields as a generic version of a personality or pattern of behavior that provides a prototype for emulation or direct copying. GM was archetypical for multinational organizational design beyond the car industry and Toyota for process integration in any business.

Many ultrasuccesses are not archetypical in this regard. Starbucks, for example, stands out as one of the most successful companies in the world, and it has transformed the routines of everyday life through the globalization of caffeine. It demonstrated the extent to which a commodity product of notorious taste and quality in the United States could be transformed into a premium branded customer experience. But it did not become a generic blueprint or model for innovation.

Many other ultrasuccesses stand out as one-time innovators, as contrasted with innovation being embedded in the fabric of the firm. They moved in surges, often marked by discrete products and dates. Microsoft and Sony can be paired here. They stand out for their blockbuster product breakthroughs: Windows, Office, Explorer, and

Kinect from Microsoft, and Triniton, Walkman, Betacam, and PlayStation from Sony.

Such firms are unlikely to become archetypes because they rely fairly heavily on preemptive strikes that few firms can ever expect to match. They are in effect playing the odds: betting on a few big bets to generate a high enough payoff to offset their failures.

They are able in the short term to compensate for or hide weaknesses that later catch up with them and show that they were definitively not archetypes of future best practices. Microsoft and Sony stand out now more for their innovation weaknesses than their invention strengths. Microsoft has a consistent record of being late to the next value opportunity and is not exactly noted for being customer-centric. Sony put together great technical teams but couldn't build a coordination capability.

It is always risky to generalize from single instances such as these and, of course, the business trade press is full of hype about individual ultrasuccesses as the Next Big Thing. The catch is that managers really do need to track the single instances to avoid being taken unaware; at the least, these instances show that some major new avenue for innovation has been opened up. Anomalies are your best alerts in this regard. The ones that show staying power need continued watching; they show that the path is one that many companies will start following.

Archetypes: Anomalies That Are Part of a Pattern

The translation from alerts and singularity to archetypes and innovation opportunities involves three tests of relevance.

1. Created an ultrasuccess through a value architecture shift:
- The firm made a leap that moved it way outside the bounds of today's best practice and achieved a dramatic level of value creation.
- The jump and its impact can be directly traced back to the forces of disturbance as the trigger and enabler.
- The ultrasuccess is explained in terms of value architecture rather than some quasi-magic ingredient (e.g., Steve Jobs' personality) or situational factor that may be unique (e.g., reliance on a single key patent as the foundation of growth).

2. Sustained and extended the value:
- The ultrasuccess turned the growth into sustained value generation for customers, itself, and its ecocomplex partners.
- It has shown the ability to make an effective change of course to exploit new opportunities or ward off threats, which

demonstrates that its value architecture enables adaptation and flexibility.

3. *Shaped a pattern*:
- Other anomalies in other choice spaces suggest that this ultrasuccess is part of a general pattern of innovation.

The logic of this filtering is fairly simple and aimed at insight rather than didactic conclusions. Creating an ultrasuccess makes news: something is happening here that's worth looking into. If it's mostly explained by, say, the force of personality of a genius entrepreneur who may or may not be able to build a solid business or a new growth opportunity opened up by some situational, political, financial, or seasonal factor, it's still news but unlikely to be replicable.

If, on the other hand, the ultrasuccess is successfully challenging a long-held business practice, and its moves can be logically traced to the forces of disturbance, then its jump shift is worth further study. Wal-Mart provides an example. Instead of money-off promotions, then the heart of the discount retail business, Wal-Mart offered everyday low prices (EDLP) for branded merchandise. EDLP was Wal-Mart's compelling new dimension, and it is noteworthy that its efforts to recover its growth surge are built on restoring this as the company mantra and focus of its renewed value narrative.

On the surface, the Wal-Mart move could be seen as just a matter of pricing strategy. Even today it is an option, not a necessity. There are many studies of what type of shopper responds to EDLP versus Hi-Lo promos, a strategy that produces most revenue increase and/or is more profitable depending on product costs and how expensive it is to move from one pricing policy to the other.

What the growth of Wal-Mart pointed to went beyond EDLP as a business model. It pointed to a need to really understand the massive untapped opportunity to attract customers and the equally massive challenge of rethinking every aspect of fixed versus variable costs, inventory management, store operations, and geographic expansion.

Leading companies such as Sears were living on their past and using Hi-Lo to optimize their own margins and supply chain, but not building customer confidence that they were getting the best deal. Others were using it to compensate for deficiencies in their operations, getting customers to pay extra for their inefficiencies. The visible value narrative shift that marked Wal-Mart's market identity signaled a value engine shift, too. Its growing integration of key processes, supply chain and store operations, and dimensions of customer service was in turn an alert that Wal-Mart was managing growth and expansion in a different way.

As observers drilled on down, new signals started to pulse, though some competitors screened them out as noise and kept their eyes firmly on the road ahead. Wal-Mart was intercepting and pushing the technology envelope, from satellite communications to point-of-sale systems to EDI and cross docking, to implement its vision of a much more responsive, low-cost supply chain. It could offer lower prices because it lowered its costs. Lower costs and lower prices meant it could grow much faster and much larger.

Again, it wasn't the technology that constituted the business alert. Kmart was ahead of Wal-Mart in many areas, and Sears was the exemplar of telecommunications management in retailing. The real message was, of course, that how a company targeted, deployed, integrated, and extended its technology resources provided a new base for creating value for customers, making profits, and growing the business.

Sustaining value in this way goes beyond news. It shows that the "something" happening is a foundation both for the long term and for going beyond dependence on the forces and factors that created the initial ultrasuccess. First, it passes a test that many growth firms fail: balancing customer value, mainly indicated by revenues; company value, which has many metrics, such as profitability, capital efficiency, and returns to investors; and ecocomplex partner value, indicated by mutual benefit from each other's success.

The initial surge of success may become old news. But when such a firm shows that it continues to adapt and transform so it can continue to grow and maintain its value balance, it becomes a likely archetype. It shows that it assumes the forces will continue to evolve, and it builds into its value architecture the ability to respond to these forces through tough as well as good times. It positions itself to be effective in adding new offers and dimensions of value. Such a company passes the archetype test. Wal-Mart is obviously such an exemplar.

The final test of an archetype for innovation is the extent to which the firm becomes part of shaping a pattern, rather than just a single instance. The shaping of a pattern indicates that the forces of disturbance are stimulating some common new perspective on innovation and that ultrasuccesses across a range of choice spaces are making the same jump-shift moves. For instance, there is more commonality between Amazon and Airtel, the Indian telecom company we will discuss shortly, with regard to pricing philosophy, cost management, asset ownership, and their branded customer experiences than there is between Amazon and Best Buy or between Airtel and AT&T.

When ultrafades get stuck in their hitherto successful patterns and are unable to make the same moves, then it is apparent that a new business-as-usual is being shaped and that it will directly affect your own innovation opportunities; the earlier you take advantage of lessons from the new archetypes, the less likely it is you will have to react defensively when they become the norm.

There is no reason to dismiss the ultrafades as irrelevant failures. They often sharpen the archetypal messages. When patterns continue to emerge from their own and related firms' success, then the fade can stand out like a stain on the wallpaper. It's worth asking how it got there, but it doesn't change the pattern. Dell moved from ultrasuccess to fade but leaves behind many lessons about capital efficiency, demand and supply synchronization, and ecocomplex relationships. The blot on the patterned wall provides extra lessons about the critical need to accommodate shifts in customer value dimensions and avoid being locked in through fixed assets or locked out through inattention to dimensions of design as dimensions of customer value.

Figure 4.1 summarizes the logic of the sequence from *scanning* to discover the archetypes that are alerts, to *interpreting* what they imply for both shifts in the business landscape of choice spaces and opportunities and *exploiting* the lessons and insights to motivate and guide the firm's innovation agenda.

This adds up to innovating in how you innovate. This is not just a play on words. Consider the firm that skips attention to the Scan and Interpret stages; it still has its innovation agenda, but that agenda is mostly defined within current bounds of industry, best practices, and value dimensions. This is how the Asset, Commodity, and Invention Traps pull companies down.

It's the newspaper and music businesses innovating in their Internet initiatives without recognizing that Amazon, Apple, Facebook, and Google were making that innovation noninnovative; they didn't adjust to the opportunities and challenges of digital modularity, variety of modes of convenience, easy and mobile access, and branding of the experience rather than the content.

The company that does include the Interpret stage but still skips Scan moves responsively to innovate on the basis of what it learns from the pacesetters, but in general it is reacting to the emerging obvious. This is the Toyota syndrome in the 1980s and Apple in recent years.

TQM had been growing in impact and scope, and Japanese car exports increased globally for several decades before the tectonic shifts that pushed, first, automakers and then manufacturers in general to rush to adopt Toyota as an archetype and even try to clone

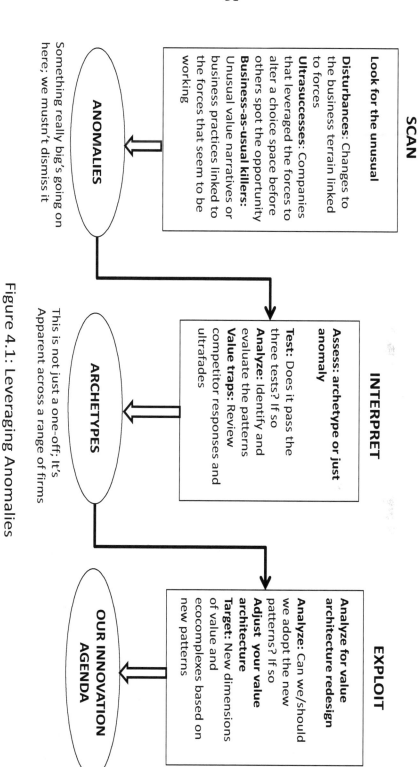

SCAN

Look for the unusual

Disturbances: Changes to the business terrain linked to forces

Ultrasuccesses: Companies that leveraged the forces to alter a choice space before others spot the opportunity

Business-as-usual killers: Unusual value narratives or business practices linked to the forces that seem to be working

ANOMALIES

Something really big's going on here; we mustn't dismiss it

INTERPRET

Assess: archetype or just anomaly

Test: Does it pass the three tests? If so

Analyze: Identify and evaluate the patterns

Value traps: Review competitor responses and ultrafades

ARCHETYPES

This is not just a one-off; It's Apparent across a range of firms

EXPLOIT

Analyze for value architecture redesign

Analyze: Can we/should we adopt the new patterns? If so

Adjust your value architecture

Target: New dimensions of value and ecocomplexes based on new patterns

OUR INNOVATION AGENDA

Figure 4.1: Leveraging Anomalies

its processes and management principles. They were largely too late and in a weary catch-up mode.

Apple had shown thirty years ago that its designs were almost always superior and elegant. Its Apple II remains one of the most outstanding fusions of form and function ever. (The Apple III is one of the "not exactly good" designs. The disk slots did melt and the chips got dislodged by all the overheating, but if you picked it up just six inches and dropped it, they usually reseated themselves.)

But design excellence didn't help Apple beat out Microsoft in PCs or compensate for its high prices, weak supply chain, and inattention to the corporate market. It was only when Apple began to pay attention to the supply chain archetypes and combined customer-grabbing design with integration of services that it became the archetype for the entire mobile choice space. It's now the True North compass setting that all other players have to steer by.

Many companies are doing well with regard to their product design features. The days of clunky phones are way past, and HTC, Samsung, and Motorola products show their recognition that new function—invention—relies on new form for them to meet the Realities of customer value. That same lesson is now being rapidly applied in the semi-clunky laptop and notebook computer choice space, with Apple's Air the reference point. Vizio, the TV maker that has had no presence in the PC market, is targeting Apple with designs that "try to avoid the industrial look."[34]

It may seem surprising that the initial reaction to the iPhone in Japan was that it was a clunky design and too slow. It took off more on fashion and "must own" status than its product features. Japan is way, way ahead of the United States and Europe in mobile technology; everything about value is comparative. The iPhone design that was advanced in the United States was ho-hum in the Japanese market.

Dell's designs became ho-hum across the consumer choice space in general. How different might its fortunes have been if the archetype in supply chain had paid more attention to the archetype in design, Apple. The problem is that design without integration of services leaves many competitors headed for the commodity trap. And those like Research in Motion (RIM) and Nokia that tried their own version of services integration have found themselves late to the game.

The problem here is that once the archetype is apparent, it's very hard to do more than match it. While another firm is innovating in response, it is doing so in someone else's established area of successful and proven innovation. It may not be too late, but it is unlikely to preempt the preemptor.

So, for instance, Nokia's and Microsoft's Lumia phone, launched at the start of 2012 specifically as a go-for-broke challenge to Apple and Android, looks stylish. It is described by Windows enthusiasts as a "hot device" and "might be just the phone to win over consumers."[35] Whether or not it does so, it's a catch-up and emulation move, rather than the result of innovators who got the Apple message years ago and used it as the base to add their own distinctive strengths.

Your own firm's sphere of innovation opportunity depends how widely you have set your alerts, how shrewdly you tease out the archetypal implications, and how rapidly and effectively you incorporate them into your value architecture. This line of sense making aims at making the best use of anomalies as alerts without misusing them to make unsupportable generalizations.

We illustrate this in the next chapters of *The Value Path* through an analysis of three very different firms that meet the three tests of (1) creating an ultrasuccess, (2) sustaining the value, and (3) shaping a pattern. These are Bharti Airtel (mobile phone services, India), Tesco (supermarkets, United Kingdom) and Google (Internet search, US-based). Different sectors, different offers, different markets, different strategies—these three companies could hardly be more dissimilar. But together they are clearly archetypal for the new generation of value architectures that have a fighting chance of both creating and sustaining success and carrying it forward into shifting markets, customers, and competitors.

5 Bharti Airtel: Owns Little, Earns Plenty

Bharti Airtel is a mobile-phone service provider, one of fifteen in India. It is part of the Bharti Group, one of the many conglomerates that are the hallmark of Indian business. It competes in a commodity market and generates less than five dollars of monthly revenue per customer, under one-tenth that of comparable US and European firms.[36] (Bharti is the name of the conglomerate of which Airtel was a subsidiary until its IPO in 2002. Airtel is its brand for its telecommunication products, services, and distribution.)

Prices drop almost by the month and have been around or below one cent per minute for several years. (The comparable average rate in the United States is somewhere north of five cents per voice minute. Because of the complexity of prepaid plans and customers paying for both incoming and outgoing minutes, the figure could easily be higher than fifteen cents.)

Airtel serves about four hundred thousand villages, two-thirds of the estimated Indian total.[37] It's perhaps possible to find a worse market to target, though hard to imagine an approach to entering it that seems less likely to succeed. The ex-minister of telecommunications is currently awaiting trial on bribery charges for the 2007–08 auction for licenses to operate in a part of the radio spectrum; the estimate of the fraud, $37 billion, which is roughly the same amount as the national defense budget, is probably just a little exaggerated.[38] Or maybe not. About a quarter of all elected members of the national Parliament are under indictment, including for arson, rape, murder, and corruption. (This is such a comforting contrast to the US House of Representatives. Or maybe not.)

This is not quite the environment that seems likely to have launched one of the most successful, admired, innovative, and well-managed mobile-service providers in the world. The driver of its opportunity was deregulation. But that was open to all players, most of them far better positioned than Bharti in terms of industry presence, resources, experience, and scale.

India has selectively opened up its markets and deregulated some industries, making practical Bharti's move from phone-equipment manufacturing to mobile services when the sector was opened up to competition in 1995. Many barriers to business expansion still remain; for instance, carriers are not permitted to consolidate, even though many industry players are losing money as fast as they launch even more price wars.

Bharti Airtel was undercapitalized in a capital-intensive industry, operating in a country where total direct foreign investment in telecommunications was just about $3.5 billion in

1997 and dropped to just over $2 billion by 1999.[39] It had no network infrastructure, no cell towers into all those target villages, no distribution system, and no customer-service base. It faced a large competitor, the government-owned BSNL, which even when the mobile market began to take off, maintained a subscriber base four times that of Bharti as late as 2005.

Now, of course, Airtel is in the same league as Starbucks as an innovator that created an entirely new value space out of a commodity. It turned every one of the disadvantages listed in the previous paragraphs into opportunities. The "of course" reflects the degree to which its value architecture is archetypal, not exceptional, as a blueprint for ultrasuccess. It corresponds fairly closely in its basics to Amazon and hardly at all to most telecommunications service providers.

Airtel built on its founder's success in manufacturing phone equipment; Bharti was the first domestic company to produce push-button phones, fax machines, and cordless phones. This body of experience qualified it as having the required telecommunications expertise to bid in the auction of licenses for cellular phones. Many potential bidders were scared away by market forecasts that, for instance, the total sales potential for Delhi was only 5,000 phones. That figure seems laughable when it took Airtel less than fourteen years to build a subscriber base of 100 million, and it was adding 8 million new customers a quarter in India, reaching the 177 million mark there and 243 million worldwide by the end of 2011.

Today, the growth opportunity of the Indian market is obvious. It wasn't at all so when deregulation largely limped into reality. This came after twenty years of jostling, entrenched positions, alliances, and "veto moves" among government and opposition parties, labor unions, and financial regulators. This was deregulation as usual, in all its messy, often tawdry, self-interest and always unresolved turmoil.

Bharti Airtel was seen as a marginal start-up player, and its intended foreign partner pulled out of its agreement. The Indian cellular phone market was slow to grow, and by the late 1990s, many of the thirty operators, each of which covered one or more "circles" of the nation's geography, were struggling. Bharti was one of the few profitable ones (reaching breakeven in 1998) with 56 percent of the then small Delhi market.[40]

Bharti Airtel chose to buy licenses in poor rural areas, instead of just the more affluent cities. The deregulation divided the country into circles roughly based on state boundaries. The circles had been designed to ensure that bidders on the cellular licenses could not "cherry-pick" only the markets with highest income and growth potential.

Bharti Airtel targeted the mainly rural "C" circles as its opportunity, despite the heavy infrastructure investment costs, especially for towers, the low population density, and the lack of even a few cents of disposable income for almost all the population. While projected to grow to $10,000 by 2039, India's per-capita income was $1,000 in 2011—just under $3 a *day*.[41] This is Airtel's primary customer base.

Now, more and more companies are copying its rural strategy. Meanwhile, Airtel is expanding into IT services for small and medium-sized companies, fiber-optic landlines, and international markets. It is moving to become a global player. It launched a move it was twice unable to consummate: a merger with South Africa's MTN in 2008–09 (MTN had close to 100 million subscribers), apparently due to the SA government being unwilling to put its weight behind the deal.[42] This did not impede its expansion, and by 2010 it was operating in nineteen countries.

In 2010, Airtel increased its stake in the fourth-largest mobile-services firm in Bangladesh, with 2.9 million customers. Its Global Wholesale Service network already reaches fifty countries. Its acquisition of Zain Africa, a company that owns mobile-service providers across Africa, is a go-for-broke claim to a position as a global megaplayer.

Airtel did not succeed by luck, riding the tide of deregulation, or muddling through. It architected its way to value. Its strategy for growth was summarized in a short presentation by its CEO in 2008:[43]

When we started our journey in the sector in 1995, we knew that we needed deep pockets for this industry. The telecom sector demands a huge amount of funding, billions and billions of dollars. We also knew that Indian customers would need to be serviced with low prices, very affordable prices...Now, these two things don't connect with each other. On one hand, we invest billions of dollars. On the other hand, we sell at very low prices.

So we thought to ourselves, how do we get over this? If we are to succeed in this sector, then let's create a new paradigm. Let's create a new business model. [Note: We would state this as "Let's redefine our value architecture."] On December 6, 2002, we had a meeting in Jaipur during which we decided that if we had to offer the lowest prices in the world, then we needed to have the lowest cost in the world. There was no choice... We initiated a huge, five-part outsourcing strategy.

Every single one of these five elements of sourcing is foundational, not secondary, for Airtel's value architecture and directly contrasts to that of just about all the major established carriers across the world. The use of relationships instead of assets and ecocomplex instead of value-chain vertical integration covers every area of operations and development.

- *Outsourcing the "entire" network* to Ericsson and Nokia: "It was the first time in the world and it took about six to eight months to convince [Nokia's top management]." Airtel buys capacity from them on a just-in-time basis as needed to meet traffic demands, rather than purchasing "black boxes." The vendors build out the network, Airtel buys the capacity only when it has customers ready to use it, and then Ericsson and Nokia operate and maintain the network.

- *Information technology*: "We knew IT was something that we didn't understand. We are not an IT company; we are a consumer company. Let's not try to do something that we don't know." The firm made an agreement with IBM that is revenue-based: IBM gets a share of Airtel's "top line" and has every incentive to maximize its contribution to Airtel's growth and control its own costs. If IBM can do the job cheaper, it gains the benefits of reduced cost and improved efficiency. Equally, if it makes investments that help add to Airtel's own revenues, IBM also benefits from this as an investment, not an expenditure.

- *Call centers*: "Now, how do we cope with it? We aren't call center experts. We went to the world's best call centers— fortunately, those BPO [business process outsourcing] companies are in India—and we outsourced to [them]."

- *Cell relay towers*: "We built passive infrastructures. We have about 80,000 to 85,000 towers in the country and we'll build many more in future. So we thought, why don't we share this infrastructure, rather than having every operator building a separate tower for itself, investing so much of resources—steel, cement, and so on. [The average cost was around $100,000]. Why don't we have three operators on the same tower and share the cost one-third each?" Airtel sold its tower company in 2007 for $1.8 billion.

- *Distribution*: "We knew we couldn't develop distribution in India. For example, today we cover 5,000 towns and 400,000 villages, and we can't establish showrooms and shops in all of them. So we said, okay, let's outsource to local entrepreneurs, guys who know the people locally..."

He summarized the choice between owning and partnering its development of capabilities: "Overall, what we have done...is outsource all expertise areas to people who are better than us. And we don't mind saying it. They are better than us...Our core competence is customer management. Brand is so important for us. We don't outsource that. People management and motivation of our people, that's our job. Financing is our job. And, finally, regulation management is our job...Everything else is done by our strategic partners, who have better domain knowledge, skills, and capabilities to help us."

In conjunction with its strategy, Airtel changed its metrics at the end of 2002.[44] Until that time it had measured success by the standard industry metric of growth in average revenue per user (ARPU). It realized that in its low-price market, ARPU was counterproductive; it emphasized gross sales at the expense of capital efficiency and cost. It moved to a focus on per-minute margins instead, with a performance dashboard made up of three graphs that measured gross revenue, operating expense to gross revenue (operating efficiency), and revenue to capital expenditures (capital productivity).

The contracts for each of the outsourcing arrangements were made under a set of principles that ensured the situation was win-win for Airtel and the outsourcing partner, that there was "skin in the game" for all players, and that the partners were incentivized to come up with new products and services. In addition, the contracts were written to support the objective of driving down the cost of the network and improving capital productivity.

Airtel moved its value architecture from a capital-intensive to variable-cost foundation and expansion. By paying Ericsson and Nokia only when the capacity is used, it avoids the traditional 30–40 percent excess capacity and related capital telecommunications that telecommunications providers build up as they try to anticipate and smooth service requirements. Airtel pays IBM a percentage of revenue every month with a guaranteed minimum, so there is no upfront capital outlay.

When Airtel contracted with Nortel for the call-center infrastructure, it paid it a monthly price per call, again with no upfront investment, and with a clause that provides a higher rate if the interactive voice response system successfully handled the call and drove down labor costs in the call centers.

"Outsourcing" seems a somewhat feeble and passive term for the creative collaborations and search for ways to build mutually beneficial value in key Airtel relationships. One example is its linking up with IFFCO, India's largest fertilizer cooperative company with fifty-five million farmer members. IFFCO brings presence and credibility with rural farmers, who together speak at least fifteen different major languages and are mostly smallholders. "Communication being the key for empowering farmers, IFFCO decided to join hands with the most admired brand, Airtel."[45] Airtel gains by winning acceptance in the remote villages because IFFCO was already there. The dealers where a farmer buys fertilizer, insecticide, and pesticide are Airtel storefronts, too.

Farmers get half-price calls between members, five free calls a day to obtain information on market prices, fertilizer availability, weather forecasts, and the like, and a free hotline for dealing with health problems in their cattle and husbandry and for other agricultural information content. Airtel strengthened the joint benefits for the ecocomplex value creation by partnering with SKS, India's largest microfinance institution, so that those farmers and others could buy their phones over a twenty-five-month period. This is an example of Airtel using its opportunity platform to add new dimensions of customer value without additional development and investment.

While outsourcing dominates Bharti Airtel's value architecture, this is not an absolute. The objective is not to get rid of activities, but to gain capabilities that will enable Airtel to grow rapidly, provide excellent service, and maximize capital productivity. The asset strategy could be more accurately termed asset-smart than asset-light, since each member of the ecocomplex owns and leverages selective assets focused on a win-win relationship within the ecocomplex. The towers, for example, were managed as a set of relationships where Airtel owned the resource but shared it with competitors and then spun it off as a separate company.

Figure 5.1 captures the key elements of the redesigned value architecture that the executive team created as an outcome of its strategy review in December 2002. What is most apparent is that it was the only sustainable foundation for the company to be able to balance value generation for all stakeholders in its low-cost commodity market.

If it offered low prices without low costs, then the company and investors lost out. If it raised prices in an intensely competitive environment, it would lose customers quickly. If it achieved low costs by squeezing partners, then their incentives to remain part of Airtel's collaborative ecocomplex erode, and eventually there would be no quality relationships left to squeeze.

The sourcing solutions, coupled with effective guiding metrics, not only drive a stronger value engine, but set up an opportunity platform for later expansion as options emerge.

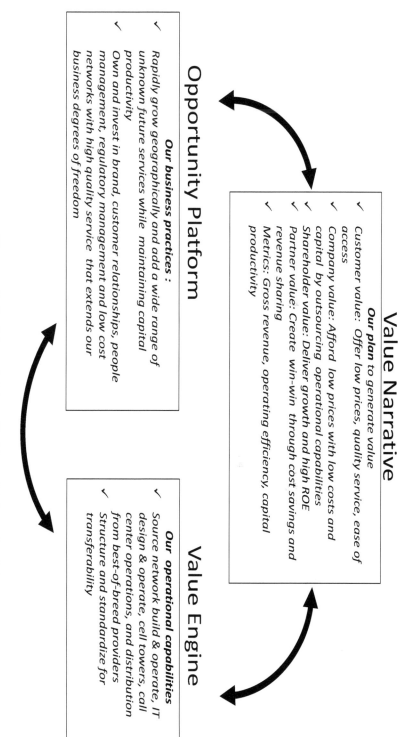

Value Narrative

***Our plan** to generate value*

✓ *Customer value: Offer low prices, quality service, ease of access*

✓ *Company value: Afford low prices with low costs and capital by outsourcing operational capabilities*

✓ *Shareholder value: Deliver growth and high ROE*

✓ *Partner value: Create win-win through cost savings and revenue sharing*

✓ *Metrics: Gross revenue, operating efficiency, capital productivity*

Opportunity Platform

Our business practices :

✓ *Rapidly grow geographically and add a wide range of unknown future services while maintaining capital productivity*

✓ *Own and invest in brand, customer relationships, people management, regulatory management and low cost networks with high quality service that extends our business degrees of freedom*

Value Engine

Our operational capabilities

✓ *Source network build & operate, IT design & operate, cell towers, call center operations, and distribution from best-of-breed providers*

✓ *Structure and standardize for transferability*

Figure 5.1: Bharti Airtel's New Value Architecture

Over the years, Airtel has received multiple and meaningful honors for its quality of service, network coverage, and business innovation, including Service Provider of the Year by Frost & Sullivan Asia Pacific in 2009 and the Telecom Centre of Excellence (TCOE) Award for "Service Provider with Customer Focus for Best Delivery of Network Services for the Year 2011."

What's behind this is more than a few simple and standard dimensions of value such as network quality and coverage. To attract and retain the rural customers who make up 80 percent of Airtel's base, it had to think differently about what value means and how to deliver it. If you've never owned a phone before and live on two dollars a day, the mobile handset, one-cent-a-minute calls, and smooth resolution of any problems you have are really big deals.

Airtel's prepaid card service means not having to make a deposit or pay a rental fee. Customers buy only as much time as they want, when they want it, and without the high premium prices most providers across the world charge for prepaid, which is often the only practical choice for those without credit. They recharge the card at any one of 1.6 million outlets, because Airtel set up a distribution and retail network that leveraged existing local merchants. They check usage on a toll-free number and finance the phone over twenty-five months through an arrangement with SKS microfinance. Most of these dimensions of value are being delivered by Airtel partners, not Airtel directly.

Meanwhile, Airtel has had to think very differently about its higher-income urban customers. It rolled out 3G service across all the Indian circles, the first Indian service provider to do so. It is expanding into such areas as corporate telecommunications services, digital TV, smart phones, and microfinance. Here it is very much moving along the same path as a Verizon or Telefonica.

Airtel: Lowest Prices but Highest Returns on Capital

Airtel's financial performance was stellar in terms of revenues and profits until the past two to three years, which have seen the pressures of commoditization, ferocious competition in a saturating market, and most of all, the challenges of financing its international expansion. In this last area, it may have gone beyond the limits of its value architecture. It has had to add substantial long-term debt, increasing its capital base to finance its international expansion. That stands in strong contrast and added risk to its long record of funding growth via ecocomplex relationships. As one of the leading stock-market barometers in India, it is very sensitive to micro- and macroeconomic fluctuations, especially foreign exchange rates.

Its major move, in 2010, was to buy the African operations of the Kuwaiti telecommunications company, Zain, in a deal valued at $10.7 billion. This added thirty-six million customers and opened up a wide and expansive new opportunity space. India's wireless penetration level is officially 77 percent of the population (although the actual active subscriber penetration is estimated to be closer to 50 percent).[46] Africa's official number is only 40 percent. India's price per minute is less than one cent compared with Africa's average of six cents, and the ARPU is almost double India's.

Africa should be an ideal market for Airtel to work its low-cost magic and export its "minute factory." Clearly, it believes that its value architecture can travel, particularly to other developing countries. The problem is that Africa is not one country. Airtel must deal with sixteen different legal, regulatory, financial, and social systems.

Before the acquisition, Airtel had $14 billion in assets and, for all practical purposes, no debt. After the acquisition, its debt was $12.9 billion with a debt to EBITDA of 2.9. AT&T's ratio is just 1.7. (EBITDA is profit before all the accounting tricks, tax moves, and noncash adjustments; it is a standard measure of short-term operating performance.)

AT&T and Verizon provide a base for financial comparison. The two US firms superficially are much more profitable than Bharti Airtel, by a large factor. They have at least a five-to-one edge on wireless price per minute—five cents in the United States versus one cent in India. According to UBS, the US wireless carriers generated an average revenue per user (ARPU) of $46.01 in the third quarter of 2011, while Airtel's was just $4.10.[47] While Airtel is adding customers at a far faster rate (eight million versus one to two million a quarter) those new customers will generate just $33 million or so of monthly revenue, far less than Verizon and AT&T will gain on a much slower growth rate.

Two numbers that are missing from the comparison, though, shift the profit picture: return on equity (ROE) and return on assets (ROA). Return on equity is generally regarded as the best measure of management efficiency in making use of all the financial resources the firm has built up from its operations. Figures from individual companies in 2009 and 2010 show an astonishing difference across the globe. Bharti's ROE was 31 percent for 2009 and 25 percent for 2010. Its ROA was 12.3 percent and 12.5 percent respectively. The world's leading mobile-service companies are all in the range of 5–15 percent ROE and 3–7 percent ROA.[48] This includes NTT and

DoCoMo in Japan, AT&T, Vodafone, Korea's SK, Verizon, and France Telecom.

Airtel spends less capital and makes double the return of the next best player. Even with cutbacks imposed by the recession, AT&T's and Verizon's capex (capital expenditures) for 2012 were in the range of $15 billion to $18 billion, mainly for investment in broadband networks.[49] Airtel's capex tripled in 2006–07 to $1.7 billion and in 2010 was budgeted at $5 billion. It continues to rely on its strategy of infrastructure sharing and co-sourcing (our term). Bharti's capital efficiency was far higher than AT&T's or Verizon's and that of the mobile and telecommunications industry in general, until its purchase of Zain Africa.

Vodafone is the largest mobile company in the world whose financial statements can be trusted. (Forget about China's light romantic fictions in many state-directed companies' published statements.) It has piled up $235 billion of assets to support its $70 billion of revenues; Bharti's asset base is one-tenth of this, for one-sixth of the revenues.

Telecommunications was always an asset game. It's now a capability game. Verizon and AT&T are earning returns above their cost of capital in their mobile but not their landline business.[50] The two other US service providers, Sprint and T-Mobile, are showing (declining) profits but not positive cost of capital returns; that's rather like earning 8 percent yield on money you invested by borrowing on your credit card at 15 percent—the "profit" is real but this is not exactly a value architecture for the long term.

Some of the leading telecommunications service firms worldwide do not separate fixed-line and wireless financial data, but the overall picture among the main mobile players is consistent. The infrastructure-heavy players don't make returns on assets that a growth industry with high risk must provide to continue to attract investor capital.

Analysts increasingly see the sector as losing its appeal. The older the asset base (France Telecom, NTT, AT&T, Verizon, Telenor), the more the ROA is just 5 percent. There is little difference in value capture for the players that have grown through foreign acquisitions (America Movil, Telefonica, Vodafone) and those that have relied on advanced technology and services for growth (Softbank, DoCoMo, or Korea's SK, which owns Cyworld, the most successful social networking site in the world in terms of the percent of the national population that is actively using it).

What's Next: Keep to the Value Path?

Could Airtel have succeeded by following a different path to value? It is hard to see that it had any chance of challenging the larger and established players through a strategy of vertical integration and capital-intensive fixed-asset investment. Can it sustain its success? It certainly cannot do so by sticking to the path that led to its dominant domestic market position. The dimensions of value are shifting, and customers have a flood of new choices. The major new wave of value creation is in handsets, where domestic Indian firms are looking to outflank the Chinese manufacturers with many adept entrepreneurs copying their low-price products at even lower prices.

The high-end market is growing and following the same pattern as in Japan, the United States, and most of Europe: demand for smart phones, music downloading, text messaging, social networking, and online gaming. The corporate market for mobile services and IT–telecommunications integration is opening up rapidly. Relaxation of government restrictions on mobile VOIP (voice over IP: Internet phone calls) is creating new players and applications.

Airtel could ride along the natural growth curve and stay with what works—until it stops working, which could well be now. There are too many companies chasing too little profit; price wars are everywhere. Airtel's main competitors' profits halved in 2009 when it cut rates down to a flat 1 paise—1.3 cents a minute to call anywhere—to respond to price wars and the coming entry of four new operators. About a dozen new entrants have acquired licenses to operate.

Airtel sustained the lowest prices in the world while returning the highest ROE anywhere. But its price edge is eroding quickly. Investors are concerned that it will be unable to ward off the price cutters, many of whom, as in the airline wars, will surely go bankrupt, but not before they have destabilized the industry, wobbling the balance between company and customer value creation. Airtel is cautiously leading the edging up of prices.

Airtel's value capture rests on maintaining strong cash flows and capital efficiency. The stock market is very alert to its adding balance-sheet risk. When it launched its plan to make a bid for a 49 percent stake in South Africa's MTN, Standard and Poor immediately announced it would review Airtel's debt rating. Analysts generally agreed that the merger made plenty of sense in terms of Airtel's expansion and was a good long-term strategic fit for the firm, but they were concerned about short-term balance-sheet pressure.

Phone calls won't make money for carriers anywhere for much longer. Landline phones are in senescence; in India, the number of mobile phones overtook wired ones in the early 2000s. In Europe or the United States, the teenagers walking along the street glued to their mobile phone are far more likely to be texting than talking. And everywhere in the world, people are paying less money each year for their phone calls.

Skype's 700 million registered users pay nothing to talk to each other via the Internet, including on their smart phone. For, say, two authors and teachers in daily conversation for five years between the United States, Singapore, Mexico, Canada, and the Netherlands, it's hard to see any value dimension the phone companies can offer that makes them a better choice than Skype (though, maybe, frequent-chatter miles?).

In Japan, DoCoMo, one of the three largest mobile carriers in the world in terms of revenues, reported a 15 percent drop in earnings in the first quarter of 2010, attributing the problem to saturation of the market and the aggressive marketing by Softbank, the newest player, whose profits increased by 41 percent and has led in new subscribers for two consecutive years. An investment analyst comments that DoCoMo still dwarfs its rival, but "as a new, hungry company (with an iPhone exclusive under its belt) Softbank is bound to attract subscribers—and there really isn't anyone else to steal them from except DoCoMo" in a saturated market.[51]

This is Airtel's challenge, of course. It can be restated as "there really isn't anyone else to steal them from except Airtel, so let's cut prices even if we go broke doing so." Welcome once again to the Commodity Trap.

Airtel's value architecture has helped it lead in just about all the new markets and to add many dimensions of customer value. The real test will be how well this architecture travels to Africa so that it can return to its high levels of ROA and ROE. Whatever the outcome, no commentators have highlighted a competitor anywhere in the world better positioned than Airtel for global growth.

6 Tesco: Lifetime Loyalty as Platform

Tesco is the world's third-largest retailer, with sales of over $80 billion.[52] Wal-Mart's revenues are more than $400 billion. The US population is, of course, far larger than the UK's: 310 million versus 62 million. Both firms now compete directly, including in the United Kingdom, where Wal-Mart's acquisition of Asda was expected to result in its inevitable dominance. Asda was number three in sales revenues among the UK's four largest supermarket chains, with Tesco the leader. The acquisition was widely expected to move it to first place, especially since it had modeled itself on Wal-Mart's processes and training. A press report summarized the purchase as the "day that many UK supermarket groups had long feared."[53]

But something happened on the way to the future. Basically, Tesco left Asda in its wake. Asda versus Tesco is now very much like Target competing with Wal-Mart: a strong performer whose options are highly responsive to or constrained by what the even stronger rival is doing.

The global superstore industry is dominated by three players: Wal-Mart, Carrefour, and Tesco, with a number of other diversified players such as Metro (Germany) and SPAR (Netherlands). The French-based Carrefour is in second place ($100 billion in a country of sixty-five million) but is falling behind Tesco in growth and profitability. Wal-Mart maintains a 15 percent annual sales increase internationally.

For all three chains, sales in their home country have been flat or eroding for the past two to three years, a combination of economic slump, market maturation, and intense competition. They are superstore-anchored, rather than just superstores, in that they all have expanded across the physical landscape to stock just about every type of product and to add a variety of formats, ranging from Sam's Club warehouses to Tesco's Fresh and Easy express stores.

The three firms are similar in their value engines; all are exemplars of logistics, merchandising, and store operations, and they all offer the same wide variety of consumer goods. They are the pacesetters in Asia, the main center of opportunity. Each has built on the superstore as its magnet for attracting customers and extending its offers.

Wal-Mart began as a discount chain, Tesco as a grocery supermarket, and Carrefour launched the hypermarket: a supermarket, drugstore, discount store, and gas station combined in one location. They differ in their dimensions of customer value and what that has implied in evolving their value architectures. Wal-Mart is noted for Everyday Low Prices as its clarion call. Carrefour states that it "has one simple ambition: making Carrefour the preferred retailer wherever it operates."[54]

The core of Tesco's value architecture is to create value for customers to earn their lifetime loyalty.[55] It's the "lifetime loyalty" phrase that distinguishes Tesco from its competitors and that, not at all coincidentally, enabled it to build a highly successful online grocery business, something no other firm has achieved. Wal-Mart's online business is just 2 percent of its sales[56] (the same proportion as Target's, perhaps its most successful competitor). Carrefour has a long history of failures in its Internet business investments.[57]

Tesco built on the store, but its opportunity platform has enabled it to go well beyond its bounds. Carrefour is in disarray and at the end of 2011 gave up on its $1.5 billion Carrefour Planet "hypermarket revamp"[58] aimed at stemming the loss of customers to specialty stores in "dire economic times." Analysts see few opportunities for it beyond a price war.

Wal-Mart and Tesco have also seen an erosion of sales in their stores; Wal-Mart's revenues dropped for nine consecutive quarters in the key industry metric of same-store sales, before improving toward the end of 2011. Its executives admitted that the firm deviated too far from its core driver of low prices and reestablished this as its priority.[59]

Tesco lost market share, albeit by less than 1 percent, in the same year. (It maintains its 30 percent position, with Asda and Sainsbury at 17 percent each.) Competitors targeted price cuts as their weapon for getting through the recession. Asda is relying on a guarantee of "a 10 percent cheaper" price for groceries as its best competitive option. This hasn't been entirely unsuccessful in the short term, though its market share dropped five months in a row from December 2011.[60] Tesco's investment of $800 million in its own across-the-board price-cutting is ironic in that Wal-Mart has always had the supply chain management (SCM) value engine to be the US price leader, but in the United Kingdom, it trails Tesco, the SCM leader.

At the start of 2012, Tesco suddenly began to look far more vulnerable. Christmas season sales were below expectations in fresh foods, and its stock price dropped 14 percent in a day, following its warning that 2012 profits would be at the low end of its forecast. Commentators point to its neglecting its domestic operations and eroding in-store service by cutting back on training and staffing.[61]

Time will tell. Many of the glitches appear to be situational, but one problem of being the archetype is that the laggards eventually get the message and begin to close the gap. As with Airtel, much of their response is price-cutting that veers near to, but has so far avoided, flat-out price wars.

One distinctive footnote in the dismal news is that while store sales dropped 3.3 percent in 2011, online revenues were up 14 percent. Tesco has integrated its online business with its stores, rather than run it as a separate set of processes, customer relationships, and capabilities, so that it is part of the opportunity platform that will help it make the generational transition to an online-plus-physical identity that is facing traditional retailers everywhere.

UK retailing is close to a disaster zone, with government putting brakes on public spending that risk halting any chance of economic growth, consumers cash-strapped, and an accelerating increase in major chains declaring bankruptcy—up 11 percent for 2011, but with an increase of 27 percent from the third to fourth quarter. GDP is estimated to have grown just 0.1 percent in 2011, with evidence that the economy contracted in the quarter leading up to Christmas.

In a sustained recession, any firm's value engine will be strained and its value narrative blurred or pushed off target. For companies with no adaptive opportunity platform, price-cutting then makes survival the only positive achievement. Tesco clearly must adapt its way out of the increasingly bleak UK economy that still hovers on the edge of recession with few signs of escape.

Tesco continues to grow profitably in foreign markets, except for the United States. All three global giants are looking for their growth in underserved markets, particularly China and India. A competitive health assessment summary is that Carrefour has large stores and a weak opportunity platform that has not opened up a value path as customers go elsewhere. Wal-Mart offers more variety in store formats and runs a historically robust platform that is very much centered on products and transactions. Tesco combines an extensive range of stores and online business with a platform that is centered on knowledge about individual customers as the base for offers.

Clubcard: Expanding Tesco's Value Dimensions

There's good reason to expect Wal-Mart to be able to outperform its competitors in these continuing dire times, and Carrefour to struggle. Tesco, however, has much more going for it. As the three companies increasingly meet head-on in international growth markets, it's worth noting that in most previous encounters, Tesco emerged ahead of Wal-Mart. It was described as "Wal-Mart's Worst Nightmare" in a much-quoted 2009 *Businessweek* article.[62] The headline may turn out to be hyperbole, but it draws attention to differences between the two firms' value narrative.

Throughout the 1970s, Tesco was a so-so performer in UK grocery retailing, with a strategy summarized in the now-clichéd mantra attributed to its founder: "Pile 'em high and sell 'em cheap." He also coined the motivational motto YCDBSAOYA (you can't do business by sitting around on your arse). Jack Cohen had established Tesco in 1919 to sell surplus groceries. It grew consistently as a follower of the market, not a pacesetter. It mainly offered copycat deals to compete with Sainsbury, the well-established and (still) well-managed then market leader. (It's now jostling with Asda for second place, with the two firms' combined market share a few smidgeons more than Tesco's.)

This changed in the early 1990s. Tesco's top management team replaced Cohen's fragmented but successful focus on giving customers a very good price and little else with a well-articulated move to establish a new image and relationship with customers: earning lifetime loyalty.

Its key move was the introduction in 1995 of its loyalty card, Clubcard. This is far more than the equivalent of an airline frequent-flier program. It was the first major success in what is now among the main priorities of most large companies in the consumer sphere: leveraging information technology to learn as much as you can about as many of your individual customers so you can tailor more and more offers to them.

Wal-Mart has long been a leader in CRM data collection, but its information has been focused on the store rather than the individual customer. Pricing is Wal-Mart's loyalty program. CRM data enables it to get the right goods on the right shelf at the right time.

It doesn't provide for enticing every individual customer by maximizing the personalized range of choices across a growing variety of offers. (As so often in the IT field, the substance stays the same, but technology and flavors-of-the-month marketing hype change the label. CRM began as data warehousing and data mining; now it has added in business intelligence and Big Data.)

Clubcard has become a form of currency in the United Kingdom and in many other countries where it has been introduced; these include Malaysia, Poland, and Indonesia, markets where it is a unique new value dimension for shoppers. It is regularly used by a quarter of the UK population. The more services a customer buys, the more data Tesco has about the *person*. An airline frequent-flyer program won't have useful information about a member's driving habits, food preferences, home, or insurance. Tesco does.

Tesco: Lifetime Loyalty as Platform

Tesco's focus is on targeting individual customer groups through data mining, described by *Businessweek* as giving it an "unrivaled ability to manage vast reams of data and translate that knowledge into sales... [and] to manage every aspect of its business, from creating new shop formats to arranging store layouts to developing private-label products and targeted sales promotions."[63]

Clubcard enables the retailer to identify specific customers and their behaviors. As with some airline programs, points earned—Clubcard "Deal Tokens"—may be used to buy insurance from a range of companies, pay for canal boat vacations, or travel on British Airways, all of which of course extend Tesco's knowledge of *this* customer.

The *Wall Street Journal* cited Tesco's "using the intelligence from the Clubcard to thwart Wal-Mart's initiatives in the UK."[64] One instance is its monitoring the impact of the introduction of Asian herbs and ethnic foods in stores with a substantial base of Indian and Pakistani shoppers. The feedback showed that the products were also popular with Caucasian customers; the program was immediately expanded.

A more unusual use of customer data was in response to Wal-Mart's acquisition of Asda, which relied on heavy marketing of its core appeal of low prices. Tesco focused its analysis on shoppers who largely chose the cheapest available item, identified about three hundred products regularly bought by highly price-sensitive consumers, and stocked them up in its stores at reduced prices; the specific aim was to keep loyal customers from defecting to Asda.

In 2012, Tesco began to use its data stores to address how to respond to competitors' price cuts. It has identified stores in more affluent areas where shoppers continue to stay with their preferred brands for some items but are moving to house brands and discounts for others. Instead of a one size fits all—or, rather, one price-cut plan fits all stores—it matches the pricing to the buyers.[65]

Neither Wal-Mart nor Asda has a loyalty card, though both firms routinely capture and analyze customer data, looking for trends and patterns. Their focus in value generation is primarily on creating products at the lowest direct cost and getting them to customers through logistical efficiency and speed. The compelling offer to customers is simply a good range of choices at the best price in the market.

Tesco's compelling customer offer is not price but choice and personalization. The BBC summarized it as rewriting the retail bible "with three simple commandments": If you want to be a supermarket superpower, (1) you have to be everywhere ("when it comes to gobbling space, Tesco leaves its rivals standing"); (2) you have to sell to everyone (a Citigroup analyst commented in 2005 that "they've pulled off a trick that I'm not aware of any other retailer achieving, that is to appeal to all segments of the market"; and (3) "thou shalt sell everything"—in Tesco's largest stores, shoppers can choose from forty thousand product lines, "anything from baked beans to bikinis."[66]

Because Tesco has so successfully built a distinctive identity that is more centered on the relationship than the deal, it has been able to expand its dimensions of value by creating offers that do not fit into the superstore categorization. In a contract with an oil firm, it built a commanding position in branded sales of gas at filling stations located near its large superstores. It launched a mobile-phone service, Tesco Mobile, in 2003 in partnership with Cable and Wireless, and a broadband service, Tesco Internet Voice, delivered over BT phone lines. Its Tesco Internet Phone is a branding of service from the Australian network provider, Freshtel.

A noteworthy element of Tesco's value in customers' minds is that many of its private-label products sell at a premium price over national brands such as Cadbury's. This is the reverse of supermarketing in general and shows that Tesco has found ways to offset price as the main factor in attracting customers. There's some evidence that this advantage backfired in the Christmas season, when Asda and Sainsbury reestablished price and discounts as their main value dimension.

One of Tesco's most distinctive successes has been in financial services, where it offers a wide range of insurance, credit, and finance deals on utility services. (Use the Tesco Compare TheEnergyShop.com platform to "compare energy suppliers and pick the best deal for you. Then switch online."[67]) It is selectively moving into core consumer-banking services, greatly assisted by not having to attract deposits at a cost of interest payments in order to fund its asset base for making loans.

A punctuation-light *Wikipedia* sentence captures the platform impacts on Tesco Bank's ability to add compelling and very new value dimensions for the customer, in words that run together in an interconnected, one-comma verbal rush—analogous to the "seamless" flow of Tesco offers. It prefaces this by pointing out that Tesco is able to use its large customer base to cross-sell financial services, with customers accumulating Clubcard points:

> This strategy is highly effective because it can be combined with in store offers which result in customers spending higher amounts of money, often on non-food items in order to increase sales across all product lines thus causing sustainable

growth which allows them to deal with competition for market control with Asda.[68]

The service "products" are ecocomplex-based. They include mini-search services under the brand of Tesco Compare that evaluate third-party deals for customers on the basis of their individual profiles and needs. TheEnergyShop.com is owned and run by a UK firm. Tesco's insurance offers come from many providers: for pets (offered by Royal Sun Assurance, branded as Tesco Pet and with a thirty-five-dollar Tesco gift card), cars (forty dollars off gas at Tesco petrol filling stations), home, health, student, travel (5 percent Clubcard discount), vacation homes, and many others.

Add in the online grocery, loans, savings, and utility services ("Search the market for leading UK brands. Pay the price you see."), and all this looks more like Amazon than a superstore. Tesco Gold Exchange pays a highly competitive rate for gold: "Collect cash, not dust...Put your unwanted gold to better use." Naturally, there's a one-point Clubcard bonus for every British pound (roughly $1.60) in value.

Tesco has been by far the most successful bricks-and-mortar retailer in exploiting technology to build an Amazon-like online business, and it stands out among supermarkets. This sharply contrasts with the failures in online groceries that include one of the largest and most famous dot-com busts of all time, Webvan. No firm has more than a marginal presence; the best known, Peapod, delivers only in a small number of US cities.

In the United Kingdom, Asda's online initiative begun in 1998 did not meet forecasts, and it has scaled back its goals. Carrefour has bombed online. Tesco has thrived. By early 2008, it had reached sales orders on its website of $2.5 billion, with profits of $190 million. By 2010, online food sales were $2.2 billion and nonfoods $5 billion. Sales growth has averaged 14 percent and profit increases 26 percent, even in the recession.[69] Tesco claims to have the world's biggest Internet grocery business in the world, and the only profitable one.

Most players have handled online groceries as a different experience from in-store shopping. The ventures were company led in the sense that they were designed to make it easy for the online operations; rather than tailor the processes to the customer, they imposed new modes of shopping. The buying process was complicated by problems of substitution for out-of-stock items, pricing, and scheduling delivery.

Tesco took the opposite approach. The online services are run through the stores, including picking and packing the items and handling delivery. Two-thirds of orders are collected at the store.

Tesco's pickup-only sites average $80 million in annual sales, at an annual growth rate of 65 percent. Customers do not have to change habits and procedures; many will order their staples online and still drop in to browse for extras when they pick them up.

Tesco's use of information technology in general reflects such customer-led principles. The formal business justification for investments involves going through a "straightforward checklist": "Is it easier for our customers, is it easier for our staff, and does it add value for Tesco?" Proposals must define clear metrics for assessing end benefits for customers, operations, people, finance, and community.[70]

One example of Tesco's focus is the "one in line" initiative put in place to reduce customer waiting time at checkout. The metric was simple: reduce the number of customers who had more than a single person ahead of them in the line. The system uses thermal imaging to scan arrivals and predict exactly when customers arrive at checkout. Additional registers are immediately opened as needed. This initiative cut the number of customers who had to wait by 250,000 a week.[71]

Both Tesco's IT and business processes are highly modularized, following a formal global expansion plan launched in 2006. Eight core processes are standardized worldwide, including in-store display, store replenishment, and distribution. This permits rapid and systematic rollout internationally. The standardization enables Tesco to handle business requirements in the UK and implement all IT development and upgrades in India. An executive commented in 2010 about the value of the standardization of processes and coordination of IT. The firm's main concern is "the capability of the people in some of our emerging markets [where they] do not have years and years of people doing modern retailing."[72]

Worldwide standardization builds an internal ecocomplex of access to the best processes and advanced IT. So, for instance, a major target in energy management is to reduce in-store carbon footprints. The main consumption of energy is from refrigerators, air conditioners, and heating equipment. All these are treated as modular components and managed centrally. Tills are being replaced for low energy usage, with IT systems to switch them on and off remotely.

"Remotely" means that a register in London and a refrigerator in Warsaw are managed in real time from the IT center—in Bangalore, India. Of course—that's what modularity, technology, and trade liberalization make practical, and once it's practical, why not do it?

Tesco and Wal-Mart: Positioned for a Tough Future

Both the product-price model of value-generation and the experience-choice model have been very successful for Wal-Mart and Tesco respectively. Each has its vulnerability, in the very fact that its sharp focus heightens some opportunities and risks missing out on others.

Tesco is struggling to maintain its record of performance in the United Kingdom.[73] However, its international sales continued their growth, with increases of 15–25 percent a year in Asia. The growth of its US Fresh and Easy chain, introduced in 2007, has also been slowed by recession.[74]

Tesco has many critics who are increasingly organizing to oppose its "pugilistically aggressive" store expansion and data profiling, which is reputedly more reliable, detailed, and comprehensive than any nation's antiterrorist databases. (There's no evidence for this claim, but it illustrates Tesco's legendary status in the United Kingdom.)

The former industry leader, Sainsbury, which Tesco had left trailing, was boosted in its sales growth in the 2008 Christmas season by a 40 percent rise in its cheap "basics" products, while Tesco had the smallest revenue increase since 1993. This helped Sainsbury position itself to close the gap on the same basis in the brutally tough 2011 retail crunch.

Wal-Mart, too, faces challenges to its value narrative of low prices. It has found it difficult to develop new store formats. In the United Kingdom, Asda stores follow the "simplistic layout" of a larger Wal-Mart store footprint; on average, they are 20 percent larger than competitors' stores, but offer 20 percent fewer lines.[75] Wal-Mart basically failed in its initiatives in moving upmarket and offering customers fashion apparel from top brands. It is criticized for its store expansions, labor practices, and anticompetitive moves.

Asda has been caught between Tesco's customer choice-experience value generation and companies such as Aldi that offer even lower prices that it does.[76] (Aldi's value narrative is very clever; it stocks branded items that it does not advertise. Let the other supermarket chains and the consumer brands spend the marketing money; Aldi customers then look out for the item on its shelf.)

The UK regulatory Advertising Standards Agency upheld a challenge to Asda's claim, long embodied in its identity and marketing, that it is officially Britain's lowest-price supermarket. It isn't, and it is not at all clear that it can differentiate its value-generation capabilities in the ways and to the extent that Wal-Mart expected.

The companies made much of Asda's CEO traveling to Wal-Mart's headquarters in the United States He would go to the United States regularly and wander around Wal-Mart stores, noting all their tried-and-tested techniques. On one trip, a store manager stopped him from taking pictures. The manager phoned the head office, and Bentonville asked to see him. "'Once they had established who I was and where I was from, they were fine. They let me copy all their stuff. Their "Roll-back" offer? We put it straight into Asda.'"77 Asda has Wal-Mart's value narrative down pat, but not enough of its capabilities.

Many companies have adopted the core of Tesco's practices; CRM software packages and geo-demographics are well-established key analytic tools for many companies, including Wal-Mart. But CRM is often disappointing in its impacts. This is because it is not the technology application or the CRM resource that generates results, but the use of the data resource to build a capability. Companies can buy the application—or copy the system—but this does not make it a value generator. Equally, while a resource can be matched or purchased, it does not make it a capability. Unless it contributes to value creation, it is just a cost.

No platform lasts forever, of course, and while Tesco continues to hold a huge advantage over all its direct competitors, Google and Facebook have even more data about more people and the ability to analyze it on the fly. Tesco is a supermarket that's now in the energy business. Could Google, which is also in energy, become the search engine for a supermarket-based ecocomplex? "Could" is obviously the wrong word. Of course it *can*. So substitute "will Google" or "when will Google." And think about Tesco as a search engine for lifetime loyal customers. For a firm like yours, perhaps. Or for a competitor.

7 Google: Focus on the User, All Else Will Follow

In Search of Value, Not Just Information

Google's founders, Larry Page and Serge Brin, did not set out to build a company. They were two computer science doctoral students at Stanford in the mid-1990s looking for a promising dissertation topic. They zeroed in on a specialized but rapidly growing area of opportunity opened up by technology: primarily the web, but also a new generation of low-cost hardware and software programming tools. This was the field of search, which had traditionally been part of the academic discipline of information retrieval (IR). The action here was mainly in journals and pilot applications that implemented new mathematical algorithms.

The leading commercial search program at the time was Altavista, developed by Digital Equipment Corporation. DEC was *the* computer ultrasuccess of the 1970s and an ultrafade by the late '80s, self-destructively stuck in Asset and Invention Traps. Altavista was one of the last of its wasted inventions. Even Google, Microsoft, and Apple have yet to surpass DEC as a culture of innovation that reshaped the impacts of technology. DEC lasted just forty years and essentially died by corporate hara-kiri, very much illustrating the more recent lessons of other ultrafades and likely to be an archetype of future ones, especially those built on a core culture of engineering and technology advancement.[78]

Search was viewed by online service firms as a utility tool and not an independent business, so many online firms outsourced it. Between 2000 and 2004, when it launched its own software after buying Altavista in addition to other search companies, Yahoo contracted with Google for its entire search capabilities.

Page and Brin began as inventors and were nudged toward innovation as others recognized the value of the software tools they had developed. Their breakthrough was to rate web page links as a measure of relevance, rather than apply standard IR indexing techniques. Their work was in and of itself a major achievement and highlights just how intellectually complex the conceptual, technical, and mathematical elements of search remain. Google's major value dimensions center on making it all *look* easy for the user: simple, reliable, fast, personal, relevant, and then simpler, more reliable, faster, and so on.

In many ways, IR thinking was based on a library conception of information: there's all this stuff accumulating on the Internet; how can we organize it so it's useful and provide fast answers to questions? Google's search engine is instead based on user behavior and relevance: there are all these people heffalumping around the web. Let's keep track of where they go and what they do and use that to establish what's most likely to be relevant to others when they make a search query. Page commented, "If you have a way of ranking things...on what the world thought of that page, [then] that would be a really valuable thing for search."[79]

It turned out to be very much "really valuable." In 1997, a year before incorporating Google, the inventors were handling about ten thousand search queries a day, which consumed half of Stanford University's Internet resources. They registered google.com and developed its technology base very much ad hoc; this was made possible only because of the recent convergence of the needed hardware, software, and communications building blocks on standardized interfaces and modularity.

Page and Brin were dedicated cheapskates and built their operations by buying used servers, taking advantage of bargain deals, and starting out in rented garage space in a 1,900-square-foot house. The software tools they used were forerunners of and foundations for today's apps (C++ and Java, the related programming languages that were designed for portability), and the Unix/IP Internet infrastructure.

By 1998, Google had become a search engine of choice in *PC Magazine*'s Top 100 Web Sites: "[Google] has an uncanny knack for returning extremely relevant results."[80] By then, a number of firms were competing in search as a utility, including Altavista, Yahoo, Excite, and Lycos.

Page and Brin did not plan to create a company: "We weren't in an entrepreneurial frame of mind back then." But they had unsuccessfully tried to license their search engine to several of these companies. The closest they got to a deal was with Excite in early 1997. The problem was their software was too good. At the time, the portals' objective was "stickiness." The longer a user stayed on the site, the more ads the portal could display. The CEO of Excite told Page and Brin "that he wanted Excite's search engine to be 80 percent as good as the other search engines." People would then spend more time on the site.

In September 1998, Google became a company, mainly because there was no other choice. No one would pay enough for the intellectual property embodied in the software, and it was attracting sufficient visitors to make Page and Brin confident that they could grow a real business. They obtained an exclusive license to their invention from Stanford in exchange for 1.8 million shares of Google stock. (Since Page and Brin were working at Stanford at the time they invented PageRank, Stanford owned the PageRank patent.)

Page and Brin were builders, with a deep commitment not just to moving the field of search ahead but also to getting their tools used. They constantly tinkered with the code, looking to make it easier to use, faster, and more helpful. Initially, they opposed cluttering up the display with intrusive ads and extraneous displays. Page later commented that "if the company failed, too bad, we were really going to be able to do something that mattered."

What mattered was to organize all the world's information and make it universally accessible and of value. For *whom* it mattered was the user. Google offered two value dimensions in a field where competitors focused on just one: usefulness *and* usability. It's this duality that accounts for both Google's early success and its flood of innovations, including its shift from being philosophically against online advertising as intrusive to making it the driver of its massive growth and even more massive profits.

Google's published Statement of Philosophy is easy to downplay as just corporate PR, but it really does seem to have been the compass setting for its navigation from its core base of search.[81] Four of the precepts stand out in this regard (out of the ten shown in figure 7.1): "Focus on the user and all else will follow." "It's best to do one thing really, really well." "Fast is better than slow." "The need for information crosses all borders."

Algorithms: The Drivers of Value

Google's prime proprietary asset was and remains its algorithms. These analyze every single search query in real time. While the original criteria for the display of search results was page rank, over the years Google has added about two hundred additional criteria to assure greater relevance.

Nagged and prodded by the venture capitalists that provided it funding, in 1999 Google developed a business plan (its first ever effort to write things down and do the arithmetic) that identified three potential streams of revenue: license the technology to other websites, such as Yahoo, to power their search; sell a packaged solution to companies to provide internal search for their firms; and sell advertising.

Page proposed a very different view of advertising that respected the user: "Our goal is to maximize the user experience, not maximize the revenue per search."[82] As a result Google set about to apply technology to advertising in such a way that the ads displayed for any

Mission
To organize the world's information and make it universally accessible and useful.

Philosophies
1. Focus on the user and all else will follow.
2. It's best to do one thing really, really well. (Do search really well and apply to other areas)
3. Fast is better than slow.
4. Democracy on the web works. (Display content voted best and leverage open source)
5. You don't need to be at your desk to need an answer. (Mobile)
6. You can make money without doing evil. (How ads are displayed)
7. There's always more information out there. (Expanding content sources and media types)
8. The need for information crosses all borders. (Global and languages)
9. You can be serious without a suit.
10. Great just isn't good enough. (Through innovation and iteration improve in unexpected ways)

Figure 7.1: Google's Mission and Philosophies

search were not *only* clearly differentiated from the search results, but were also relevant to the user.

Google's first ad system, launched in early 2000, was keyword based. The advertiser bought keywords, and Google algorithms would display ads relevant to the customer's search request based on them. This means that to the best of Google's ability, the "relevance" of the ad is entirely determined by the user ("Focus on the user and all else will follow.") and by search ("Do one thing really, really well.").

Google built new dimensions of value on this solid foundation. It described the value for advertisers: "The result is a highly targeted ad that appears only if a user enters the same keywords or phrase that an advertiser has purchased, ensuring advertisers will be delivered a prequalified visitor and will not pay for 'off target' impressions."

The ad typically included a link to the advertiser's website, but in the initial system, the revenue collected was based on cost-per-impression—an impression is a unique appearance of an ad on a web page. The ads were sold by a traditional sales force on a traditional basis for an online version of a traditional product. Cost-per-impression had become the standard for online ads when Yahoo owned the screen and corresponded in logic to the rates for newspapers (paid circulation) and TV (viewing audience).

It took two more revolutions of Google's innovation engine to really monetize search. The first was the launch of AdWords in October 2000. This catered to small firms and enabled them to purchase ads online. With it, Google also made its first step into displaying ads based not just on keywords and price, but on ad quality as determined by user response: either clicking on the ad or ignoring it.

The second and bigger step was the launch of AdWords Select. A history of online advertising states that "Google had two moments of pure brilliance. The first was PageRank. The second was introducing relevance into the pay-per-click auction model."[83] Here, relevance is a dimension of both user value and advertiser value.

Google engineers leveraged and advanced two concepts created by Bill Gross of GoTo, another search engine of the time that later became Overture. These ideas (which Gross had somehow failed to patent) were to charge advertisers based on cost-per-click-through, where the advertiser only paid if the user clicked on the ad rather than being charged at a rate of cost-per-impression, and to auction off the keywords rather than charge a fixed price.

Google took these ideas to a new level, however. Google's auction is based on the advertiser paying only one cent more than the next higher bidder and building other parameters, such as context and quality, into the equation to assure relevancy. In 2002, Google's revenue surge began, fueled by its introduction of the "clickthrough" rate to the AdWords Select algorithms.

The old auction system meant that an advertiser might bid its way to the top listing, but if few users clicked on the displayed ad—that is, if it was irrelevant—then no one benefits from it: not the user, the advertiser, or Google in terms of longer-run growth. In effect, Google's shift created a dynamic quasi-market economy of online advertising. As user behavior shifted, so did the ads, on a sub second basis. By contrast, a fixed price for keywords led to some being overpriced and some underpriced—that is, their relevance changed.

Advertisers no longer own keywords, and Google runs a new auction every single time a user makes a query. Ads are posted, and the order in which they are displayed is determined by the keywords the advertiser has selected, the words the Google search algorithms assess as most relevant to this user, the advertiser price bid, and an algorithm-based rating of the quality of the ad.

One of the striking features of AdWords Select is the extent to which advertisers are made an integral part of the "look after the user" rule. The ecocomplex is elegantly balanced to produce, by and large, a win-win-win relationship, where value for the customers, company and partners does not come at the expense of each other. The scheme does have its critics, of course, especially among disgruntled small company owners: "I have my campaign budget at $3.00 a day. Yesterday they [Google] ran up $4.53 in charges for impressions, they don't understand what the word 'budget' means. I had $0.57 left in the account this morning that it burned up...It's no wonder they make billions when they rip off their customers like this."[84]

Google continues to expand the dimensions of value it offers to both users and advertisers around search. For the user it has always been about relevancy, speed, and price (free). But Google not only continues to enhance these dimensions, but also extends other ones, such as personalization, media types searched, translation, and access beyond the desktop. We have tried to capture the essence of this in figure 7.2 with some examples. Our guess is that most people who use Google every day are not aware of even this limited list, but the dimensions and their continued expansion is why they rely on Google every day.

Of course, many of these features that compose the value dimensions are offered by other companies. One of these is Microsoft, which explicitly targeted Google in its stronghold through its Bing "decision engine," a search tool that aims to cut out junk and

Value Dimension	User Value Drivers
Price	✓ Free
Relevancy	✓ Started with page rank rather then key words ✓ Added over 200 other criteria over the years to assure relevance
Speed	✓ Constantly improving search algorithms and technology infrastructure to drive speed of response ✓ Added features like "Instant Response"
Ease of use	✓ Simple Web page ✓ Clean, simple tool bar readily available ✓ Perfecting everyday language search (non Boolean) ✓ Results as you type ✓ Spell check as you go ✓ Translation function
Personalization	✓ Tailored results based on individual search history and geographic location
Media searched	✓ Added search engines for video, blogs, images, books, academic, news, product, document, e-mail, etc. in addition to Web and then pulled them all together under one search ✓ Tools for Web site developers to describe non-text content through XML so that it becomes part of Web search ✓ Created News and Blog services, expanded YouTube content, and scanned books to expand media content
Advertising – necessary evil to support free search	✓ Non-intrusive, relevant ✓ Incentives for Advertisers ✓ Clear delineation of advertisements from search results
Ease of Access	✓ Incentivize providers like Dell, Apple, and Adobe to put tool bar on devices ✓ Special tools for mobile phones and tablets ✓ Development and distribution of Android
Translation	✓ 506 matched language pairs

Figure 7.2: Examples of Search Dimensions of Value for Users

so help the user focus on making the most informed decision. It has matched Google's search features for most practical everyday purposes and reached a market share of about 15 percent. It powers Yahoo's search, which adds another 16 percent. The figures remained stable throughout 2011, and Google has maintained its 65 percent share. Bing is losing $1 billion a quarter, and Yahoo is in fire-sale status.[85]

TechCrunch summarizes the contrast between Google and Bing. "Bing is not a bad search engine... [but] you're likely not thinking to yourself: 'Oh, I'll Bing that.' No, no, no. You Google that sucker. Because Google is a verb. And Bing is not."[86]

Innovating Every Day

Preserving, protecting, exploiting, and expanding the dimensions of value that make up this brand advantage obviously involve continuing innovation. Maybe Bing won't succeed in eroding Google's dominance, and maybe Apple's iAd mobile advertising will continue to look like a bust, but there's always another innovator looking to exploit the same forces and opportunities as Google did. This helps explain why Google has positioned for innovating on an everyday basis.

Many observers question if there is a coherent plan in its choice of—and often gambles on—new market segments, software products and services, technologies, and media. The strategy is proactively and very publicly opportunistic.

Google launched about five hundred improvements just to its search algorithms in 2010. These improvements required twenty thousand "experiments," each of which was scientifically tested with data from raters and real-world users. The objective was to improve each user's experience: speed of response, personalization, and ease of use, down to details of correct interpretation of misspelled words and even interpreting and responding to hesitation in keying the next letters.

With all its focus on the user's dimensions of value, it is easy to overlook that Google is an engineering-driven company. Make no mistake about that. It's as apparent as entering a marine base and sensing that this is not a gathering of rock groups. Normally, engineering cultures deliver new technology, not enhanced and expanded dimensions of value, at least not from the customer's perspective.

Think of all the times you have cursed your remote control for all those buttons or have tried to find a simple feature in PowerPoint, knowing it is there because you found it just a week ago, but even if your life depended on it, you could not find it today. Why not use the help feature? Stupid question. It is typically ill-organized geek-speak that will only raise your blood pressure.

In this context, Google seems like an anomaly, to date at least. That is because the flow of feedback from users provides a constant push toward simplicity, ease, and speed. Google is not only engineering-driven but also a data-dominated culture. Almost nothing is done unless the data proves it is right. With its vast troves of data and expansive, active user base, Google can determine in an instant whether a change will enhance the user experience or hurt it. Its technical teams propose, test, and learn every day, and then live by what the data tells them.

In passing, it is worth noting that there are many ultrasuccesses that grew through a core competence of engineering and faded when it became a frozen core culture. DEC, the progenitor of online search, was packed with many of the very best, most creative, energetic, and committed engineers that MIT and Carnegie ever graduated. Sony's and Nokia's problems partly reflect how excellent its engineers are. Google has been able to recruit and develop the diversity of skills and perspectives it needed to maintain the primacy of the user experience in its value creation. So far.

Both the primacy of the user experience and Google's much-publicized and often-challenged claim to "Do No Harm" increasingly push up against its—and Facebook's—tracking of personal data and intrusions in more and more areas of privacy. Will customers accept this because it adds to their value dimensions of relevance and personalization? Or will it be seen as detracting from their value in order to increase Google's?

The company announced in the spring of 2012 that it will integrate users' information across sixty of its services and combine it with third-party data. The justification is couched in terms of adding value by offering "a simpler, more intuitive user experience" and enabling Google to do a lot more "cool things." As a proactive move, it is the natural and perhaps inevitable next step in the evolution of speed, personalization, and ease of use. Conversely, it may affect customer choices by forcing them to make a personal trade-off between two potentially, or even already, conflicting dimensions of value.

Google's leaders have tried to maintain the challenge of encouraging both a freewheeling creativity and a focused discipline in its innovation processes. Its 70-20-10 rule was implemented within its technical community: "Googlers" should dedicate 70 percent of their time to the core business (search and advertising),

20 percent on projects "adjacent" to the core, and 10 percent on projects unrelated to it. The press naturally focuses on the 20 percent and 10 percent projects because they are new and more newsworthy. They also often question the soundness of the 10 percent ones because they don't fit into the core.

They do fit into the opportunity of the expanding choice space, though. An underlying assumption behind all of Google's most radical innovations is that information is the constitutive element of every service customers will come to value. That is entirely different from the competing assumption of Facebook that communities, not information as such, are the driver of online value.

Facebook's chief operating officer said in 2012 in a *Wall Street Journal* interview, "Our vision is that industries get disrupted and [they get] rebuilt with people at the center. The gaming industry has been really impacted by these social gaming companies like Zynga and Playdom. By putting people at the center, they took a totally different approach to gaming. We think this will happen to every industry."[87]

The Google equivalent here is that by putting information at its center, it takes a totally different approach to mobile phones, software, TV, digitizing all the world's books, and even driverless cars. These are all part of expanding existing choice spaces for consumers and opening up new ones.

Google has to be a presence in them since they are the base both for its own expansion and for competition that will try to siphon off customers. That would erode its advertising revenues. It has chosen to build its position in these markets primarily by exploiting the partnering opportunities and filling the space rather than controlling it.

The logic here is that if Google can help expand the choice space, it will be able to leverage its own growth through the growth it makes practical for others in its ecocomplex. It then does not have to be directly profitable in its own innovations that target that space: "Google contended that there was a holistic aspect to its activities: the companies it bought, the new areas it colonized, built a bigger ecosystem. Google would often point to a putatively unprofitable area and claim data that showed a positive impact on search and subsequent clicks on its ads."[88]

Mobile: New Choice Space and Value Dimensions

Android is the open-source (meaning it's yours to use, change, and improve on as you like) operating system for mobile phones and

Google: Focus on the User, All Else Will Follow

other devices that Steve Jobs of Apple threatened to go "thermonuclear" to destroy. Understandably. By making Android its gift to the world, Google turned the mobile choice space from a set of competing proprietary domains into a free-for-all ecocomplex-rich savannah plain. Apple's fenced-off game reserve is now surrounded by a host of roaming wildlife.

Putatively, mobile communications in general and Android specifically constitute a very unprofitable initiative by Google; it had failed in an earlier effort to launch a branded phone. Giving Android away free turned out instead to be one of the most far-reaching innovations in modern business history, almost literally priceless.

It's been apparent for well over a decade that at some point wireless telecommunications would move from an add-on service to becoming the driver of communications in the widest sense of the term. In the transition phase, mobile phones dominated market growth, though it is worth noting the unobtrusive emergence of Wi-Fi, now as indispensable in everyday life as umbrellas and TV remotes.

Motorola and then Nokia dominated the mobile-phone terrain. Motorola's market share was close to 40 percent, but fell when it misread the historical direction of technology as a disturbing force; its leaders were insistent that mobile phones would remain phones and that phones meant analog not digital transmission. Nokia passed it by and became the dominant global player.

Nokia grew through technology leadership and the same attention to design as a new value dimension that Apple has. It viewed mobile phones as a fashion accessory, whereas Motorola's devices signaled functionality and power talk, not "chat." Nokia invested heavily in R&D. In the early 2000s, over 60 percent of its worldwide employees were in research.

Nokia identified multiplayer mobile games as its major revenue growth opportunity and made a large profit from texting and downloading of ring tones. Most profitable of all, it built by far the strongest manufacturing asset base in the industry, able to turn out a hundred million new handsets to meet demand in just about any market, flourishing across the world, especially in developing economies.

It also invented the smart phone. It launched its Communicator line in 1996 with a stream of firsts: first web browser, first color screen, and first built-in camera. Its operating system, Symbian, led the market from 1996 to the first quarter of 2011, when it dropped to second place behind Google's Android. In 2009, Symbian had a 51 percent share to Android's 2 percent. According to the technology industry research firm Gartner, by the third quarter of 2011, Android had 52.5 percent of the market and Symbian 16.9 percent.[89]

Microsoft was the other dominant player, with a 23 percent smart phone market share in 2004. In 2010, that had fallen to under 2 percent. Apple introduced the iPhone in 2007. It obviously changed the innovation game, but Nokia and Microsoft had thrived in the invention game and missed the shifts in the innovation playbook.

Google recognized that the expanding mobile space was both a threat to and a natural extension of its value architecture. This was about as fragmented an industry as could be. The core technology itself varied widely, with "incompatibility" everywhere. Incompatibility is a long-established euphemism for "logically, this ought to work with this, but it doesn't; sorry about that." Recall that incompatibility is one of the most frequently cited reasons for couples filing for divorce because of irreconcilable differences. It is also the reason your $40 printer turns into a $1,000 a week inkaholic.

So, GSM, UMTS, IS-95, Wimax, LTE, HSDPA, Wibro, EV-DO, EDGE, OFDM, and a few hundred other standards all address how to deal with the central issue of mobile communications: efficient sharing of the radio frequency "spectrum" and creation and transmission of usable signals. They affect which US phones don't work in Europe, international roaming charges, the networks that the iPhone can run on, and why China assembled 90 percent of the world's 3G phones but had no domestic 3G networks. (It delayed issuing licenses in the hope of imposing its homegrown standard on the global market and ended up creating three companies for three technologies and their individual customer bases.)

The core transmission differences were compounded by proprietary operating systems. Each device maker had its own OS, and all the major networks required that these be tailored to their own technology. A handset maker in Japan would have to modify its software for each of the competing carriers and also design for Europe's and North America's providers.

In addition, each OS does different things with the hardware it runs on, including power management, loading apps, tethering, virtual machine compilation, NDC, dithering, Bluetooth HDP (Health Device Profile), page rendering, back buffering, and—well, just make up your own phrase; it will be plausible, even if not factual.

Android: Modularity for All–Except Apple

In mid-2005, Google bought the small firm Android with its staff of five people for an estimated $50 million. Google's CEO, Eric Schmidt, had stated the goal pretty clearly a year earlier: "We're not going into the phone business, but we're going to be sure that Google is going to be on those phones."[90] At the time, he meant that what would be on the phone was Google search and advertising, not a Google operating system.

Android's founder had planned to create an open-source operating system for the carriers (Verizon, Sprint, AT&T, etc.) to save them the roughly 20 percent of the unit handset cost they paid for the software OS. This would have given them a significant degree of control across ecocomplexes of choice spaces.

Instead, when Google announced Android, it opened it up for any player in the mobile space to adopt, on the logic that what was good for the web was good for the smart phone handset makers, which was good for the networks, which was good for independent service developers, which was good for Google's mission to access and organize all the world's information, which was good for users.

Android's open-source system is part of the genealogical family tree that began with Unix that begat Linux (via GNU), the direct progenitor of Android. There are some slightly weird nephews and nieces. Meamo hopes to inherit part of Nokia's trust fund (it's aiming to be more "finger-friendly" than cousin Android) and Tizen is being groomed for stardom by Samsung and Intel. Android's parent, Google, seems to have got a touch of the Frank Zappas in naming the kids as sweets—Cupcake, Honeycomb, and Ice Cream Sandwich. Amazon's Kindle Fire is built on its own version of Android 2.3, Gingerbread.

Naturally, Android chose Linux as its core. The entire evolution of Google's technology platform, from the garage to the era of its server farms and cloud computing services, rests on the principle of SIMCap. SIMCap is an awkward neologism that we introduce here to save continuously writing "standardized interfaces to modular capabilities."

Whenever the firm has needed additional technology capability to leverage its business capability, it added more modular hardware units linked together through an ever-evolving set of standardized Internet interfaces. By contrast Apple's value architecture rests on PIMCap—proprietary interfaces to modular capabilities—to assure control and the highest degree of integration of services and components in its products, such as the iPhone tied to iTune services and more recently to Apple-only apps. By keeping Android open source, Google in essence made SIMCap the base for an entire reorientation of the mobile industry.

A plurality of technical commentators view Android software and devices as inferior to their Apple equivalents in many dimensions of design, though others see this as a matter of minor differences between two excellent options. But most comparative assessments highlight some detail where Apple is still a little ahead of Android in, say, how apps display on a smart phone screen.

Let's assume that they are indeed correct and that Apple's proprietary operating system is at the least the better between two equals and perhaps still the gold medalist. The obvious question then is why did the not-quite-best Android so quickly overtake Apple when other competitors had failed?

Figure 7.3 suggests some answers. It shows the value dimensions of the Google offer to both its close business partners and its new ecocomplex allies, noncompeting firms, and even competitors. (Amazon has exploited the open nature of Android to develop its own implementation for its Kindle Fire tablet.)

Many analysts completely underestimated the impact of Android because they assessed it in terms of just technical measures of both customer and company value. Gartner was one of the optimists and forecast in October 2009 that Android would "surge" from its 2 percent of the global smart phone market to 14 percent by 2012, in second place behind Nokia's Symbian. So much for that forecast. It is nowhere near Android's actual leap, which has captured half the choice space. Symbian has been all but abandoned.

Android lost a few percentage points to Apple's IOS in the Christmas quarter of 2011 but gained from Amazon's Fire tablet taking 10 percent away from Apple's iPad. In 2011, Google generated $2.5 billion from mobile advertising, up from $1 billion in the previous year.[91] Current estimates are that could more than double in 2012 and double again in 2013. Where might Google be without the value architecture and opportunity platform thinking that made Android an evolution rather than a revolution in its innovation?

The companies that had most thrived through their proprietary technology platforms added their own assessments. Here are two comments from the CEOs of Microsoft and Apple, the dominant proprietary platform owners, about the two main open-source alternatives, Linux and Android:

- Steve Ballmer, Microsoft: "Linux is a cancer that attaches itself in an intellectual property sense to everything it touches."[92]
- Steve Jobs, Apple, on "grand theft Android": "I will spend my last dying breath if I have to, and I will spend every

Value Dimension	Android Business Partner Value Drivers
Additional Revenue/Margin Potential	✔ Provide software platform that will enable device makers and service providers to get to market quickly with phones that can compete with iPhone and RIM with higher margins than non-smartphone ✔ Device maker can modify user interface for competitive advantage
Total Cost of Ownership	✔ Android code is free; Google maintains and services it ✔ Open source and the Open Software Alliance mean others will enhance at no cost to any one device maker
Ease of Implementation	✔ Can implement without modification
Ease of Customization	✔ Many developers available that can modify Linux-based open source code
Support	✔ Google will enhance and maintain ✔ Everyone benefits from contributions made by Open Software Alliance member
Quality	✔ Android is Linux-based which has quality reputation ✔ Open source means development community can all contribute to fixing problems ✔ New releases are tested with one chip maker and one device maker before release

Figure 7.3: Examples of Android value dimensions for Business Partners

penny of Apple's $40 billion in the bank, to right this wrong...
I'm going to destroy Android because it's a stolen product. I'm willing to go to thermonuclear war on this."[93]

To this may be added "P.S. Patent theft lawsuits to follow." The entire mobile operating system field has become a battleground of buying up patents, enforcing patents, making accusations about patents, suing and countersuing for patent infringement, and working around patents by rewriting code. Of course, the open-source advocates are as courteous and circumspect in their own views, as the mere 2.6 million Google hits on the search term "Microsoft + Evil Empire" indicate.

Central to Google's ability to pull together and deliver all its dimensions of value for users, advertisers, and business partners is what has been traditionally referred to as its technology platform: the infrastructures, tools, and massive operations base that in effect are its development and distribution system.

The technology determines what is practical to create and deliver as a digital service. The platform design shapes how the services can work together, provides a base for continued expansion, and opens up new areas of potential value. The technology is an enabler of value, but it's how it is designed and used that creates the dimensions of value and opens up customer choices.

Google and Apple are at two ends of a spectrum of technology design principles that has very practical implications for just about every aspect of their value architectures. It is hard to imagine how Google would have been able to build its technology platform on anything other than SIMCap principles, given its stated mission to organize the world's information.

It is also hard to imagine Google being able to crack the wireless walled garden with a proprietary system given Apple's huge lead at the time, Apple's proprietary design principles that would have locked Google out, Symbian's strong established occupancy across the market, and Google's desire to enable search and advertising across the entire mobile world. What is also becoming very evident is that it would have been a disaster for Google had it not been able to open up the mobile world. Its growth would have been bounded, and its market cap capped.

The question for you and your firm is what is the basis for your technology design principles: SIMCap or PIMCap, and why?

The New Archetypes: Beyond the Business Model

How clear is your own firm's value narrative? How well does its value engine support it today, and is it likely to hold up well in the anticipatable near to medium term? That time frame is about three to five years for many sectors where markets are mature and new infrastructures take time to build or where customers, by and large, seem fairly content in shopping around for options. But in many others, it must seem more like three months. A long-range plan in digital media is out of date before the next news ripple across the blogosphere.

If the forces of disturbance make that future more and more uncertain, what is your company doing now to make that unpredictability a source of opportunity? To quote from the inestimable Kurt in the TV program, *Glee*, it used to be enough just to have a dream, "but now the future has the nerve to show up, and it's expecting us to do something."[94]

Individually, Bharti, Tesco, and Google are outstanding companies, and they have found highly innovative value paths. Clearly they are very different from comparable competitors in how they have innovated and sustained their growth. This ranges from their assumptions about the extent and nature of value shifts, balance between asset ownership and ecocomplex relationships, and market expansion and intrusion on other industries' established territory.

In many regards, there is nothing new here, in that the three historical forces of disturbance have always been at work, and ultrasuccesses leverage them ahead of other companies. They locate a new value path that exploits the opportunities an expanded choice space opens up and that avoids their becoming locked in by what was once an effective—even the most effective—way to go.

It's not the differences that are relevant for other firms, though, but the extent to which these point to common patterns and *why* the patterns have emerged. Each of these three companies has found an effective way to address the new realities of an ever-changing environment. What jumps out as a general pattern underlying the very different specific innovation strategies of the three anomalies is that they look ahead to add an additional organizational balancing act that weights their resource investment between meeting today's opportunities efficiently and positioning for tomorrow's, often inefficiently in the sense that their current operations do not benefit from the extra cost, planning, or organization.

So, for instance, Google could have used proprietary technology, as Apple did, to optimize its operational performance, maintain control, and impose terms for connecting to its products and services. Instead, it chose to position its opportunity platform to increase the variety and extent of potential ecocomplex relationships.

Bharti's asset-light value architecture is a highly opportunistic contrast to that of telecommunications service providers over past decades. It avoids the Asset Trap of being locked into the networks that were highly profitable when customer choice was limited, new entrants were blocked by regulation and investment demands, and technology was stable and affordable only by large firms. It exploits the opportunity of ecocomplex relationships enabled by all three forces: deregulation/trade liberalization that opened up options in markets, customers, and partners; technology that provided a new coordination base and drove entirely new types of service, delivered in new ways; and modularity that facilitated a building block approach to operational capabilities.

The relevant terms here are all conditional, rather than causal: opportunistic, enabled, opened up, and facilitated—not caused, required, or produced. It's *all* about the choice space. As that shifts, innovators like Bharti, Tesco, and Google begin to move away from established practice and exploit the Value Realities of buyers determining value, value shifting, ecocomplexes extending, and entrepreneurs creating new dimensionality.

At some stage, their own value architectures become the blueprints for new practice, often morphed, extended, adapted, and tailored from the original. The anomaly was the stimulus, and the specific value architectures that enabled a range of ultrasuccesses were the end result.

Google is unique, but its exploitation of modularity is becoming general. Tesco is just another retailer in some regards, competing as such, but it is more general in showing that if the customer experience increasingly drives value, then you can't design and target it unless you know the customer as an individual.

Bharti Airtel is interesting as a telecommunications company in a country of bewildering variety and flux where the word "average" does not apply to anything. But more generally its value architecture principles are rapidly becoming a norm for the average company, especially in enabling a low-cost structure that helps it afford low customer prices and high service levels.

The three anomalies are thus illustrative of specific innovative responses that point to broader shifts. They are not absolutes; how your own company exploits the opportunity of the patterns rests on its assessments of time past, time present, and time future. Time past determines its legacy of accumulated assets, its assumptions about customer value dimensions, and most of all how much its existing value architecture is built on stability. In general the stronger and longer this heritage, the more its value architecture will provide flexibility within a range of value dimensions and the less across dimensions.

The question for your firm that emerges from the three archetypes is: do we need to navigate rapidly from time present toward a far stronger time-future focus via a strategy built on the changes in management focus to:

- Move away from overreliance on fixed assets?
- Actively look to build new ecocomplexes and interface with partners to cosource capabilities and resources?
- Shift branding from product to experience and relationships?
- Assume an accelerated and unpredictable shift in what customers value and who offers it to them?

Of course, if the answer is a "yes" in any of these areas of value, then the firm will need to adapt or even transform its capabilities to meet the demands of change. How the ultrasuccesses and superextenders achieve this is the topic of a later section of *The Value Path*. The point to be made here is that if the firm accepts that the signals from Bharti (assets, ecocomplex), Tesco (branding, value dimensions), and Google (interfacing, ecocomplex, modularity, value dimensions, branding) are relevant to them, then they constitute the starting point for innovation.

The patterns that emerge from the three illustrative archetypes are so clearly apparent that they cannot be left aside for decision by omission or default; they must be factored into any firm's thinking, if only because they are certainly being considered as archetypes by likely competitors positioning for innovation through architecture.

8 Three Value Narratives within an Industry

In this chapter we look at value narratives that leveraged opportunities opened up by the forces of disturbance. The three companies we chose for review are all in the apparel "industry." They responded to the same shifts but picked different value paths, each of which made them an ultrasuccess. One has maintained its success and is a superextender (Li & Fung, Hong Kong), one slid badly back down the value path and is an ultrafade (Gap, USA), and the third seems likely to continue to grow, although there are elements of its value architecture where today's strengths could limit tomorrow's extension (Zara, Spain).

Each of the firms preempted competition in ways that redefined its competitive arena. A resonant general lesson here is that the more open the choice space, the wider the opportunities for a distinctive value narrative.

The first company is Li & Fung, the intermediary that integrates the logistics flows between producers and retailers. It has been a standout in growth and profitability in a market where low margins and high losses are the norm. Very few companies have grown to so dominate an entire global sector. Its narrative is built on coordination of the global supply chain on behalf of producers and sellers, optimizing all parties' costs and logistics.

Li & Fung built its ultrasuccess without any capital commitment to production facilities or even to owning its office buildings. Key terms in its narrative are network orchestrator, smokeless factory, dispersed manufacturing, and removing the "soft three dollars" of logistics costs incurred along the supply chain for every one dollar of manufacturing cost. It sustains its growth by leveraging the assets and capabilities owned by others in fusion with its own financial and organizational strengths. In turn, it has built on these to move into other competitive sectors, including toys and household items.

Its sales growth has averaged over 20 percent for two decades. Its return on equity was 24 percent in the difficult period 2006–11 and over 30 percent for the preceding decade.[95] Over that time frame, the US consumer price index rose 30 percent while apparel prices fell by 10 percent.[96]

Gap and Zara are the world's largest fashion clothing chains, with Inditex, the company that owns Zara, having taken over the number one position in sales revenues from Gap in 2007.

Zara's value narrative is built on its offering high-fashion items at low prices in stores that are attractive to shop in and easily accessed. It generates high margins: 55 percent gross margin, compared with Gap's 40 percent.[97] Its value narrative is built on offering instant "runway fashion" through very tight control of most elements of supply chain and branding of the customer shopping experience.

Zara's profits grew even in the recessionary period of 2009, though at a slower rate than in previous years. Analysts commented that it had held up better than most clothing retailers, "due to its focus on selling catwalk styles at knock-down prices."[98] The priority of superb design and up-to-date fashion has shaped its supply chain coordination, with an emphasis on localization rather than the global sourcing Gap helped pioneer and Li & Fung makes its fortune from.

Gap had been Zara's 1990s equivalent in growth and success as the retailer that "invented casual chic" and "changed the way the world dressed." Its erosion has been sustained and is likely to continue. Its strong value narrative has lost focus and it is caught in the Asset Trap, with limited flexibility. Its operating profit in 2009 was the highest in a decade, but only because of short-term cost cutting; this followed a 9 percent drop in sales in 2008, but a 17 percent increase in profits. It continued to struggle to reestablish its identity with customers.

Gap's rise, plateau, and continued drift illustrate how quickly a firm can lose its dominant market position when customers are totally in control; there is no other industry so marked by competition, variety, design, price and quality options, channel choices, specialty providers, cycle time, and fashion.

Gap built a unique identity by offering a new type of value to its target market though design and the global sourcing of production of high-quality casual clothing at a reasonable price. Its troubles came when it lost that identity and became unclear about who its customers were for its three main and very different chains of stores: Gap, Old Navy, and Banana Republic. At the same time, other retailers learned how they could leverage those same global sources of production to offer high-quality apparel and lower prices.

So far, Zara has been clear in its identity and distinctive offers of customer value and has superbly engineered its value engine to optimize its own cost and profit balance. Li & Fung similarly has been outstanding in not only generating value for its customers, itself, shareholders, and partners, but also showing that it can transform over time.

Li & Fung is clearly in the superextender camp. Its value narrative has enabled it to continue to transform by leveraging the market forces as they evolve. Zara is in the "we don't know" category. It has a compelling narrative today. Time will tell if it has the opportunity platform to continue to adapt and grow.

Trade Liberalization: Policy Makers Plan, Innovators Exploit

The global apparel industry illustrates the three forces of disturbance at work in all their unpredictability. When the choice space opens up, the impacts are not linear and causal but highly dynamic. In this instance, after decades of debate, negotiation, and sophisticated policy analysis, world trade in textiles and apparel was liberalized, with the expectation that the results would be smooth and fairly incremental. (This is like the weather forecaster on TV news: "We are expecting the warm front moving across our area to veer out to sea this evening...The tropical storm is now a Category 4...Authorities have issued an emergency warning for Hurricane Bert.")

The markets had been governed by the Multifiber Arrangement (MFA), established in 1974 as an intentionally short-term agreement among forty countries.[99] This pact strictly governed export quotas, with the stated intention of making the global market quota-free in due course. Due course ended up being twenty years and four renegotiations of the MFA later, followed by the 1995 ATC (Agreement on Textiles and Clothing) that provided for a ten-year phaseout of quotas.

Each country naturally wanted to protect its apparel and textile producers, especially the developed nations that foresaw the inevitable growth of low-cost imports. But even after the phaseout, tariffs remained; importing countries could impose them or ask exporting ones to do so voluntarily.

Quotas or not, the landscape changed rapidly and turbulently. In 1975, 88 percent of all apparel sold in the United States was made domestically and 12 percent imported. By 1999, the figures were almost exactly reversed.[100] It was well understood in developed nations that the migration of apparel and often the related textile production to the new choice spaces of lower wages was now unstoppable.

Technology reinforced the shifts. The piecework nature of apparel-making encouraged modularity through standardization of thread counts, sizes, colors, buttons, and so on. The 1974 MFA limited the number of garments of a given type that could be exported by a country—men's cotton shirts, women's rayon/stretch lace/tricot undergarments, and so on.

Entrepreneurial instincts led companies to find ways around the complexity of the rules. They sourced and performed individual pieces and tasks across various countries, assembling and shipping the finished goods from the location that offered most advantages in tax, quotas, export licenses, and shipping. New industry players emerged on the scene, and modularity began to rule.

This was in direct contrast to the established value architecture of vertical integration. As recently as 1990, the US textile and apparel industry employed a million workers. By 2004, the figure had dropped by two-thirds. Now those look like the good old days.

In 1960, Burlington became the first textile firm to reach $1 billion in sales; it was the largest textile company globally and the forty-fifth biggest US corporation. It achieved another first for a textile firm when it hit $3 billion in revenues in 1981. It invested heavily in assets, including foreign acquisitions. By 2000, it operated forty-five manufacturing plants in the United States and Mexico—exactly forty-five more than Li & Fung. In 2001, it filed for bankruptcy.[101]

By then, the mass-market retailers had figured out that they did not need the US manufacturers. In 1987, the five largest fashion chains accounted for 35 percent of total national sales. This almost doubled by 1995; the top five merchandisers had 68 percent of the market.[102]

The retailers, not the producers, now owned the supply chains, from design through to sales. As they rationalized and integrated them, thus passing more power from manufacturer to retailer, firms such as Wal-Mart fueled a hollowing out of the apparel industry, with just the giants and small fashion boutiques surviving, and the midsized ones driven out.

Marks and Spenser in the United Kingdom and Gap in the United States were already dominant on the high street and in the mall. They extended that position to tighten the links in the supply chain. They worked closely with their leading suppliers to help them improve standards and productivity. The retailers' central procurement offices, with their skilled and often aggressive buyers, were increasingly in control of contract terms and prices. The very same manufacturers that the quotas were designed to protect were increasingly cut out of the picture. The retailers, coupled with offshored producers, could carry out all the activities from design to closing the sale.

They also began to leverage technology and standardized interfaces. Sears was an early and heavy investor in point of sale and the emerging new digital telecommunications technology. Players such as Wal-Mart transferred data captured by their point-of-sale systems to leading suppliers; between 1988 and 1992, EDI (electronic data interchange) linkages grew fivefold. Wal-Mart and others built highly automated distribution centers. Kmart bet $3 billion on IT as the core of its effort to catch back up with Wal-Mart.

Ironically, all these innovations not only eliminated hard-to-copy local supply chains, but established new ones that were easy to copy—plug and play can become unplug and play elsewhere. Little by little, but also further and further, faster and faster, and cheaper and cheaper, supply chain coordination and integration moved from innovative option to operational necessity.

Trade liberalization made and unmade players. Li & Fung, for example, had been a traditional broker up until the opening of the Chinese market. It was the first company to be granted a Chinese export license. Its strategic location in Hong Kong, the gateway for Chinese business, made it a natural hub.

The value chain of Burlington and European retailers, with its reliance on domestic manufacturing for sales to domestic stores was loosened by NAFTA and later the WTO's renegotiation of the Multifiber Arrangement. Technology and modularity just added fuel to the furnace of change. Wal-Mart, which had boasted about its Made in America commitment, became one of the main drivers of the China manufacturing surge.

The 2005 liberalization of the entire industry can be summarized as "We Didn't Plan for This" (policy makers), "Didn't Expect This" (the establishment mass producers), "Don't Know How to Handle It" (most of the domestic manufacturers that the policies were intended to protect and who survived only by offshoring production), and "We *Really* Love It."

The really-love-it group is the wide range of players that exploited liberalization, technology, and modularity very creatively. They include entirely new types of player. Nike, Liz Claiborne, and Reebok were 1970s start-ups that owned no manufacturing or stores and focused their value narratives on design and marketing.[103]

Specialty retailers such as The Limited bypassed domestic manufacturers and expanded their relationships and coordination capabilities to source manufacturing from Asia, Mexico, and the Caribbean. Private-label and store brands grew from almost nothing to half of US retailers' imports.[104] (The patterns are directly equivalent for Europe.) Such retailers expanded their value engines to add new modes of self-sourcing, including design, fabric selection, and remote monitoring of manufacturing.

This further modularized the traditional value chain to improve speed, quality, product variety, and fashionability, while streamlining costs and efficiency. The modularity directly enabled the trading-network companies that began as brokers and expanded into every area of supply chain coordination.

But this modularity did more than just fuel the launch of the new network orchestrators. It enabled economies of coordination. Without it, each retailer would have had to invest in the resources to manage the quota systems and supply chains on its own, especially in meeting the complex individual national and international compliance rules. Li & Fung stands out as archetypal in its success and sustaining of value creation, but it's just one among many opportunity-based innovators in an industry that had been almost frozen in its structure and dynamics.

Most of this innovation and variety of new value narratives was unplanned and can't be explained in terms of just policy. It's *all* about the choice space, and the more unpredictable the policy impacts are, the more unpredicted will be the new value narratives that make a claim to a place in the foreground of the landscape as viewed by customers. If these value narratives are supported by a powerful value engine, then these are companies that will jostle to become ultrasuccesses. Those that balance the drivers for growth today with investments in their opportunity platform will benefit from the next waves of disruption.

A few will put all these elements of the value architecture together. Li & Fung is one instance.

Li & Fung: The "Network Orchestrator"

Li & Fung deserves to be compared with Toyota as a firm that redefined its industry, with Amazon as an example of how an integrated opportunity platform and operational capabilities built around coordination can build a franchise of relationships, with Airtel as a blueprint for creating new value in underdeveloped areas of the world where capital for investing in traditional infrastructures is not available, and with Dell in making supply chain the competitive driver and differentiator of an entire industry.

At one level of perspective, Li & Fung may seem to be in a different business from Gap and Zara. The bulk of its apparel operations are centered on factories with low-paid workers in China, Vietnam, Thailand, India, Mauritius, and other countries in Asia, Europe, Latin America, and Africa. Zara's and Gap's operations mainly center on operating stores in Europe and North America.

Li & Fung has no stores. Its contribution to shoppers' value comes from its relationships with retailers. If you buy a garment at Kohl's, Liz Claiborne, Wal-Mart, Target, The Limited, Abercrombie and Fitch or Laura Ashley, or from chains such as Seiyu in Japan, Coles Meyer in Australia, or Mexico's Soriana, it will not be a Li &

Fung product, but it will probably be produced through Li & Fung. (If you stop off next door at Toys"R"Us, the same situation applies.)

Equally, if you are any of these chains of stores, you have many staff working on logistics all over the globe. Your success depends on keeping the two sectors of apparel manufacturing and retailing tightly connected and coordinated. In many instances, you may conclude that it makes more sense to hand over responsibility to Li & Fung rather than manage the supply chain internally.

An example from the company's top executive, Victor Fung, shows just how complex the art form of apparel supply chain management has become and also what it is that the firm brings to its retailer customers in handling that complexity:[105]

> Say we get an order from a European retailer to produce 10,000 garments. It's not a simple matter of our Korean office sourcing Korean products or our Indonesian office sourcing Indonesian products. For this customer we might decide to buy the yarn from a Korean producer but have it woven and dyed in Taiwan. So we pick the yarn and ship it to Taiwan.
>
> The Japanese have the best zippers and buttons, but they manufacture them mostly in China. Okay, so we go to YKK, a big Japanese zipper manufacturer and we order the right zippers from their Chinese plants.
>
> Then we determine that, because of quotas and labor conditions, the best place to make the garments is Thailand. So we ship everything there. And because the customer needs quick delivery, we may divide the order across five factories in Thailand...
>
> Five weeks after we have received the order, 10,000 garments arrive on the shelves in Europe, all looking like they came from one factory, with colors, for example, perfectly matched...We're not asking which country can do the best job overall. Instead, we're pulling apart the value chain and optimizing each step— and we're doing it globally.

This statement was made by Victor Fung a decade before the Internet had morphed into the coordination technology platform it is today.

In many regards, Li & Fung is directly analogous to Amazon. Both began with a core focus on a market segment: apparel manufacturing and book retailing. They both *evolved* a platform rather than *built* a company: an expansible infrastructure of integrated ecocomplex relationships, technology, processes, and services that can be customized to manage order fulfillment and supplier coordination based on customer requirements. Li & Fung has in its database fifteen thousand factories around the world that it calls on to produce components of a retail customer's orders, and Amazon has close to two million sellers connected to its website.

They have each extended the reach of their platform into new services and segments. Li & Fung has moved into toys, shoes, and hard goods, and it has broadened the array of services it offers to customers. Amazon is a player in dozens of areas of everyday consumer life. Both have single-mindedly built this value from the customer back to the organization. Amazon's branded customer experience is built on dimensions of personalization, variety, information, shipping, and retention and is coordinated through its technology platform. Li & Fung relies on its innovation of "Little John Waynes, " managers of about two hundred divisions with the expertise and authority needed to, in effect, coordinate Li & Fung on behalf of the customer.

Li & Fung globally sources a wide variety of consumer goods for a retailer or product-brand owner as, when, and where needed, and on a customized basis. It does so more efficiently than most of its customers can or want to commit resources to and, like Toyota, relies on continuous improvement in cost, quality, and speed.

Initially, its sourcing was confined to apparel, the focus of this chapter, but its opportunity platform has enabled it to extend into toys, fashion accessories, furnishings, handicrafts, and many other consumer goods. As it exploits the new opportunities created by the expanding consumer base inside China, it opportunistically finds it smart to build and own some distribution facilities, just as Amazon invests in fulfillment centers as coordination hubs. Both shifts are enabled by the design of the two companies' opportunity platforms.

Li & Fung's most distinctive capability is in driving down the overall end-to-end supply chain costs through coordination, often in creative ways that may actually increase the costs of individual steps and elements. For example, in some instances it may be cheaper to ship items in full containers with Li & Fung taking on the added expense of consolidating partial shipments, while at other times it may be better to ship partially full containers to avoid the cost of unpacking and repacking at the receiving end.

The firm built relationships with thousands of factories but did not take any ownership position. It also limited the fraction of each manufacturer's capacity that it contracts for. In both instances, this reduces the control of and dependence on each party in its relationships with the other.

Li & Fung takes responsibility for optimizing end-to-end logistics and has a coordinated view of the entire ecocomplex. This set of services and guarantees leaves the brands free to focus on design and marketing and the retailers to concentrate on the store and customer service. They place their orders, and Li & Fung handles the rest; the goods are made and store inventories replenished with no involvement by the retailer. Li & Fung will even handle the design of the products. It has also selectively purchased brands and turned them into private labels for retailers.

Given just how complex and time-sensitive the apparel industry is, this coordination on behalf of the customer turns the largely commodity service of a broker/intermediary into a premium capability that can be refined and extended and tailored to specific new markets. It makes Li & Fung in effect an interface that connects to all the players. It thus incorporates the customers' own processes and systems in the dynamic ecocomplex. Similarly, they can make their own "late-cycle" decisions to adjust orders to meet shifts in demand at short notice; this alone has reduced buying-cycle time by 60–70 percent.

The single most distinctive element of Li & Fung's value narrative is its targeting "the soft three dollars." This figure equals the expense and markups along the supply chain for every one dollar of manufacturing cost. This is waste; it reduces, not adds to, value. By eliminating it, or rather by coordinating it into extinction, Li & Fung cuts its own costs, is able to pass on the savings to customers, and boosts the efficiency of the manufacturers who are at the same time its suppliers and also its customers.

The value captured by Li & Fung's ecocomplex is in striking contrast to the financial performance of apparel manufacturers and most retailers. Its customer base grew 300 percent in a decade, from 350 retailers to over 1,000 between 1998 and 2008. Suppliers increased by 60 percent, from 7,500 to 12,000. Li & Fung amounts to 30–70 percent of most suppliers' total business. Its compounded sales growth has been over 20 percent a year since the mid-1990s, with a total increase of 775 percent from 1998–2008. Its percentage return on equity averaged more than 30 percent from 1995 to 2007. With the global financial crisis, it fell to just below 20 percent in 2008 and 2009.

The 2009 decision by Liz Claiborne's CEO to sell the firm's entire sourcing operations, which handled all aspects of production from material selection to manufacturing, to Li & Fung illustrates Li & Fung's value path for future relationships and acquisitions.[106]

Liz Claiborne has struggled in the recession that produced a "battered retail landscape." It must bring to market high-value fashion clothing on an ever-faster time schedule. It has a limited international presence in the countries where key suppliers are located. By selling off its sourcing arm to Li & Fung, to whom it will pay a commission for its own orders, it can focus on design excellence, its key capability. This is a general feature of the new sourcing relationships: while more and more items sold in the United States—apparel, consumer electronic, golf clubs, furniture, phones—are made abroad, they are largely still designed at home.

Li & Fung illustrates the blended asset-sourcing mix that seems to be a natural evolution in the maturation of many fast-surge, long-growth companies where the assets and capabilities are spread throughout the ecocomplex, each company providing what it is best at. Li & Fung adds value to the companies it buys through its operational capabilities today and making them part of its infrastructure and process base. Value is generated by focusing and coordinating all those capabilities on behalf of the customer. It appears very likely that this will be as much the blueprint for expansion as vertical integration was for so many large companies for a century or more.

Li & Fung Viewed as an Opportunity Platform

Li & Fung can be viewed as an opportunity platform just by tracking where it is now, versus where it began and how it made its way to sustaining its future as a superextender. The traditional value-chain company is largely linear in its growth; it's a freight train moving along the track. The platform company, of which Li & Fung is a physical instance and Amazon, Google, and Apple newer digital exemplars, looks more like a map of the night sky. It is part of an expanding energy source that reaches out to new stars and planets—its ecocomplex relationships and customers—and moves on into new constellations and business galaxies.

Li & Fung started out very much on Planet Earth, Hong Kong station. It expanded in terms of reach to new ecocomplex partners and customers and then to new markets and choice spaces. Today, it comprises three network structures:[107]

Trading network:

- The largest global sourcing platform, reaching fifteen thousand suppliers.
- Sources 30 percent of the brands found in an average US shopping mall.[108]
- Extended from soft goods (garments and apparel) to hard goods (toys, home furnishings, footwear, and health and beauty products).
- Tailored demand chain for each customer order, from design all the way through to delivering the finished product.

Logistics network:

- Physical movement of goods via one hundred distribution centers.
- Menu of modularized solutions, from warehousing to transport, repacking, customs brokerage, freight forwarding, consolidation, etc.
- Value-added services, including supply chain analytics, value engineering.

Distribution network:

- Three pillars: private labels, proprietary brands, licensing of brands.
- Focus on design, sales and marketing, distribution, supported by supply chain management.
- Started in United States, moved to Europe, and is now the platform for its entry into the Chinese consumer market.

Li & Fung's expansion was a fairly natural evolution that built on its capability base while getting off the freight-train track. It is not diversification in the style of conglomerate firms looking to accumulate a portfolio of companies. Instead, it balances a core "same" and starburst "different" coherence. The three networks all exploit its sourcing, logistics, and coordination core, but they move into a variety of new areas: private-label clothing, customs brokerage, toys, shoes, logistics, design, and warehousing. And along the way, its new markets: United States, Europe, Japan, China. These are its starbursts.

This points toward the need for platform companies to focus their resource management strategies to achieve the coherence and not the conglomerate effect. There are some common patterns among archetypal ultrasuccesses in this regard, which we use in the final chapters of *The Value Path* to answer the obvious management question: what do we *do*?

Part of the doing is to exploit modularity and asset blending. This provides organizational and market flexibility. But the pieces don't fit themselves together automatically, and modularity is useless without the platform, which in turn doesn't come prepackaged. The picture for assembling this business jigsaw puzzle is created by executive leadership.

Li & Fung's top management planning process is well documented, through Victor and William Fung's outstanding book, *Competing in a Flat World* (2008), and a variety of case studies. The formalized planning process for direction- and goal-setting takes place every three years. This time horizon is shorter than might be assumed, given that the issues are long-term in their dynamics.

This suggests that platform companies can afford a slightly shorter perspective than the asset-intensive firms, which must constantly consider how to preserve their investment, and a longer one than those companies that have to constantly work out how to react to change rather than take charge of it through their platform as an innovation launchpad.

"My job is to manage our company for the next hundred minutes and position it for the next hundred years." This is the (as always) insightful epigram of Bill McGowan, founder of the original MCI, the company that transformed the entire value narrative of telecommunications and directly drove the divestiture of AT&T. (MCI was sold after his death to one of the more notorious corporate crooks of recent decades and became an ultrabomb.)

McGowan's leadership statement is an apt summary of the ethos of platform companies such as Li & Fung. How does the conceptual value narrative get turned into practical results, as measured by the metaphorical next hundred minutes? The answer is "through operational capabilities that leverage the firm's resources."

How do those same capabilities help position the company for the next hundred years? The answer must be "through the development of an opportunity platform that coordinates existing and new resources for launching expansion and innovation in times of uncertainty and hence unknown opportunity."

Victor and William Fung take the long view in planning but run the company on operational excellence today. They anchor their meshing of the views through the three-year process they began in 1989, with the goal of setting stretch goals that would double operating profits over the coming three years; this financial target has become the main plot element in the company's evolving value narrative.

Meeting these goals requires balancing revenues and costs to ensure increased margins. Li & Fung must expand its value dimensions to avoid the Commodity Trap and create offers that command a premium price: "Nobody is going to pay you more unless you do more."[109]

The "more" initially came from organic growth with some acquisitions. For 1990–92 and 1993–95, the priority was to consolidate the base: dispersed manufacturing, expanding the supplier network, and creating dedicated customer teams. In recent years, Li & Fung has expanded both its markets and sourcing options through an aggressive acquisition program: four major deals and ten smaller ones in Q1, 2011, alone.

The acquisitions and growth in the number of relationships and scope of operations led to an organizational innovation that added a new dimension of customer and company value. This was the establishment of the new cadre of customer relationship managers:

"Little John Waynes" (LJWs). They act as entrepreneurs to develop and manage each customer relationship and the customized demand chain for that customer. They have unlimited pay potential, build their own teams, and operate with complete discretion in designing the services and terms of the relationship for their customers.

This enables Li & Fung to build the human capital capabilities that reinforce its value dimensions of ecocomplex relationships, technology, and financial structures. The LJWs can concentrate on the customer conversation knowing they are backed up by a powerful and consistent set of coordinated capabilities.

By the end of the 1990s, Li & Fung had about sixty business divisions; this number has grown to over two hundred. Each is headed by a Little John Wayne who is running a $20 million–$50 million operation. Modularity enables the LJWs to manage complexity. Their formal role provides a way of avoiding the problems of fiefdoms, territoriality, and the necessary narrow focus of the many units that comprise the ecocomplex in everyday action.

Victor Fung is very clear that the company's value architecture rests on growing and extending its ecocomplex as a platform. The goal is to build, maintain, and extend what he terms the customer demand chain: "The network orchestrator starts with the customer and builds the chain to achieve the desired result."[110] This means that cost-efficiency comes from the orchestrator, not any individual unit. This is his rationale:[111]

> At Li & Fung we think about supply chain management as "tackling the soft $3" in the cost structure. What do we mean by that? If a typical consumer product leaves the factory at a price of $1, it will eventually end up on retail shelves at $4.
>
> Now we can try to squeeze the cost of production down 10 cents or 20 cents per product, but today you have to be a genius to do that because everybody has been working on that for years and there is not a lot of fat left.
>
> It is better to look at the cost that is spread throughout the distribution channels—the soft $3. It offers a bigger target, and if you take 50 cents out, no one will even know you are doing it.
>
> So it is a much easier place to effect savings for our customers.

One impact of this strategy is that any new acquisition or supplier relationship both adds to the overall capabilities of the ecocomplex and also benefits from them.

Here is a short summary of the sequence of Li & Fung's three-year plans in this new century:[112]

- *2002–04*: License premium brands, such as Levi Strauss's Signature line; expand value-added premium services to include product design and development.

- *2005–07*: Focus on onshore expansion to service the US market; add private-label and proprietary brands to the ecocomplex via licensing, to complement the premium ones; extend sales, marketing, and distribution capabilities; expand into order analysis (to help reduce markdowns and process inefficiencies), contract shipping, custom clearance. All this positioned Li & Fung to build its distribution network base.
- *2008–10*: Expand onshoring to Europe; acquire IDS (Integrated Distribution Services) as the core for the third network: logistics. The focus here is on helping US brands get their products to retail stores in China.
- *2011–13*: Extend onshoring capabilities to Asia, especially China.

The natural evolution of business modularity and ecocomplex development is "plug-and-play." This is a term taken from the computer hardware field, where it refers to any gizmo, such as a USB, that can be plugged into a system where it is automatically recognized and activated so it plays without having to be configured, installed, specially wired, tested, with prayers then invoked and curses inveighed before trying again.

Victor Fung uses the phrase plug-and-play to describe the platform approach to back-office functions run by its OSG unit (Operations Support Group). He rejects the option to outsource them:

The ability to build and tailor a plug-and-play enterprise is a core competency of Li & Fung. It enables the company to grow and acquire new firms, facilitate sharing information, and keep loosely linked businesses aligned with overall corporate goals.

In building its plug-and-play platform, Li & Fung's OSG systems are so integral to the success of the enterprise that they need to be directed from inside the company.[113]

There is a fairly consistent move by superextenders today to centrally manage and standardize processes that they can plug-and-transfer to their acquisitions to provide a strong coordination capability. Tesco and Bharti are examples; they manage key resources critical to the evolution and exploitation of their opportunity platforms as core to their company "way." Corporate finance, human resource policy, and IT are the main areas.

Victor Fung summarizes the goal as the creation of "an open culture that allows for differences under a common 'umbrella [enterprise] culture.'"[114] So, for instance, overseas offices develop their own management processes, while the umbrella culture handles remuneration, incentive schemes, and compliance.

Three Value Narratives within an Industry

An old TV cowboy series was pithily titled *Have Gun—Will Travel*. Li & Fung can be summarized as "Have Platform—Will Travel." Travel where and when? Pretty much anywhere and soon.

9 Two Ultrasuccesses: One Fades, One Sustains

Gap: From Fun and Trendy to Bland and Big

Gap was a successful but relatively small specialty retailer, reborn in 1983 under the leadership of Mickey Drexler, an industry superstar. His strength was his intuition and ability to spot fashion trends early. The relaunched Gap was built to exploit this by introducing new items in stores every six to eight weeks and getting customer reaction quickly.[115]

The offer was basic casual apparel: sturdy, colorful cotton clothing such as jeans and sweaters. "Everyone can wear these [Gap] clothes...We want to provide the basic pieces for anyone's closet."[116] The Gap's value architecture was designed to produce high-quality goods at a low cost. Its market identity was reinforced through heavy promotion and advertising, the highest in the industry.

Quality rested on its in-house capabilities in the design of clothes and choice of materials. Low cost came from leveraging the market forces to operate a manufacturing sourcing network that spanned fifty countries; it was very early in exploiting trade liberalization and the resulting new supply chain choice space.

The firm made all the decisions on sourcing and quality and coordinated the supply chain. It faced many pressures from public advocacy groups to ensure compliance with rules on labor conditions and to ensure worker safety and well-being, a responsibility it is generally seen as having met well.

The Gap was a phenomenon of growth up through the 1990s, comparable to Starbucks's later success in terms of business innovation and cultural impact. It bought Banana Republic and opened Old Navy to expand its market segments. However, from 2002 on, the story was one of contraction. Same-store sales increased in only one year in the last decade. The adjectives applied to Gap were increasingly ones like "struggling" and "disappointing." Drexler was fired in 2002, as were his successor as CEO in 2007 and other senior executives in Gap's main companies over a number of years.

Gap remains a force in retailing, but it has been unable to adapt to shifts in customer value by delivering new, attractive offers that they will seek out in the expanding apparel choice space at a price that allows Gap to capture new value for itself and its shareholders.

Initially, customer value seemed to give it an almost unbeatable competitive identity. Increasingly, it lost that identity—and customers. Its value engine fueled much of that erosion. It got trapped along a winding path where to provide customer value, it had to speedily provide variety, fashion, and choice while its operational capabilities relied on cost control and scale. Its value architecture tilted out of balance and has remained so.

Like Starbucks, Gap's initial growth came from its creating a new space where customers could fulfill unmet and even unknown needs. It turned jeans and white cotton T-shirts into—well, jeans and white cotton T-shirts, but with a difference: an appeal to a new generation of shoppers (the gap in its name).

It began as a localized specialty store in San Francisco, stocking just Levi jeans and LP records. Its founder, Donald Fisher, was a real-estate developer. His business grew to 566 stores. But he was not a merchandiser. The products were ho-hum and the stores shabby. Gap stumbled along until he hired Mickey Drexler in 1983.[117]

The legendary Drexler had a remarkable sense of trends and how to target customer segments. He made changes quickly and radically, transforming the Gap's value narrative. His vision was one of "basic, with attitude." He got rid of private labels and dumped all non-Gap products, except Levi jeans. Those, too, were eliminated in 1992.

He repositioned Gap's capabilities and hired a team of designers with the directive of creating only what they themselves would choose to wear. They picked their own materials, and Gap began to monitor the producers to assure their quality.

Drexler renovated the stores and began advertising heavily to build the new Gap brand. He set a policy of changing clothing styles and colors every six to eight weeks. It is not clear that the designers were ever able to achieve better than eight to ten weeks, but the stretch target focused their efforts, and they were far faster than the industry multimonth averages.

Gap became an ultrasuccess almost overnight. It sustained its trajectory for well over a decade. When Drexler was fired in 2002, sales had reached $14.5 billion, up from $480 million at the end of 1983, a 3,000 percent increase. Gross margins had reached 38–45 percent, and net margins were 15–18 percent. They have dropped below 10 percent since then.

Gap sizzled whenever it found the right wavelength to excite customers. When the workplace went casual in the 1990s, it offered new selections of khaki pants. Sharon Stone wore a black Gap mock turtleneck to the Oscars; stores literally couldn't stock the item fast enough to meet the surge in demand in the following weeks. Models graced the cover of *Vogue* in white Gap jeans and shirts. "Retro celebrities" added flair to Gap's heavy marketing blitzes.

Two Ultrasuccesses: One Fades, One Sustains

Old Navy's "breathtaking" growth was built on "silly ads, lively stores," and inexpensive fashions sold in "industrial chic" stores, with the "simple yet revolutionary goal to make shopping fun for middle-income families." Its tenets were "fun, fashion, and value."[118]

It was even more successful than Gap itself and reached $1 billion in sales just four years after it was set up as a "markdown version" of its parent firm; customers could buy jeans for $22 versus $34 for the Gap brand. At one point, it accounted for 40 percent of the company's total sales.

Gap's 2008 annual report rhapsodizes that Old Navy had "entered the retail market with a wink and a smile and became an instant hit with its irreverent advertising." Banana Republic, the third of the main Gap chains, began as a high-end, travel-oriented store with a safari theme. It offers "accessible luxury" clothes that provide higher margins than the other groups; it was noted for its "eccentric" catalog and attracted young professionals.

The very language that commentators use to describe the glory years of Gap's growth is full of words that highlight vibrancy and color. The words got duller as time went on. What stands out in Gap's history is that its growth was built on creating new dimensions of customer value. In each instance—Gap, Old Navy, and Banana Republic—it targeted a specific type of person with a distinctive new offer that was more about the shopping experience and sense of self than just the product.

That somehow all got lost. Again and again, commentators contrast its early attributes with such opposite criticisms as "a saturated market and fashion missteps along the way,"[119] "pursuing fickle teenage customers and alienating its over-30 customers,"[120] "we're watching to see if Gap can mend its brand,"[121] and "a very tired brand that does not resonate with the public."[122]

What seems to account for the change in adjectives from ones about fun to blandness is that Gap's value narrative rested on Drexler's intuition of fashion trends and his ability to anticipate what customers would choose in the next season. Its value engine rested on costs, and costs rested on mass production and supply chain rationalization. That killed any concept of rapid fashion response, because its supply chain was not configured to handle it.

Even though new items were moved into the stores every two months or so, they were variants on existing designs. The design-to-product delivery cycle was more typically nine months. If customers did not like the new products on offer, there was no way to move the merchandise, plus all the goods still on their way along the pipeline, except through price discounts and remaindering.

Gap was an innovator in the evolution of the shopping mall as a social and psychological nexus, which gave it advantages of location. That meant being everywhere. According to the *Wall Street Journal*, "Gap pioneered the strategy of developing a popular store and expanding it to every viable shopping location in the U.S.—then beginning the process all over again with a new brand."[123] Today, Gap still operates over three thousand stores, mostly in the United States, though it has been closing domestic namesake stores. By the end of 2013, it plans to have 34 percent fewer US outlets than in 2007. So much for the value of stores as assets.

Long-term debt increased to finance the growth surge. Gap's relative advertising expenditures were twice the average of its competitors. Obviously, all this increased the need for financial capital and put pressure on earnings. Gap's expansion coincided with the opening of China as a manufacturing giant. It exploited the opportunity and established a supply chain that provided scale, but at the cost of speed.

The decision to launch Old Navy rested on the single issue of supply chain management. Gap's supplier base of garment factories needed to produce a lower-priced line of products using less expensive fabrics and finishes for it to make a profit on Old Navy's much lower prices. It couldn't do so over the long term as the same manufacturing options became available to its competitors.

Gap did not solve the problems of flexibility and speed versus scale and cost, and its operations suffered. It became heavily centralized. One commentator summarized the result as "[Gap] have become so process-driven that it is not about product any more. It is more important where they get those one million units made than what those units are."[124]

An example of the impact of increased centralization was the decision by the new CEO in 2003 to launch a company-wide plan to remake the supply chain. One major goal was to consolidate purchase of fabrics across the main brands: Gap, Old Navy, and Banana Republic. So, for instance, since all three used denim bought from multiple suppliers, large central purchases would cut costs and speed the merchandise flow from design to store.[125]

The result was the use of a lowest-common-denominator fabric of one level of quality, one weave, and one weight. The three brands all made jeans, but for entirely different market segments. A single material might fit all customers but certainly did not appeal to them all. Designers resigned themselves to being unable to anticipate fashion trends and opportunities to launch new products. After three years, the plan was abandoned entirely.

Another failure in the remake was in how test samples were handled. These are the bridge between design innovation and market success and a key capability in turning invention into innovation. The prototype designs had previously been made at studios in the Manhattan Garment District, a hub of small firms that compete on creativity and speed.

The CEO moved the entire sample-making to Asia, where the majority of Gap's suppliers are located. The coordination burden became an overload. Designers had to create patterns, send them to Asia, wait for the samples to come back, make changes, and reiterate the process again and again. The logic was to cut costs. Instead, the plan produced decentralized fragmentation and delays, plus centralized control and rigidity; all overnight shipments from New York to Asia required senior corporate-level approval.

One ex-Gap designer summarized the result as it "made you less nimble." With all the loss of speed and coordination, "we'd go back and forth, and change, and redo, and then we'd be out of time before orders had to be placed or stores would have empty shelves." Staffers fell back on lowest-common-denominator items, with bland styles they hoped would be acceptable to enough customers "but risked pleasing no one."[126]

It's not clear whether Gap lost touch with the shift in what customers value, or if it focused too much on capturing company value in the form of short-term profits. The industry consensus places the blame mainly on erosion of the customer value that Gap was able to generate. The examples above suggest that the firm's short-term drive to make money got in the way of the customer relationship, product innovation, and design excellence; there was a growing contradiction between the mass/scale/cost priorities of company value and fun/style/personal value priorities of the customer.

In either case, Gap did not, and still does not, have a value architecture that enables it to adapt and change in response to the continuing forward disturbance created by the market forces.

In comparing Gap and Li & Fung, there are some very apparent commonalities and some stark contrasts. Both are sourcing globally. Both are minimizing cost while delivering quality goods. Both are process driven, but their processes and supply chains are structured to deliver very different value. Li & Fung's supply chain is built around giving customers anything they want with a rapid response time (mass customization). Gap's is built to deliver the same products for all (mass production). Li & Fung may be contributing to Gap's problem. Other retailers, such as Kohl's, can now easily source merchandise through Li & Fung that is similar in design, quality, and cost to Gap's.

Zara: Fast Fashion via Virtual Vertical Integration

Zara is as "hot" as Gap was at its peak. Gap's offer to customers was high quality and low cost, and up-to-date fashion: casual rather than trendy. Zara's is medium-quality goods and the very latest fashion. Its primary focus is on the customer experience through its store design, which is based on a waste of space, lack of variety, and minimization of inventory, even at the risk of stockouts. Put that way, all this sounds like a weakness, and it would be so for Gap.

But it fits Zara's value narrative. The firm's identity is built on offering fashion-conscious buyers a fresh assortment of the latest designer-style garments. Its stores are in prime locations for its target customers, who are likely repeat buyers. The idea is that they can drop by the store and look for new items that grab their fancy. They had better buy the clothes quickly, because those goods probably won't be in stock the next time they come in. The store layout draws their attention to what is on offer *now*.

Some 75 percent of Zara's merchandise turns over every three to four weeks, and it introduces eleven thousand new products a year, compared with two thousand to four thousand for most fashion apparel retailers. Wear the clothes ten times or so; they are not designed or manufactured to be durable.[127] Why should they be? Why add extra cost that would get in the way of Zara offering a relatively low price for the very latest fashions? One industry analyst comments that at any point in time, it has less variety of products on offer than, say, Gap, but more over time.

The most distinctive element of Zara's value engine is that it sources from the low-cost global producer ecocomplex only 40–50 percent of the finished items it sells.[128] It makes the rest itself, handling weaving, dying, and cutting of material through several dozen highly automated factories it owns in northern Spain. It then relies on a local ecocomplex of assemblers to finish the work.[129]

This balances the lower costs of using external firms with the speed and flexibility of local and in-house production. Zara offsets the higher overall costs by not offering price discounts, avoiding markdowns, and not spending money on advertising and marketing. The store is the ad, and word of mouth and repeat buyers are the effective promotion.[130]

Speed is Zara's strategic capability edge, which runs through all its operations. Lead times in apparel manufacturing vary widely, depending on the product, location, and so on. A survey of Indian producers in 2009 provides a benchmark for comparing Zara with the overall industry.

The survey estimated an average of three to four months for manufacturing a new product.[131] Typically, additional time for handling design development and testing and shipping extends this to six to nine months before the goods hit the store. Zara's cycle time from design to store is four to five *weeks*. It uses batch production of small lots. After testing customer response, modifications take two weeks for restocking.[132]

Retailers used to plan their products for an annual season and sign advance agreements with manufacturers for production. Now the average chain precommits for about half its forecast volumes, making adjustments to meet fluctuations in demand. The main risk here is that even a small gap between programmed supply and decidedly nonplannable fluctuations in demand results in either a stockout—an industry adage is that a lost sale is a loss forever—or a markdown. Zara is as close to real-time in matching supply and demand as any firm could be. Only 15 percent of its products (as measured by dollar sales volume) are precommitted.[133]

A 2007 study shows how Zara makes more money on lower prices through speed from design to sale. A specialty store competing with Zara may offer a black dress for $100, with an initial margin of $70. It is typically able to sell 50 percent of its inventory at the full price. By contrast, Zara moves 85 percent of its inventory at its 15 percent lower price of $85. This translates to 50–60 percent higher net margins and 30 percent more sales per square foot of store space.[134]

The figures in many surveys capture Zara's balance between the value created for the customer and the value captured by the company. Shoppers visit their Zara store seventeen times a year, versus three to four times for its competitors. And they pay full price; Zara generates only 15–20 percent of its revenues from markdowns. Its leading European peers are in the 30–40 percent range, and their marketing expenses average 3–4 percent of sales; Zara's are 0.3 percent. It does almost no advertising.[135]

Value narratives are in themselves a sort of autobiography: how some aspect of an individual entrepreneur's or small team's experience and insight intersect with the forces of disturbance to create an opening for them to exploit. At some point it becomes crystallized and forms the core mission of the firm. In retrospect, it can seem almost like a simple Archimedes-in-the-bath "Eureka!" or Newton getting bonked on the head by a piece of fruit knocked off a tree (probably by one of those nuisance squirrels again).

Examples are Michael Dell's insight that the personal computer would become a commodity and that companies like IBM and Compaq would not be able to afford their expensive overhead, so he'd better invent the Supply Chain era, or Larry Page's observing how tracking which sites users visited would solve most of the issues of identifying relevance in Internet search queries.

The folklore of business "thinking outside the box," creating a "new paradigm," or other well-worn clichés includes Taiichi Ohno wandering around a US supermarket ruminating on Toyota's problems obtaining supplies during the post–World War II occupation of Japan. He observed how shelves and fridges were replenished on a just-in-time basis and *zowie!*—lean production, kanban, TQM, and Six Sigma launched into global orbit.

It's never that easy or instant, of course. It took Ohno a full decade to deploy just-in-time inventory management. Howard Schulz stopped for an espresso in a "great theater experience" Milan coffee bar where the barista was "pulling shots with a smile stamped on his face" many years before he expanded his Starbucks coffeehouse beyond Seattle and began his caffeination of the galaxy. However brilliant the insight, ultrasuccesses need a value engine, and the reverse applies, too; however great the value engine, it needs the insight to keep ahead of the pack when change becomes the norm and the opportunity platform to make the move.

Inditex, Zara's parent company, illustrates the dynamics of such entrepreneurship. Its founder, Amancio Ortega Gaona, set up his first garment manufacturing firm in 1963. He had long wanted to make quality clothing for more than just the wealthy and had become a student of the apparel industry's processes and costs in the manufacturing-to-retail cycle.

He expanded to four factories over the next decade, relying on distribution across Europe through independent contractors. A large cancelled order pushed him close to bankruptcy. His only solution was to move integration forward. He opened his first store, exploiting his situational advantages, which became a structural component of Zara's value architecture: location and pulling in customers.

He sited the store near one of his factories and next to one of the town's best known upmarket department stores. He summarized his Ohno/Dell insight as, "You need to have five fingers touching the factory and five touching the customer."[136] That translates to: control what happens to your product until the customer buys it.

His first store featured low-price look-alike versions of popular higher-end clothes and was very successful. In the next decade, he expanded throughout Spain, focusing on its larger cities. He evolved his value architecture to drive down cycle time from design to sale, a process he called "instant fashion." In Italy, Benetton was moving in exactly the same direction.[137]

The narrative was clear and crisp. Zara's target customer base was sixteen- to twenty-four-year-olds. It offered fashion goods rather than branded products. Ortega monitored the fashion shows and press to get their opinions and alerts about the latest trends. He did not need the outside fashion houses to create original designs for him; he simply and rapidly copied what was hot, manufactured the goods, and moved them quickly to his local stores. He replenished stocks from his nearby factories, making sure he was always able to use available materials.[138]

He not only gained the advantage of the fashion houses' expertise without their heavy costs, but also then beat them to market with his own lower price and lower-cost products, because they followed the traditional seasonal cycle, which meant up to a one-year gap before their creations hit the stores. Ortega was on both sides of the street, in his phrase: making high fashion fast fashion.

He was quick to recognize the value of computers in the late 1970s, because his success rested on spotting what was selling in the stores and moving fast to adjust production. Excellent and up-to-date though his information was, automation of sales records made it more accurate and timely.[139]

He expanded outside of Spain, balancing organic growth and acquisitions. His value architecture evolved very much along the same path as Li & Fung's, though the network orchestrator helped retailers loosen the five fingers and coordinated the integration of their demand and supply chain.

Zara did the same for its own internal coordination and integration that tightened the fingers: replenishment twice weekly based on demand, distribution center hub-and-spoke logistics, quick store feedback, rapid design and manufacturing, highly automated factories using CAD/CAM, meticulous store site selection, and localization of materials supply and product assembly.

The main difference between the two firms is that Li & Fung's opportunity platform seems more open to adaptation and expansion across new choice spaces, while there are a few hints of rain clouds on the Zara horizon. Because everything is distributed from Spain, even items sourced from China and to be sold in China are hubbed through the Spanish facilities. Since all remote stores are replenished twice weekly, goods must be shipped by air, not sea. To maintain margins, Zara charges higher prices in the markets that are far away from its Spanish base, with Japan incurring a 50 percent premium and the United States 60 percent, for instance.[140]

Its value narrative and sophisticated value engine remain solid. Customers show with their purses that they love the dimensions of value on offer today. But remember that this is the fashion business, and fast fashion is the Zara differentiator. The question remains unanswered: when will another firm come on the scene with new dimensions of value that customers shift toward, and when—not if— they do, does Inditex have the opportunity platform to respond?

The Value Path is not a thesis on the death of assets and vertical integration. It is, though, a challenge to what may be termed asset thinking. We have selected our three examples from the apparel industry to span a spectrum of an asset-light to an asset-heavy operational base.

Li & Fung is at the asset-light extreme. It took over the entire handling of global logistics for retailers, without itself owning a single manufacturing facility. Gap is in the middle. It maintains tight control of most designer-to-producer-to-consumer activities while outsourcing basic manufacturing. On the surface, Zara is at the opposite end of the asset/control versus relationship/sourcing spectrum from Li & Fung. It combines two major historical traditions in retailing, getting the best of both. This is a clever value narrative that so far has enabled it to escape the failures of each approach to adapt to the forces of change, especially globalization and trade liberalization.

Zara is vertically integrated for its in-season, high-fashion products. It maintains tight control of every activity for the 50 percent of its goods that add up to 85 percent of its sales revenues. But an adjective is needed here; it is a *virtual* vertical integrated company. While it owns a few dozen factories and almost all of its stores, it relies on an ecocomplex of over five hundred local producers that assemble the goods it makes.

It may be no coincidence that Zara began operations (in 1975) in northern Spain. European apparel manufacturing and retailing have been built on "fast fashion." The Italian *pronto moda* and French *mode de la rue* (street fashion) rely on highly localized small firms that make design their edge.

A 2005 US National Science Foundation report on how to save the dying US industry pointed at the displacement of the vibrant thousands of New York City *mode de la rue* equivalents centered in Soho and the garment district as a missed opportunity. Half of these US "cut and sew" manufacturing operations had fewer than twenty employees.[141]

Each of the three companies in our analysis had its own rationale for choosing its balance of make/buy and own/access resources. Our main point in comparing them is that the question your firm has to ask in harnessing the forces is what will be your offers and to whom? Then and only then can you address the issues of the blended asset/sourcing mix. It thus makes sense for Zara to push toward control given that its offers are marked by a constant flow of new designs, rapid response to very short-term fashion shifts, and "buzz" rather than cost or quality.

Gap's offer was casual and trendy clothes at a low price; this pushed it toward a wider and larger supply chain complex built on economies of scale (cost) but also flexibility and individualization in the supply chain (trendy). Li & Fung's offer is unseen optimization—any of the elements of any aspect of supply chain capability optimized on behalf of the customer without the retailer having to know how it is all done.

Zara's offer is still gaining customers. In 2012, the disastrous year for Spain when its banking system came close to collapse and unemployment was over 20%, Inditex reported a 15% increase in sales with higher margins and became the largest company in the nation in terms of market capitalization. Keep in mind that Inditex gets 25% of its sales from Spain and another 45% other European countries, some of which were not in a whole lot better economic shape than Spain. Zara's platform was able to deliver what customers wanted in a time when their wishes had changed dramatically. Speed plus adaptability are a powerful platform combination.

10 The Innovation Cube

Resourcing the Business

Innovation has to start somewhere in the firm, but it can't end up being stuck there. Leadership is obviously a key element in setting direction and priorities, but the innovation agenda will remain just a goal unless the leaders' plan goes beyond vision statements, mandates, and exhortations from the executive suite.

Equally, innovation gets shut in a box when ideas that come up the management hierarchy from employees get blocked, not necessarily by "bureaucracy" or "resistance to change," but by their being impractical right from the beginning, given, say, the firm's asset base, information technology, marketing processes, or other organizational constraints.

When firms get stranded along their value path, it's always tempting for insiders and outside commentators to focus on the need for stronger leadership or culture change, rather than on the interplay between the two. Leadership certainly enables leaps in innovation: the big, bold moves that help turn a firm around. This is innovation as an event. The everyday challenge is the next innovation. And the ones after that. And after that.

That's where culture comes in. A well-resourced, well-managed culture can keep a flow of innovations coming from all over the organization—for decades in some instances. But today that innovation must be based on *if*. The "if" contrasts with "given" and lies behind the new archetypal value architectures. The "if" is based on unbounded innovation in an environment of change and uncertainty, whereas the "given" is based on bounded innovation in an environment of stability and predictability.

The value chain companies that thrived in most of the last century built organizational structures and cultures that were efficient for their todays, *given* stability in the structure of the industry and corresponding choice spaces and value dimensions. They were also built to innovate for tomorrow, but again, *given* that the choice space wouldn't change too much or too fast and that the dimensions of value on which customers based their decisions were also not likely to move too far outside the bounds of the organization's capabilities.

Many of the most admired firms of the *Fortune* 1000 thrived on the givens, and they motivated, developed, and rewarded innovators. The leadership provided the guiding narrative, and the culture responded. Every day. Examples are Proctor and Gamble, Shell, GE, IBM, Pfizer, Delta Airlines, and many others. For many decades, these companies were models of management practice and seemed likely to remain so.

It's when the given becomes iffy that this doesn't work so well and often winds down to a crawl. "Our priority for next year is to increase customer retention" means "We have the capabilities we need and know what we want to achieve. We just have to focus our efforts, and we will achieve this. As long as things stay the same as now."

Add: "But if they don't stay the same, then..." Then what? Once a firm accepts that "if" may soon turn out to be "when," both leadership and culture must become much more adaptive. The leadership value narrative, the vehicle for communicating the direction, will become more future-focused, rather than history-based. It will demand getting away from a narrow product, industry, or distribution viewpoint.

The organization will be marked by increased turnover, fewer guarantees of promotions and pensions, more urgency, and much more diversity of skills, services, and collaborative relationships. There will be a series of asset-reduction programs. Incentive systems will be redefined to encourage cross-functional teamwork and a shift in balancing revenue/profit/cost goals.

But where does the culture fit in as this evolves? Perhaps it will become more nontrusting, with everyone in it looking at change from their own personal and job perspective. By contrast, it could become more energized, with risk takers given a new freedom to act. It may largely shape itself as pressures and opportunities encourage different behaviors and personalities.

In some instances, the signals from the top of the organization will push it in any one of many directions that make it narrow, open, aggressive, short-term results oriented, collegial, or insular. In others, a new leader finds that he or she has relatively limited influence, however much lip service subordinates respond with. So leadership is critical to innovation but may run up against culture. Culture is key and may be affected positively or negatively by leadership. There's a missing middle here between the leadership that sets the agenda for innovation and the culture where the work gets done.

Resource blueprints bridge the gap. If the people don't have the appropriate resources to leverage their work and collaboration, there is no way they can execute the innovation agenda. The Asset Trap is an example of inappropriate blueprints; the world is moving along a new trajectory, but the firm's facilities or corporate infrastructures block the culture from changing course. The Commodity Trap amounts to all core resources being tied up in areas that generate less and less value over time.

Resource decisions are the *only* discretionary vehicle for managers to enable innovation. They can make offers to customers, make a case to investors, and motivate staff, but in each instance, they can only influence the results, not control them. They do control where funds are spent and contracts made to increase this influence.

They had better get these resource commitments right. Established industries tended to equate "right" with "the same as everybody else but a little bigger, newer, or better." For many decades, the Big Three automakers moved along parallel lines; they built factories, invested in their dealer networks, and juggled the mix of the R and the D in R&D. Global multinationals such as Shell, Unilever, and GE invested heavily in management development. In telecommunications, most firms strengthened their resource base through acquisitions, to the degree that many have highly leveraged balance sheets and heavy debt-repayment schedules.

A firm's value generation rests on its capabilities. Those in turn are a function of its resource base. How skillfully that base is created, adapted, and matched to the leadership value narrative and the culture of work is pivotal for the value architecture. Research decisions can have a long tail, in that a commitment made now may pay off only over the long term or lay a curse on later generations of managers.

The decisions need to be structured and focused differently in an "if" versus "given" world. One example of the given/if shift is once again the move away from reliance on assets to exploiting relationships. The logic is this: given that things are likely to remain pretty stable, then we will invest in our productive asset base, but if that is not the likely case, then we had better rethink this and better leverage ecocomplex relationships. If the leadership team does not support a win-win partnering environment, that option will be off the table for the culture. It requires a redrawing of the blueprints for managing corporate assets and ecocomplex relationships.

All the many organizational resources that are under the control of management—as opposed to the external forces of historical disturbance—fall into the following six categories:

- *Human capital:* The skills and experience of employees, partners, freelance specialists, and people who come as part of an acquisition.
- *Branding:* The processes and capabilities that establish the company's identity with customers, as well as employees, and add a distinctive differentiation to its offers in the market.

- *Corporate assets:* These comprise all the items that are proprietary to the company, most obviously its physical facilities, equipment, and other items that appear as part of the asset side of the firm's balance sheet. In addition, and often more importantly, these include intangibles such as patents, information, systems, and other fungible sources of market advantage.
- *Financial:* the metrics and planning and management processes for capturing value in terms of capital returns, operating margins, net profits, shareholder value, and cash flows. These provide the financial payoffs from the company's value generation and fund its future.
- *Ecocomplex relationships:* The variety, benefits, and contribution to growth provided by partnerships and collaborations.
- *Technology:* For all companies, their information technology, more appropriately thought of as coordination technology, which determines their reach—which customers and ecocomplex partners they can link to—and their range—the processes, data, and transactions they can directly interface to and from. This technology is increasingly generic, but there are also many additional business- or sector-specific resource-management subdomains, including manufacturing technology, chemical, and materials.

As we analyzed the anomalies to find archetypical patterns in their resourcing, several jumped out at us. The patterns are in the value narrative and opportunity platform, not the value engine. This is in sharp contrast to the industry model where, for all practical purposes, everyone had the same value narrative. And since the marketplace of the past was relatively stable, there was little need for an opportunity platform. As a result, a company's value-generating ability was determined by its choice of industry and differentiation within a narrow range of operational capabilities.

Of all the patterns, those relating to the opportunity platform were the most pronounced. To illustrate what we found, we created what we call the Innovation Cube: a plastic cube where each two-inch-by-two-inch face represents one of the resource domains. The faces list the guiding blueprint for new best practice, derived from our superextenders, such as Tesco, Bharti, Li & Fung, and Google, and longer-established superextenders such as Southwest Airlines, Wal-Mart, and the recent Apple (whose forty-year history also illustrates how close to disaster it has so often been, very much because of its neglect of the need to maintain a balance across the face of the Innovation Cube).

We show the patterns without much comment, since we have addressed each of them individually in early chapters. We do not provide any cookbook recipes for implementing them. There are many approaches, and most companies will have experience and expertise available to use, say, training, process analysis, incentive schemes, and many other vehicles. The list is an alert and an agenda for action; until you get the alert, there is no agenda, and until there is an agenda, there's no basis for action.

The Innovation Cube is a tool to help managers visualize the patterns that have emerged that are integral to improving, building, sourcing, and acquiring operational capabilities in the face of the onward march of the forces. (In the next three chapters, we look in more detail at how superextenders address the management of these resources.)

The Innovation Cube is depicted in figure 10.1. Figure 10.2 shows the resource blueprints that emerged as patterns from our analysis of exemplars. We make no grandiose claims for the Cube. Managers seem to find it useful and often report that it alerts them to gaps in their organization's value architecture. It is simple and captures the major resource-management base their organization must have to achieve the innovation goals of its value model.

Because each resource face is so different in nature, skills, language, professional expertise, cost dynamics, and many other dimensions, they can easily be seen as an independent part of Flatland, where inhabitants make sense of their one-dimensional world without even knowing there are other dimensions out there. (A silly analogy? Maybe, but if you're in marketing, finance, or HR, just ask yourself what are the key design elements of your company's enterprise IT architecture blueprint? If you're in IT, tell yourself exactly what are the firm's finance and corporate assets blueprints. Are these dimensions outside your view?)

What is key about the resources and the development of the right resource blueprints for you is their role in the missing middle between the leadership innovation agenda and the creation of an innovative culture.

For any firm there is one and only one reason to choose how and where to invest in resources: to build or acquire operational capabilities. These are clusters of activities that drive value for the company and its customers today, the next hundred minutes.

A simple test of whether a cluster of activities in your own firm is a capability rather than just a set of operational activities is to ask yourself if, in today's context, a 20 percent improvement or decline in that cluster's performance relative to that of leading competitors would have a marked impact on the company's ability to generate

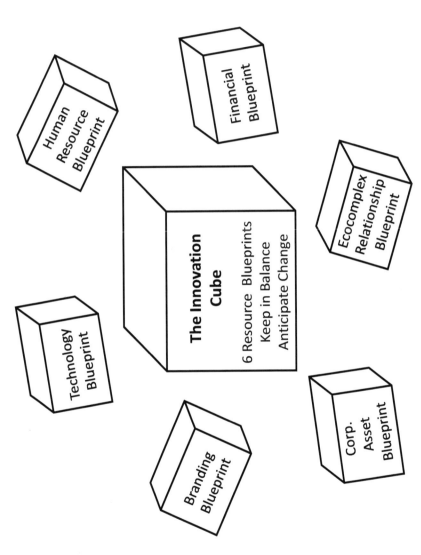

Figure 10.1: The Innovation Cube

Domain	Blueprint
Human Capital	Build the culture to drive and reward innovation centered on customer dimensions of value Anticipate major skill shifts and respond through both internal development and ecocomplex relationships
Branding	Build customer relationship on value dimensions, not products Integrate all components of your offer to create a seamless experience Target innovation to create compelling new dimensions of customer value
Corporate Assets	Decide which physical assets you must own Modularize all physical and intangible assets Exploit standardized interfaces for ecocomplex innovation
Financial	Transform capital efficiency Make smart asset/relationship investments to balance risks, performance and adaptability Create low cost structures to afford low customer prices and high service
Ecocomplex Relationships	Build win-win partner relationships Source for expertise and flexibility while reducing costs and capital Strengthen coordination capabilities
Technology	Define an enterprise architecture built on standardized interfaces Establish formal justification and governance systems focused on business value dimensions not technology cost control Exploit any technology capability that enhances customer/ partner value dimensionality

Figure 10.2: The Resource Blueprints

value. If the answer is "very much so," then this is an operational capability.

If the reply is, "This would not enhance value creation; it's overhead, administration, or a support function," then it is just a set of activities. Activities are costs that consume resources. Capabilities tie up the same resources but put them to productive use in such a way that they generate value. Some activities are intrinsically just that; it is difficult to see how, for example, office cleaning and maintenance can be leveraged to generate business value unless, of course, you are in the office-cleaning business.

Then ask: given the direction and pace of change dictated by the historical forces, will this still be a capability three to five years from now? Will it enable our company to seize new market opportunities? Will we be able to extend, reconfigure, or reinvent it so that it can? Can we build or source new ones as the need arises?

If the answer is no to these questions—which is the case for most companies—then you have a problem, because the world is neither constant nor predictable. If the answer is yes, then it is more than likely your company has a platform perspective. So without the right resource blueprints, the leadership team's innovation agenda will be asking the culture to do something that falls somewhere between very difficult and impossible.

With the missing middle identified and some ideas on how to fill it, we can now return to the innovation agenda that gets set and communicated through the value narrative. Here, the patterns among the new archetypes include being truly customer led, sometime almost to an obsession. Costs are managed to lower customer prices rather than increase operating margins. Ecocomplexes play a growing role in ensuring operational capabilities. Companies brand the customer experience, rather than products and services.

While the superextenders' value narratives include common elements, their individual narratives differ significantly, unlike in the era of the industry itself as the well-defined choice space. The Big Three car firms of GM, Ford, and Chrysler; the Big Pharma giants that included Merck, Pfizer, Hoffman Laroche, and Glaxo; the main airline carriers across the world; or the petrochemical power houses of Shell, Exxon, Mobil, and Amoco—all these firms competed mainly through their value engines: their innovation focused on how they could operate more efficiently, gain an edge from their R&D, or increase their market share a few percentage points.

Don't even try to think that way if you are in the field of digital media, retailing, telecommunications, energy-equipment manufacturing, software, or financial services. The archetypal value narratives here are very fluid, continuing to evolve with the three forces of disturbance and defying the ability to put business model labels on them. As the forces drive on, archetypes leverage them to create compelling new dimensions of value, rather than being caught off guard by entrepreneurs doing do.

At the simplest level of use, the archetypes provide a checklist of points to consider: are we strong here, have we paid enough attention to this, and do our initiatives in one domain directly affect any of the others? More strategically, since these are archetypal and drawn from the experiences of superextenders, should we be moving in this direction, and if so what do we need to do? If not, why? There may be a sound reason for diverging from this value architecture navigation path, but that should be a decision by commission, not omission.

You Can't Buy Culture off the Shelf

Fit the pieces together—all the elements of a value architecture to thrive in an "if" world—and you will have an innovation culture. We go more deeply into how three companies have managed to create such a culture in our next three chapters.

One is almost venerable, FedEx, a company that created a new "industry" and continues to change its opportunity. The second is no longer a dot-com ultrasuccess but the superextender that sets the terms of competition and even survival across the retailing landscape, that is one of the main platform players in digital anything and is reshaping publishing. This, of course, is Amazon.

The final exemplar may seem a surprising pick. It is a nonbusiness agency with a track record where mediocrity would have seemed an unattainable ambition just a decade ago. Now, the word "best" is routinely attached to it. The title of a book that chronicles its transformation seems judicious, not hype: *The Best Care Anywhere.*[142] This is the Veterans Health Administration (VHA). We chose it to illustrate that any organization can be turned around and that the dynamics of transformation are part of the same patterns as in start-ups that become ultrasuccesses and move on to be superextenders.

Any discussion of corporate culture immediately triggers associations with people: inspirational leadership, motivation, values, passion, willingness to take risks, beliefs, language, rituals, and the like. Culture is very elusive and "tacit" in that much of it is unconscious, the result of accumulated learning. It becomes the correct way to think and behave if you want to be part of—well, the culture.

Culture is often picked out as the main explanatory factor in histories of companies' rise and fall and in studies of great and failed business leadership. It's the call to action for firms in a time of change. We really don't quite know how to define it, but as with Supreme Court Justice Stewart's phrase about pornography that is a near-immortal cliché, "I know it when I see it." Just about every commentator on the subject knows that it is very hard to change. Lou Gerstner, the CEO hired to turn around IBM, summarized his challenge as "culture isn't just one aspect of the game—it *is* the game."[143]

You can't buy culture off the shelf, and it's not pixie dust, though at times executives and management experts seem to view it that way. Many of the spells for making cultural magic are based on variants of three ingredients: creative nonconformists, "intrapreneurial" champions, and inspirational leaders.

The potion has to be strong enough to counter the debilitating contaminants of the status quo. These include functional routines, process regimentation, hierarchy, budgeting, and resistance to change—that all-purpose label for dysfunctional behavior analogous to attention deficit disorder or adolescence.

At the extreme, that says if you are not creative, if you like being part of a team that is productive and reliable, and you are content to be a manager, professional specialist, or loyal subordinate, then you are not an innovator. You are definitely outside the magic circle if you work on the boring stuff, such as making sure that the planes have fuel in them and the engines work or that the innovative new product is actually in stock when people want it.

Surely, any view of innovation that sees the organization as the blockage is creating a self-defeating circular argument. It amounts to saying that the problem in building an innovative corporate culture is that corporate cultures are not innovative. And if it's innovative, it's not corporate culture.

This assumption lies behind the recurrent calls for revolutionary approaches to breaking the rules, adhocracy, skunk works, and radical reengineering. It has been encapsulated in the, at times, gleeful use and the misunderstanding of the term Creative Destruction. This evocative phrase has a long history, beginning with Marxism, for which the focus was on destruction: the forces of capitalism move forward through "financial barbarism" that wipes out existing wealth and economic orders.

Joseph Schumpeter made Creative Destruction an influential idea by highlighting the creative element of renewal in a market economy.[144] So, for those who believe that radical times need radical innovation, Creative Destruction is the very essence of progress. In less dramatic accounting-speak, it's a glossy excuse for "Restructuring Expenses" and "Other Extraordinary Items" on the firm's income statement. These all amount to a statement that we can't continue on our current value path and are going to blow up a part of the business and move in a different direction.

It's great to be on the creative side of this innovation equation, but not much fun to be part of the destruction. Your job has just been blown up, too. Schumpeter was not exactly a cheery business booster. He was convinced that the forces of socialism would overwhelm capitalism and that the necessary creative destruction was undermining its own frameworks and sustainability.

Maybe there's a somewhat less frenetic view of innovation, one of its being based on management, not magic, and on evolution not revolution. Here, the archetypes of innovation are a useful guide. By definition, a superextender has been able to evolve its innovation capabilities and to do so by management, not luck and happy accidents. Ultrafades and players caught in the Asset, Commodity, and Invention Traps innovated but didn't institutionalize their ability so as to continue to innovate and innovate and innovate.

The value narrative is the starting point in this process. It is the mobilizer for just about everything that can sensibly be seen as part of the resource base for building an innovation culture. If the narrative is not customer-led, then innovation won't be, either.

If it doesn't attract a particular type of talent—designers in the Apple class; Google IQ-in-the-sky engineers; Little John Wayne entrepreneurs; risk takers; self-motivated, street-smart, independent thinkers; team players; and other not-as-usual people for not-as-usual business—then the firm will need to scale down its ambitions.

If the narrative is not convincing in its claims to create new customer value or enter a new choice space, investors will not provide the funding for the resources needed to support rapid and expansive growth. And if it announces a reliance on building an asset base rather than relying on ecocomplex advantages, then it has placed a strategic bet on its internal capabilities providing the most effective path to value and has narrowed its financial flexibility in the expectation that it will have advantages of scale and efficiency.

All in all, the value narrative focuses the innovation agenda—not in details and certainly not in terms of just a business model for now. It sets the direction and establishes momentum.

Work is done at the level of operational capabilities, and given a clear blueprint, all decisions can be directed to turning blueprints into action. That is innovation as part of everyday business life. At the management planning level, innovation is more of a process of enabling than doing. The task of executive management is resource planning. That is innovation for tomorrow. At the executive leadership level, the framework for guiding research investment is the value narrative. That is innovation for today, tomorrow, and thereafter.

The six faces of the Innovation Cube are largely disparate programmatic priorities for executive action. Each needs individual attention in this regard. HR has its own language, mission, and business case. So, too, does finance. The cube facilitates fitting them together so they are kept in balance. What is apparent in ultrafades is that each face is not considered in equal depth and as an equal potential priority and that they often do not mesh.

It is rare for IT specialists in technology to be brought into the customer experience and human capital blueprint discussions, for instance, and it is notable how often an apparently collaborative and innovative culture led by product, technology, and marketing talent turns out to have been conflict laden and driven by stock options rather than the espoused mission; when the options are "under water," the culture drifts into the mists.

There is no hierarchy in the faces; that is why the list is not numbered. A cube has no starting and end points, just six faces. Pick it up and place it on the table; it is stable and won't fall over. The top face will be most visible and draw attention. The bottom face is hidden. If you hold it in your palm as you review any one face, you will naturally rotate it, move between the faces and perhaps stop to focus on one that seems of new relevance as you progress. There is no one face that drives the entire innovation process. Nor, obviously, are the blueprint priorities we list universal; they are pointers, alerts, and reminders. Your own company may differ in its own specifics.

Nevertheless, it does not make sense to ignore a face. Many meetings and plans will begin with a focused gaze on the customer-experience face placed on top, while the one on the bottom—the financial blueprint—is left for later, even though each shapes the other. (For telecommunications companies, the capital-investment cost of attracting and serving a new customer may dwarf the operational revenues, for instance, and a management squeeze on capital-asset spending in and of itself has just affected every aspect of the firm's technology blueprint.)

Similarly, for the firms that highlight financial restructuring, the opposite face of the cube—branding the customer experience—is literally out of sight and probably out of mind. This makes the organizational conversation—the mobilization of skills, experience, and perspectives—incomplete and often conflicting. We would place a bet on this happening again and again in your own firm; we ourselves have never been involved in a high-level management project where this is *not* the case.

You can test it for yourself. If you are in marketing and helping define new product targets, how much general awareness and discussion is there of the technology and human capital blueprints? What does the IT staff working on the complexities of data-center rationalization and virtualization know about the finance blueprint for capital expenditures? Has someone from corporate finance ever been invited into a meeting on customer-relationship planning and innovation?

Everyday Innovation: Creating Compelling New Dimensions

There is much discussion in the press today about business model innovation. The contrast is with product innovation and process innovation as the innovation priority. The latter two focus primarily on *better*, while the first intentionally targets *different*. The problem is that if you asked most employees how they would implement business model innovation, they wouldn't have a clue.

What we have repeatedly heard in business discussions and in the classroom is that only the top executive team can effect business model innovation. What if, by contrast, the value narrative were clear as to how the firm plans to create value over the next hundred minutes and for the foreseeable part of the next hundred years? Suppose that at the same time, the opportunity platform provided a way for the business to identify opportunities created by the forces, and, in addition, the resource blueprints enabled the building of the desired capabilities?

It would then be logical to ask everyone to focus on new compelling dimensions of value within the opportunity space and the value narrative. That is far more empowering and productive than asking people to create new business models or simply make better today's capabilities that won't travel to tomorrow.

Contributing to new dimensions of value are within everyone's grasp, no matter where they are in the organization. Our next three chapters show how this is made to happen.

11 Don't Go There

Somehow it doesn't seem quite right to have a "chapter 11" in our book. We hope to make a small contribution to helping you never to be anywhere near it.

But...here are a few US firms that filed for Chapter 11 after being among the most noted innovators in business. Just FYI.

AMR (American Airlines): The dominant player in the use of information technology to transform customer service, relationships, travel agent ecocomplexes.

Blockbuster: Reoriented the family weekend.

Bloomingdale's: Set fashion and style in New York City for decades.

Borders: Along with Barnes & Noble, redefined the bookstore.

Circuit City: The first high-quality, low-price, nontechie consumer electronics retailer.

Kmart: Preceded Wal-Mart as the low-price seller of branded goods. Dominated the mall.

Kodak: The global film and cheap-camera proliferator that pioneered digital photography.

MGM: Boasted of its brand as iconic studio; unforgettable filmmaking; leader in digital entertainment platforms.

Napster: Broke open the closed space of the music industry and created an entirely new technology base—peer-to-peer—for community sharing of digital content.

Nortel: The technology leader in fiber-optics network equipment.

Polaroid: Changed the very nature of photography.

Psychic Friends Network: No comment.

Samsonite: Is there any better or better-known product in rugged luggage?

Tower Records: Pioneered many in-store innovations in customer service and technology and grew and grew with the CD boom.

12 FedEx: A Customer-led Platform Company

FedEx provides an exemplary and archetypal example of an opportunity-platform company. Its founder began from a value narrative that laid out a very different path than the established firms used. His thinking began from the viewpoint of what services he could offer to his target customers and then worked back to the capabilities he would need and the resource investments that would enable and leverage these capabilities. That is very different from the value-chain approach that implicitly reverses the sequence to: if we invest in these resources, what services can we offer?

Fred Smith's thinking began the creation of a new industry that has morphed from package shipping to an integrated global logistics set of ecocomplexes. In the beginning he lacked many of the resources now readily available, especially in the area of technology, where FedEx was an early and much-admired pioneer, although at great expense.

With no modular web to use as its foundation, FedEx had to build proprietary tracking systems, make its own deals for international satellite communications access, and build databases that pushed the limits of software, hardware, and storage—building from scratch tools that companies now take for granted. It was asset intensive in its reliance on owning its airplanes instead of relying on the established ecocomplex of badly coordinated relationships between shippers and commercial airlines. That meant that it was cash-flow negative for a full thirty years, even as it grew to dominate not the industry but the expanding ecocomplex of customer–vendor relationships that depended on impeccable and immediate coordination of goods and information.

Logistics costs in the United States decreased from 16.5 percent to 9.5 percent of GDP from the late 1970s to the early 2000s, thanks in large part to companies thinking differently about inventory: "It's a waste, and we don't want it. Firms like FedEx can help us shrink it."[145]

At one level, these historical factors make FedEx very different from Amazon, which exploited the Internet as its technology foundation, stands out for its asset-light growth, and as a result has a level of flexibility not available to FedEx for most of its growth. But probing deeper, they look increasingly similar and are converging. FedEx's opportunity platform enabled it to move very quickly to interface its proprietary systems with the Internet. It did not even need to advertise the launch of its Internet tracking service; the value was immediate and obvious.

Similarly, Amazon's platform design has enabled it, like Li & Fung did, to add assets on a smart basis: fulfillment centers and acquisitions. Both FedEx and Amazon were able to ride through some potential disasters, such as FedEx's heavy investment in Zapmail, international fax service by satellite, and a number of Amazon's acquisitions of online specialty retailers at the peak of the dot-com surge.

Whenever these companies came up against a powerful competitor that thought in traditional industry terms, they slaughtered it. Their competitive threats now come from companies that bring a customer-led, not industry-inherited, value narrative to the arena.

For FedEx, the dominant pioneer in air cargo, Emery Air Freight is gone, along with a large number of courier services, freight forwarders, and shippers. Its competition in logistics comes from firms with powerful technology platforms, such as UPS, which repositioned itself to exploit an area that FedEx's value engine was not originally designed to handle: items of different size, shape, and weight, and options for slower, cheaper delivery than overnight service.

Thinking "Industry" Is Dangerous to Your Innovation

One of the words to be wary of in every area of your innovation agenda is "industry." It comes with so much history that it generally focuses your thinking in advance and substitutes "of course" assumptions instead of "how about" fresh perspectives.

Part of the problem can be quickly summarized. If your company sees itself in, say, the utility industry, Google doesn't; it is offering many of the same services but in the broader context of new customer value, outside traditional utility dimensions. If it is part of the newspaper or music industries, there are a whole lot of firms that simply don't think in such terms as they look to exploit the opportunity of customers wanting news and liking music. If you define yourself as in the construction industry, then you will calibrate innovation largely in comparison with other such firms and benchmark industry best practice. By that very fact, you are likely to overlook effective new practices.

Amazon famously demolished Barnes & Noble's future. Amazon's own competition is entirely from companies that don't fit into an industry or those that invented a new one: Google, Apple, Netflix, and now most likely Facebook, to name just some obvious players.

160

FedEx: A Customer-led Platform Company

Does the success of Amazon or FedEx rest on the industry they chose to build in and around? How about Li & Fung, Tesco, Google, or Bharti Airtel? Do the corresponding ultrafades and failures of competitors reflect the industry losing its attractiveness? Does that explain Blockbuster, Barnes & Noble, DEC, Gap, and AOL?

The moment you put an industry label on your market, competition, product and service strategy, and business model, you have by default chosen most of your value narrative, identified best-practice targets for your value engine, and minimized the need for an adaptive and explicit opportunity platform.

You also put the customers of tomorrow way off in the background of the business landscape. You risk losing sight of them as they move around, often going outside the scan of your industry panorama. The realities of value shifts add up to a metareality that might be termed "your problem, not ours." Customers care less and less about what industry your firm defines itself as a member of.

Industry is a supplier concept. Customers wander all over the place—*their* place—in a world where they expect expanding choice spaces, new value dimensions, a growing provider focus on branding the experience, and a widening selection of digital options in shopping, services, and relationships. In some instances, the industry label may carry an implicit value dimension of trusted history, established track record, or brand advantage that leads them to choose to stay. But do you really want to bet your future on the industry's past rather than the customer's future?

If you live by the industry, you will die by it. In effect, you have opted into the industry's core narrative. If you opt out and offer something that points to a different value path, then you really, really need to think platform, not just engine.

For decades, firms didn't just live by the industry business model, they thrived. The industry business-model tradition, which relies heavily on the concept of a value chain, is a foundation of modern business that held up well in general in an era where it could be assumed that markets were fairly anticipatable, and while change was continuous, it was largely a matter of more or less—more of this, such as cost inflation or technical improvements, and less of that, perhaps industry growth or average development time to market.

All these shifts posed equally continuous challenges, which meant that firms invested their resources largely in their value engines. This made plenty of sense so long as the value narratives were pretty much stable, with each of, say, the Big Three US automakers, the international airline flag carriers, or television channels in the same basic business. There was no need for an opportunity platform since the stronger the value engine, the firmer the foundation and the bigger the advantages to be gained from it.

This viewpoint is firmly established in management thinking on corporate strategy and still flavors much of the language in everyday use and hence many "of course" assumptions. The classic and still influential encapsulation of the industry perspective on competition and value was formulated by Michael Porter in the 1980s. Here are a few of his comments:

> Competitive strategy is the search for a favorable competitive position in an industry, the fundamental arena in which competition occurs.
>
> Two central questions underlie the choice of competitive strategy. The first is the attractiveness of industries for long-term profitability and the factors that determine it. The second central question in competitive strategy is the determinants of relative competitive position within an industry.
>
> Industries become more or less attractive over time, and competitive position reflects an unending battle among competitors.
>
> A few firms construct contingency plans as part of the strategic planning process, in an attempt to test strategies against major sources of uncertainty. Contingency planning is rare in practice...[146]

This just doesn't explain a FedEx or Amazon. Of course, there are instances where the industry space and its competitive range of options is fairly constrained; the arena in which competition takes place has a limited growth potential and in many instances there are few incentives for new entrants to commit heavy investments. Wendy's, McDonald's, and Burger King are in competition with each other in fast food, and until one decides to become a full-service family restaurant, they can be directly compared to and calibrated with each other.

They will innovate, but the industry provides the basic value narrative for doing so, and value engines will tend to be very similar in design, processes, and use of technology. Developments by one company will be quickly spotted and duplicated, and opportunity platforms will address the foreseeable rather than the contingent.

In this regard, Porter comments, "The firm postpones resource commitments that lock it into a particular strategy. Once the uncertainties begin to resolve themselves, a strategy that fits the scenario that appears to be occurring is chosen, taking into account the firm's resources and skill."[147] That's just what Barnes & Noble did.

Figure 12.1 summarizes the shifts in value architecture from the industry business model plus value chain to the extender's platform-enabled ecocomplex and platform.

In no way was the industry model "wrong" twenty to forty years ago. But the forces of disturbance have since undermined it as archetypal for competitive strategy. It isn't just ten- to fifteen-year-old firms such as Google, Amazon, and Facebook that have defined new norms for innovation, but thirty- to forty-year-old value path beaters such as Wal-Mart, FedEx, and Apple.

Yes, Apple is that old (1976), just five years younger than FedEx, and for decades it was an industry model firm and a pretty bad one: all narrative, no working engine, and an undirected and mishmash platform. It needed the complementary skills of Tim Cook and Steve Jobs to make the company the innovation machine it now is. Cook took on all the boring stuff, such as supply chain, and, as a book on Apple's culture of secrecy, compulsion, and leadership narcissism indicates, enabled Jobs to be creative by being the opposite.[148]

You can run your finger down the extender's Value Architecture list in Figure 12.1 and put a tick on each item for "Yes, that's Apple." If you do the same for Microsoft, you'll find your eye wandering to the Industry column, with ticks for "Yes, that's what got Microsoft to dominance, and, yes, that's why it got stuck and has been living very much on its heritage."

FedEx It: One of the Great Verbs in Business History

Heritage is an heirloom of worth if its inheritors continue to build on it. FedEx remains one such company. It has passed its fortieth year in operation and has grown consistently, even though the forces of disturbance have often favored new rivals that were heritage-free and made many of FedEx's areas of strength obsolete.

For example, e-mail has shrunk the market for overnight document shipments. UPS was better positioned to offer two- and five-day ground shipping of the assorted shapes, sizes, and weights of e-commerce, whereas FedEx's capabilities were optimized for overnight delivery of small packages by air. The Internet opened up opportunities for companies to catch up on FedEx's legendary IT systems for coordination, tracking, and real-time information management in creating logistics services.

FedEx has had to move outside its areas of organizational strength in making acquisitions, facing new turmoil from its pilots and contract truck drivers in labor relations. But it remains a benchmark company and shows up not just on lists of most-admired

	Industry Value Architecture	Extender's Value Architecture
Determinate of success or failure of a firm	Competition	Value produced
Value narrative: Search for a favorable position	Within the industry	Within an expanding choice space
Choice of competitive strategy/Value narrative	1. Attractiveness of the industry 2. Competitive position within the industry	1. Attractiveness of opportunities 2. Capabilities to generate value from the opportunities
Primary forces companies focus on	5 Industry forces that determine industry profitability	Historical forces of disturbance that shift the choice space
Customer's perception of value	How it impacts the buyer's value chain	How it compares to other offers in the customer choice space
Value engine construct	Value chain (owned capabilities)	Ecocomplex (owned and sourced capabilities)
Competitive advantage	Value chain differentiation within an industry	Value architecture differentiation (narrative, engine, opportunity platform) in an expanding choice space
Resource management	In support of existing operations (primary activities that create, deliver and service products and services)	A platform for investing in current opportunities and seizing future unknown ones
Rate of change	Slow - Over Time	Fast: Over Night
Dealing with change	Threats managed through scenario planning	Opportunities leveraged through an opportunity platform

Figure 12.1: Value Architecture Shifts

firms, but in the category of most widely assigned subjects for business school students where you can get away with cheating; there's an Internet mini-industry of term papers on FedEx, essays, and strategic SWOT/Five Forces analyses.

The company really is a foundational archetype of modern business and illustrates the many facets of the superextender. The cheat-sheet downloadable papers cover many high-level aspects of its strategy, mergers and acquisitions, global expansion, and organizational development, and also many nuts-and-bolt topics, such as advertising, service management, IT, and culture. The pieces all fit together and have largely moved together. This was a platform company well before the era of the Internet that made the term part of business thinking.

The value architecture of FedEx also reflects a consistent and forceful leadership heritage, starting with its founder, who remains CEO. Fred Smith's vision of a small-package delivery service is part of business mythology, with a fable that he himself puts in the "I don't really remember" category: that he drew up the idea for a class paper at Yale, but got only a C grade because the professor found the idea improbable.

It was indeed improbable within the constraints that bounded the air freight industry at the time. The sector was tightly regulated, though there were growing signs of a shakeup coming when he launched the company in 1971. (It was then Federal Express; it adopted the FedEx name in 1994.) What Fred saw was that as "society automated,...society and the manufacturers of the automated society were going to need a completely different logistics system."[149] Traditional inventory management, warehousing, and order fulfillment could not adapt naturally to the demands of time-based competition and global operations.

The largest incumbent company, Emery Air Freight, was profitable but limited in its capabilities and customer-value dimensions. Regulation blocked shippers like Emery from buying their own cargo planes, so it relied on commercial airline services for moving goods. In essence, the carriers handled cargo as a way of filling up space on commercial flights, rather like standby passengers. Emery was able to book capacity—reserve seats for packages rather than people—to sell to commercial customers, but it had no flexibility in its options and operations. This posed many problems in terms of value narrative. It could ensure delivery, but there was no way to provide a value dimension built around "on time," "overnight," and "guaranteed."

Emery's capabilities were based on scale and efficiency. It operated three distribution terminals and was building a fourth one in 1971; none of these were run on a hub-and-spoke basis. It was a technology leader, with the industry's first computerized online tracking system, launched in 1970 with 170 workstations. This system provided rates and routes for eighteen thousand points, linked to airline schedules, and provided a running diary of the movement and location of shipments.

But that did not mean Emery could deliver on time. Few companies in the industry made any money in the period 1946–80. They couldn't even be dismissed as fly-by-night companies, since only 10 percent of commercial flights took off after ten at night. Some 60 percent of all commercial air traffic was between the twenty-five largest US cities, but only 20 percent of air shipments moved between them.[150]

Emery was known as the "tallest midget" in the industry and held up fairly well for close to forty years as the largest freight forwarder, but then it collapsed as FedEx and others took over. It suffered from competition from small firms with low prices (but slow delivery) and depended on the airlines' cooperation. When fuel prices increased, the airlines cut back on cargo operations; they saw freight companies as much as competitors as customers and forwarders as middlemen nuisances. This was a dysfunctional ecocomplex.

Emery could not balance small and large/heavy item shipments in its operations. Its purchase of Purolator to add package delivery to its operational capabilities was not exactly seen as a masterstroke: "a limping company had bought a sick, if not mortally wounded one, for synergistic ends."[151] Emery ceased operations in 2001. It had been defined entirely within the framework of the airline industry via a series of adjustments to those business models and structures.

Smith saw this very clearly. He stated emphatically in a 2004 interview that Emery had the wrong corporate asset base. "They were trying to use an infrastructure built around mostly passenger air transportation—the airlines—which wasn't designed to handle it at all. So they were force-fitting the rapid movement of high-value-added and high-technology products into a transportation system that wasn't designed for it."[152] Not owning the planes virtually guaranteed that Emery could not create the customer-value dimension of next-day delivery.

Smith began from the customer perspective, not the airfreight viewpoint. He saw an opportunity to create a service for the many companies, such as IBM and Xerox, that needed to move small shipments of goods quickly and could not afford or manage distributed inventories of parts and products. They were poorly provided for by the air cargo companies. And so, as Christopher

Jkelgaard wrote in *Flight International* in 1981, Smith created a new value narrative:

> Smith proposed a concept new to the air cargo industry. Have one carrier, and only one, responsible for a piece of cargo from local pick-up right through to ultimate delivery, operating its own aircraft, depots, posting stations and delivery vans. To ensure accurate sorting and dispatching of every item of freight, the carrier would fly it from all of its pickup stations to a central clearinghouse, from where the entire operation would be controlled. According to Smith this was simple reasoning: "It was a systems approach to a systems problem."[153]

Fred Smith was anticipating that the forces of disturbance were moving in a direction that would soon start opening up opportunities for his new way of thinking. This forward-looking perspective has marked FedEx from its start, and it has generally been ready to move earlier and faster than rivals.

The forces were very much Smith's ally. Deregulation would permit FedEx to become a carrier, operate its own fleet of planes, and build its hub-and-spoke complex of highly efficient shipping operations. Technology would enable him to create dimensions of customer value built on information about the package and its movements. Modularity was part of what stimulated his initial ideas. The need to coordinate multiple components of products was driving new types of process in inventory management, maintenance, and repair in the computer business and a need to move small components quickly.

Airline deregulation was implemented in 1978, as well as the federal government exempting some types of publications and documents from the Postal Service monopoly. In 1979, restrictions on the size of cargo planes were lifted and landing rights extended. (Between 1973 and 1979, FedEx had exploited loopholes to fly its own air taxis.)

While the company is generally associated with shipping documents overnight, from the start Smith was defining the company in terms of inventory management for its customers; the core logic was to replace stocks of products with parts on demand.

And so we have the start of the FedEx opportunity platform, which was based on the ownership of a number of physical assets deemed important to servicing the customer. Smith blended the asset base on the basis of balancing customer value and cost. He hired delivery drivers and leased the trucks from Hertz. He built a hub-and-spoke distribution center modeled on the Federal Reserve Bank's clearinghouse. He bought Dassault Falcon planes, which qualified as air taxis, not cargo carriers. The firm operated within a roughly twenty-five mile radius around airports.

As early as 1975, FedEx had commissioned an independent study that showed that FedEx's Priority One packages arrived next day 93 percent of the time, versus just 42 percent for Emery and much worse for the two other companies in the analysis.[154]

One impact of the corporate asset blueprint was in the financial domain. This would be a very capital-intensive business, contributing to FedEx's first three decades of negative cash flow. "But we needed to build a global network," its CFO stated, "we needed to get to economies of scale, and we had to have market share to get the gain productivity."[155]

To reach scale, FedEx grew organically, but also made some key acquisitions: In 1984 it bought Gelco Express, a worldwide courier that gave it services to eighty-four countries. In 1989 it acquired Flying Tigers for $895 million, which brought it overseas routes and landing rights in twenty-one countries, including Japan; a fleet of twenty-one 747 planes; and expertise in international airfreight. This opened the door to Asia and positioned FedEx to exploit the coming surge in trade. From a purely operational viewpoint, the purchase was not needed at the time; it was a platform investment.

By 1990, FedEx had 350 aircraft, qualifying it as one of the world's largest airlines. It owned 20,000 vans and 2,000 large trucks in the United States and another 6,300 vehicles abroad. It had 1,530 staffed facilities worldwide and served 119 countries.[156] It seems natural to ask: isn't this just another capital-intensive business and what is so unusual about its resource blueprints? To answer that, we go back to a comment Fred Smith made in an interview with *Businessweek* in 2004:

> It occurred to me very shortly into this proposition that it was self-limited if we couldn't constantly improve what we were doing. If people were going to use FedEx in lieu of having incalculable amounts of money tied up in inventories, it "absolutely, positively" had to be there when promised. The business had to operate with a level of precision and reliability that heretofore had not been possible in the service business.
>
> And that led to the very simple recognition that we had to use information technology to an extent that had never been done before. We had to basically create a whole industry to do that. [157]

Those last two points about a very simple recognition and basically creating a whole industry added up to an entirely new value architecture. That architecture depended equally on new principles of technology research management and building new organizational capabilities, but it wasn't the technology that made the value.

That is apparent in the move by another Smith, Roger, the CEO of General Motors, to join the technology-is-our-future movement. He spent about $54 billion, when a billion was a big number and not the contract size for the next NBA superstar, on buying technology companies. He could have purchased the entire Japanese car industry, including Toyota, for a mere $35 billion.

GM had a technology resource as a strategic add-on to its organization. FedEx had a technology platform as an integral source of capabilities in its value architecture. The standard practice in large companies at the time was to deploy existing technology support or automate individual activities, generally to reduce both organizational and IT costs. Few firms tied these together as an enterprise architecture and business platform. As the senior VP of information and telecommunication for Federal Express was quoted as saying in the late 1980s:

> You can view technology as a wave in the ocean washing up debris. Most people concentrate on the debris that floats in. "Oh isn't that neat!" they'll say of some device. "Where can I use it?" And that is where I think they mess up.
>
> I view technology as the wave itself, not the individual things that are brought to shore. We knew what we wanted to do ten years ago, but the technology wasn't there. So we were waiting for the wave and constantly prodding manufacturers to create what we needed as the wave rolled in.[158]

FedEx's technology deployment was very much in the flow of the tide and integral to all business activities. Many of its innovations are part of the IT Hall of Fame. They are archetypal:[159]

- *1979:* Package tracking system (COSMOS)—pushing limits of database management.
- *1980:* DADS (Digitally Assisted Dispatch System) computer in vans to communicate needed pickups and routes.
- *1984:* Customer input and package tracking (PowerShip). The company gave free PCs (over 100,000) to customers for self-service.
- *1985:* Sequential bar code labeling—first to introduce in the ground transportation industry.
- *1986:* Handheld bar code scanner: SuperTracker.
- *1989:* Satellite for vehicle tracking.
- *1996:* Web tracking.

Fred Smith and his executive team clearly understood the need not only to continuously make the value engine better, but to work from a technology blueprint based on constantly pushing the state-of-best-implementation envelope. So, as Linda Grant said in a 1997 *Fortune* article: "Smith figured out two decades ago that FedEx was in the information business, so he stressed that knowledge about cargo's origin, present whereabouts, destination, estimated time of arrival, price, and cost of shipment was as important as its safe delivery. He has therefore insisted that a network of state-of-the-art information systems—a sophisticated melange of laser scanners, bar codes, software, and electronic connections—be erected alongside the air and vehicle networks."[160]

And so FedEx was also simultaneously beginning to build an ecocomplex blueprint, first with technology partners to push the limits of the business-technology choice space and then with customers so they could self-manage most of the processes, enter their own information, and track packages. This was initially done through the PowerShip program, in which FedEx gave PCs to customers because there was no Internet. Its ecocomplex relationships were later expanded to include the contract driver home-delivery network.

The Human Capital blueprint is foundational to the value architecture, and certainly central to FedEx. But we need to back up to the early days to get a good picture of its underpinnings. Two of Smith's early policies laid the foundation for much of the innovation that came from FedEx staff. He started the company with no-layoff and guaranteed fair treatment (GFT) policies, where employees could escalate problems above their manager if they felt they had not been treated fairly. A major goal here was to give people the freedom to innovate, not just concur.

When FedEx was founded, there were not enough packages to keep staff busy, but the focus was on growth rather than cost control. Not only did everyone do everything, including pilots making sales calls, but employees were also told to use their imagination to "get the packages."

Many early stories show imagination on the part of employees who felt empowered to solve problems and serve customers. One is about the tracing clerk who located a woman's missing wedding dress in Detroit on a Friday afternoon. It was supposed to have been delivered to Wilmington, Indiana. She was getting married the next day. The tracing clerk rented a Cessna and lined up a pilot to fly the dress three hundred miles that afternoon. As it turned out, a manager for a local plant whose business FedEx had been trying to get attended the wedding and heard the story. Two weeks later, guess who gave FedEx the business it was seeking.[161]

Smith lived his principles. FedEx was widely admired as a place to work. (It still routinely wins Best Places to Work awards.) The organizational logic was expressed as People–Service–Profit (P-S-P). If you take care of the people, they will provide the right customer service, and profits will follow. The no-layoff policy and guaranteed fair treatment were part of this.

High quality of treatment demanded high quality of commitment and performance, and the policies were amended to add management by objectives, performance by objectives, and bonuses strictly tied to performance. Almost meeting a target did not result in getting almost all your bonus; if you missed one, you lost the other entirely.

Years later, implementation of the PowerShip system, which enabled customers to enter their own airbills, schedule pickups, and trace packages, eliminated twelve hundred jobs. Instead of being laid off, the people in those jobs were placed in other jobs throughout the organization, such as helping customers deal with the new technology.

These examples show how policies and decisions surrounding one resource have implications on other resources, as depicted on the cube. If the tracing clerk had been reprimanded or fired for renting the plane or the twelve hundred people had been laid off when PowerShip was implemented, innovation by the rank and file would have been inhibited, with radiating implications on future technology decisions, process improvements, and customer relations.

The tracing clerk's boss initially did reprove her, but after the customer reported her delight, he saw the light quite quickly and vividly. The story says a lot about FedEx's P-S-P culture that was getting established. Michael Basch, who was the VP at the time, and the clerk's senior manager, says that after he finished a call from the bride on her honeymoon, who had phoned to thank Diane, the tracing clerk, and a senior manager, he went to Diane and said, "Why on earth would you charter a plane for a wedding dress?" Her response was, "You said 'GET THE PACKAGE' and for me that meant you give great service and solve the customer's problem. Then they talk about you, and you get more business."

Basch responded: "Come on, Diane, if we spent three hundred dollars on every package we'd go bankrupt." After a couple of minutes of her attempting to vainly to explain what GET THE PACKAGE meant, she finally blurted out in total frustration: "I figured we're going bankrupt anyway. What's the difference?"

Basch says: "There was obvious truth in that statement, and so I let it go. Being people first meant honesty, and Diane was no stranger to our financial situation." After the RCA plant in the bride's hometown began shipping twenty packages a day, Basch says, he returned to the clerk with his metaphorical tail between his legs.

Operational capabilities feed back into the value narrative, which needs refreshing and refocusing as times change and opportunities emerge. Initially, FedEx's target customer-service level was set at 95 percent of all shipments being error-free, on time, and meeting the promise to the customer. The assumption in the narrative was that that was the right balance between customer service and cost. It was an ambitious goal at the time and well above the level for service businesses. To go higher than 95 percent was cost-prohibitive, and prices would have to increase. Below that would cause loss of customers.

But one day, Fred Smith challenged the "95 percent rule." Just as happened at Bharti Airtel, he gathered the executive team together for a pivotal meeting, with the assignment of figuring out a way to drive the value engine to a higher level of service. He reasoned that if FedEx handled a million packages a day then using the 95 percent rule meant it would mess up fifty thousand packages and a hundred thousand customers (the sender and receiver would both be unhappy).

The executive team created what he called a hierarchy of horrors: a list of the worst thing FedEx could do to a customer, followed by the next worst thing. The purpose of the analysis was to develop new operational capabilities to avoid the horrors. This led to the SQI (Service Quality Indicators, pronounced "sky") metrics and associated incentives. The operational goal was to significantly improve the daily SQI number while growing the daily package volume. A senior executive owned each of the twelve indicators. These included abandoned calls (weighting of 1), lost package (10), and missing proof of delivery (1).

Teams were assigned to improve each indicator, and the metrics were tied to performance, determining a third of each manager's bonus. The other performance indicators were the SFA (Survey Feedback Action) on employee satisfaction and achieving 10 percent operating margins on the domestic business. An instructive addition was that the firm's corporate executives were rated as a group by the employees. If the evaluation was less favorable than last year, no bonus. None. By 2003, FedEx's on-time delivery had increased to 99.7 percent, from 95 percent in 1989.

This whole venture was more about making the value engine better, rather than different. It required that the entire organization be trained in quality-management methods and tools. While the executive team owned the SQI components, results depended on thousands of employees in quality teams to identify problems and find solutions throughout the company. Without FedEx's human capital blueprint based on P-S-P, no layoffs, and guaranteed fair treatment, and management by objectives, it is hard to believe it could have achieved the results it did.

What is apparent in stepping back from the details is the coordination of all the blueprints to drive the branded customer experience: on time, all the time. Corporate assets are selected based on the need to provide a desired customer experience. The technology, along with the technology partners, is essential to the brand; FedEx's ads did not discuss the package or price, but the branded dimensions of value: time and reliability.

The human capital is incentivized to not only serve the customer, but to continuously innovate to improve that experience. The capital investments and budgets enable the branded experience.

Now the question was, could FedEx leverage its opportunity platform to expand its customer-value dimensions? As Smith explained in another *Businessweek* interview in June 2005: "Back in the mid-'90s we recognized that our customers wanted us to broaden the things that we did for them. They particularly wanted us to be in the ground package business, they wanted us to be in the freight business—so we made some good acquisitions, and I think we engineered their absorption into the FedEx system well."[162]

The acquisitions he referenced included:

- *1998:* Caliber Systems, for $2.7 billion. This put FedEx in the small-package ground and freight business. Caliber Systems included a small-package ground carrier with 13,500 trucks and was run on a contractor model. This grew into FedEx Ground, with independent operators who own their own trucks.
- *2000:* Towers Group International, specializing in customs clearance and end-to-end transportation around the globe.
- *2001:* American Freights, a less-than-truckload carrier that covered central and eastern United States to complement Viking, part of the Caliber acquisition. This became FedEx Freight.

By 2000, FedEx was operating in 210 countries, with 648 aircraft, 60,000 vehicles, 10 million square feet of warehouse space, and 200,000 employees. At first, the acquired resources were not well integrated into the business, at least not from a customer experience perspective. Federal Express, RPS, Roberts Express, Viking Freight, and FDX Logistics initially operated as separate subsidiaries, managed independently and responsible for their own accounts.

In 2000, the parent company FDX was renamed FedEx Corporation, and all the businesses were brought under the FedEx brand. The services were divided into companies that operate independently yet compete collectively: FedEx Express, FedEx Ground, FedEx Global Logistics, FedEx Custom Critical, and FedEx Services, which provides the marketing, sales, and services for the other companies so that there is one face to the customer.

Also in 2000, FedEx launched FedEx Home Delivery to provide business-to-residential service in the US market. This service was based on the contract-driver model developed by RPS. But for it to work within FedEx's branded experience, it needed to expand its ecocomplex relationships to the contract drivers, supported by a complex technology platform and FedEx's sophisticated processes.

The drivers were used to simple and autonomous running of their truck as a small business. Now they were part of this giant company. What does "part of" mean here in terms of resource blueprints? The answer remains blurred, and FedEx has faced many problems in its driver relationships.

Overall, though, the opportunity platform continues to fuel integrated growth. As Fred Smith said in 2004, the company worked hard to fit all the pieces of the business and all its capabilities together:

> We have a unique strategy: operate independently, compete collectively, and manage collaboratively. This means each of our core operating companies—FedEx Express, FedEx Ground, FedEx Freight and FedEx Kinko's—gears its systems and processes to the particular segment it serves. When it comes to our markets, one size does not fit all. So each company tailors its service and operations to its specific customer needs.
>
> At the same time, our operating companies compete collectively under the trusted FedEx name. That means certain standards are met, no matter which service a customer is using. For example, all our team members—couriers, contractors, service reps on the telephone—are asked to keep the Purple Promise to our customers, that is, to give them the best experience possible any time they use FedEx.[163]

FedEx has continued to evolve its opportunity platform. Today, it runs a state-of-the-art modular services-oriented architecture (SOA, which has become a standard term in the IT field). That means its processes are far more modular and flexible than they were ten years ago. The company has held fast to its human-capital policies and people-service-profits. During the recession that started in 2008, all employees received a 5 percent temporary pay cut so that no one would be laid off. Full pay has since been restored.

FedEx: A Customer-led Platform Company

Which element of FedEx's strategy, organization, technology, HR policies, process designs underlies its ultrasuccess and ability to superextend? In many ways the answer is "none of them." But it is also "all of them." This is archetypal for, well, you name it: service, growth, customer-centric, technology for competitive advantage. It seems appropriate to summarize the fusion as an innovation culture or as a value architecture. They are the same thing.

13 Amazon: Building a Platform in the Web Era

In the beginning, Amazon created an online bookselling value narrative based on broad selection, the convenience of shopping from home, and no sales tax. It built and continued to improve its value engine to turn that narrative into action. But its opportunity platform was the key to Amazon's growth and success from the very start. It illustrates a focus on the customer experience that is like a laser in its precision, a strobe light in its illumination, and a diamond drill in its deep rock penetration.

There is nothing vague, undefined, or casual in the links between Amazon's value narrative, engine, and opportunity platform. This especially shows up in how it has evolved its technology base. It is designed, like Google's and Tesco's infrastructures, to enhance and enable dimensions of customer value. That sounds bland. What company would ever design its technology to get in the way of creating customer value?

Well, how about Starbucks? One of the puzzles for many years was why it lacked information about its customers, provided limited loyalty programs, and was not moving to personalize the relationship. It was far removed from Tesco, Google, and Amazon in terms of technology, despite having been as focused as it was on building the customer experience. It had also been a pacesetter in providing free Wi-Fi service in its stores and was a leader in expert systems software for its coffee research and automation of production. So there was plenty of technical skill in the company.

But, it seems, not much management attention was paid to the Technology face on the Innovation Cube. As late as 2008, its point-of-sale systems used a pre-Windows operating system. Because it handled credit-card payments, the system software blocked employee uses for other applications, including e-mail. It took six weeks to train an employee to use the single PC allocated to each store. Executives spoke of the firm piling up a technology "debt" during its growth years—investments it was deferring. That's one way of putting it.

Catching up on the debt became overdue, and in recent years, the company has repaired much of the damage, including in business intelligence, customer-relationship management, and use of social networking. These seem to be helping it recover its lost growth, but it's very much a matter of catching up on best practice, not keeping ahead. Starbucks lost a lot of opportunities for innovation by lacking a customer-centered technology resource plan.

Amazon is positioned to take just about any opportunity that has a digital element to it. Bear in mind that the company began by adopting the open, standardized web infrastructure and tools that were a free gift from the forces of disturbance to every dot-com entrepreneur then and for *any* firm just about anywhere now. Amazon made a management difference in exploiting the technical infrastructure of the web. A piece of tech-speak captures the essence of its Technology resource blueprint:

> Our technologies are almost exclusively implemented as services: bits of logic that encapsulate the data they operate on and provide hardened interfaces as the only way to access their functionality...Service-oriented architecture—or SOA—is the fundamental building abstraction for Amazon technologies...
>
> Our e-commerce platform is composed of a federation of hundreds of software services that work in concert to deliver functionality ranging from recommendations to order fulfillment to inventory tracking. For example, to construct a product detail page for a customer visiting Amazon.com, our software calls on between 200 and 300 services to present a highly personalized experience for that customer.[164]

How many business executives in your firm can think like this about the interrelationship of its business choices and technology decisions? Or even know what on earth this Amazon geek is talking about?

The geek is its CEO and founder, Jeff Bezos, and the quote is from his 2011 letter to shareholders. It's a business message that captures his recognition from the start that the entire role of the technology was to create new dimensions of customer value at a cost that would permit Amazon, like Southwest Airlines and Bharti Airtel, to afford low prices and high service.

Bezos's thinking was consistently platform driven. Here is an extract from an early (1999) shareholder letter:

> At a recent event at the Stanford University campus, a young woman came to the microphone and asked me a great question: "'I have 100 shares of Amazon.com. What do I own?" I was surprised I hadn't heard it before, at least not so simply put. What do you own? You own a piece of the leading e-commerce platform.
>
> The Amazon.com platform is comprised of brand, customers, technology, distribution capability, deep e-commerce expertise, and a great team with a passion for innovation and a passion for serving customers well.[165]

Bezos follows up in the next paragraph to address the ecocomplex impacts of the platform: "Our vision is to use this platform to build Earth's most customer-centric company, a place where customers can come to find and discover anything and everything they might want to buy online. We won't do so alone, but together with what will be thousands of partners of all sizes."

Amazon began as the e-commerce poster child of the dot-com era. Its core was transactions, not relationships. It needed a site for customers to place orders, operational capabilities in managing supplies of books and fulfilling orders, and a reliable payment system. There were many doubters in the investment community and business press that it could go beyond that. The skepticism has evaporated, though there are still commentators who disagree with Bezos's insistence that the company will invest for the long term and accept low margins during periods of infrastructure investment.

The headline of a *Wall Street Journal* article in February 2011 captures Amazon's success: "Retailers Struggle in Amazon's Jungle."[166] It sets the rules of emerging competitive games, along with the other online platform brands: Google, Apple, and Facebook. It enjoys the advantage of a value engine that radiates out from online business across consumer choice spaces.

It has maintained and extended its strength as an e-commerce giant by balancing its resources to create capabilities that parallel Google's philosophy: "Look after the user, everything else will follow." The Amazon equivalent is "Make it easy for the shopper and everything else will follow." It selectively blends its asset base to exploit its core reliance on ecocomplex relationships with fulfillment facilities that provide advantages of scale and coordination, and it further enhances the customer experience by selling its technology and fulfillment services to its ecocomplex partners.

When easy, convenient, and fast also means lower price, the Amazon customer relationship edge increases. The *Journal* story points out that for a representative basket of products, Amazon was 19 percent cheaper than Wal-Mart, 28 percent lower in price than Target, and 30 percent below specialty retailers.[167] A year later, at the end of March 2012, a survey conducted by William Blair analysts concludes that even if sales tax and shipping were added in, Amazon prices would be nearly as low as Wal-Mart and 7 percent below Target.[168]

Many consumer electronics retailers that do not directly compete with Amazon are nonetheless being pushed onto the defensive by it. Bloomberg News reported in late February 2012 that "Amazon Gained Brand Value at Best Buy's Loss"; Amazon grew 32 percent in brand value while Best Buy dropped 11 percent.[169]

Much of the business Best Buy is losing is going to Amazon, both because of the Amazon price advantage, its massive range of items on offer, and its superior order fulfillment. A growing problem for bookstores and Best Buy is people "showrooming." They stop in the store to look at products and then pop out and order them on Amazon.

Amazon is cheaper and often easier to deal with. Best Buy's handling of online orders and items that are not in stock in the store was summarized in a fairly typical customer evaluation: "Over-promised, under-delivered seems to be the theme."[170] That is certainly not a tag applied to Amazon.

Amazon's revenue in 2011 was $48 billion. Of that, $26.7 billion was in the United States and amounted to 13.7 percent of total US online consumer sales. Amazon offers more than ten million products across eighteen categories and partners with over two million sellers. The data-management tools and linkages between software-components technology make it easy to search through and evaluate this cornucopia of choices, which would otherwise be impossible for customers to find their way around or for Amazon to coordinate.

This SOA architecture that Bezos referred to is absolutely critical in all these elements of making it easy, and is an alert that business choices and technology decisions have often very far-reaching impact on each other, so keep rotating the Innovation Cube and make sure that technology planning and customer branding are consonant and not cracking at the corners of each face. As with Google and FedEx, the technical architecture is a unique application of general principles that are followed by many vendors and IT organization, but with a little bit of genius added.

Perhaps the most useful analogy here is your smart phone. All those apps and links you enjoy using are the services and the SOA architecture makes them all work together. You may see just a dozen or so apps displayed on your screen and be playing around with two or three, but there are hundreds of components handling millions of combinations of software and data bits and pieces at the same time. Amazon's SOA essentially is an apps-management universe.

Amazon has added many new services and value dimensions across its offers and deals (Gold Box Daily deals, Lightning Deals, Warehouse Deals), Your Browsing History, Amazon Betterizer ("Improve your shopping experience by telling us which things you like"). It has extended the value dimensions of relationships, such as the Vine reviewers who choose about six items a month to evaluate and keep for free and provide a rich range of ratings and opinions, as well as Sell on Amazon, and Independently Publish with Us.

Amazon is now one of the leading players in cloud computing, an arena where it is ahead of the natural candidates, including leading software companies and managed IT service providers, and is a major player in fulfillment logistics. It remains the largest seller of e-books, despite a heavy challenge from Apple that is the subject of antimonopoly suits brought by commissions in the United States and Europe for Apple's price-fixing collusion with publishers who oppose cheap books.

This seems to be a business form of if you can't beat 'em, yell "unfair competition," and then if you can't regulate 'em, cancel all the "we believe in the free market" PR stuff and gang up fast. In late spring 2011, the Justice Department came down hard and heavy on the publishers, who caved immediately. It's noteworthy that the publishers still argue that Amazon is the one that's anticompetitive, not them.

Amazon now sells more e-books than physical books. It is one of the pacesetters in the online music and video business. It is so far the only company to mount an effective challenge to the iPad in the tablet market. It has cleverly positioned its e-book reader along a spectrum of low prices—the equivalent of a Subaru or Honda line alongside, but not in direct competition with, Apple as a BMW.

Amazon is moving to fill most of the operational capabilities provided by the traditional publishing business, including editorial services for self-published writers, who also get access to a distribution and marketing resource that the establishment offered to very few authors. (The average book sells fewer than two hundred copies, and 80 percent never reach a bookstore.)

To understand how all this produced a profitable and still expanding flow of innovation, we need to analyze the evolution of its value architecture and, in particular, its opportunity platform. But first we'll step back and examine the forces that started the online commerce earthquake and its aftershocks across the business terrain.

Amazon's success is not because of the web, but because of how technology thinking is embedded in its value architecture. After all, every dot-com had access to the same technology base as Amazon. If you look at Amazon only in terms of what it did by being an e-commerce firm, you are likely to ignore what your own firm will need to do to exploit the stream of emerging web services and online ecocomplexes that include Facebook, Twitter, Groupon, and myriads of new players/partners.

Amazon is archetypal in how the business/technology dialog is factored into the innovation conversation. In many firms, corporate IT is increasingly marginalized, a primary target for outsourcing, viewed as an operating cost to be reduced rather than as a business investment, and lacking in needed skills. Surveys in 2012 show that well over half of organizations report that they severely lack IT talent.[171] IT is not included in the value narrative discussions; business innovation is detached from technical efficiency. Amazon has skills for every flavor of IT and for every nuance of IT interdependence with the faces of the Innovation Cube.

The Web: From Information Network to Business Resource

Even though the Internet as we know it can be traced back to specialized academic and scientific networks such as ARPAnet in the late 1960s and NSFNet in the 1980s, it was not until the early 1990s that it took shape as a useful and then essential business tool. Up until that period, the network was run by the National Science Foundation in the United States, with access restricted to government agencies and organizations receiving government research funding.

It was opened up for commercial use by Congress passing the High Performance Computing Act in 1991. The World Wide Web Consortium's making the web available free, with no patent restrictions or royalties, cleared the stage for its open interfaces and protocols to become the standard. In 1992 the Supreme Court ruled that retailers were exempt from collecting sales taxes unless they had a physical presence in that state. (Supposedly this was one of the reasons that Bezos located Amazon in Washington state—a good supply of talent but not that many buyers.)

The invention of the World Wide Web enabled people and organizations to link information across the Internet and thus provided the key tool for making the Internet an infrastructure. It created SIMCap: standardized interfaces. The very language of the web is one of interfaces: hot links, apps, APIs (application program interfaces), JPEGs, RSS, and many others. It's an interface tool kit.

The proliferation of the PC extended the modularity and interfacing through the invention of intuitive graphical browsers, beginning with Mosaic. Web use gathered momentum and critical mass through Netscape and was brought to market permeation through Microsoft's Internet Explorer (with the browser choice space expanding with the open-source Mozilla Firefox).

Later, the creation of search engines added what amounts to a find-and-link interface. Customers could now have access to the information with which to make choices. Companies now had a pervasive communication system on which to expand customer relationships and their brands. They did not have to build a proprietary infrastructure, as FedEx did. They were able to leverage the medium to build and coordinate ecocomplexes.

The Internet was now an open technology platform available to all. Most dot-com entrepreneurs latched onto one of the new e-business models as their opportunity (portal models, B2B auctions, information intermediaries, etc.). They largely created value narratives with little differentiation. Most failed to build or even respect the need for a value engine. They made a claim on *future* value creation, then burned through *present* cash and went out of business.

Most established companies added an e-business venture, typically an e-commerce portal, without an opportunity platform for doing so. They largely assumed, as the dot-coms did, that leveraging the fundamentals of the web would create a value narrative by default. Over time they integrated the web into the business as another channel of sales or service, but were never able to differentiate themselves.

Even Wal-Mart has not quite leveraged its online operations to mesh with its store business, and for many other companies, Internet transactions are an add-on feature to their services, rather than a driver of innovation opportunity. Many of their value dimensions are comparative alternatives to their mainstream operations and services. For instance, is it cheaper to look on walmart.com or go to a Wal-Mart store? Will it be faster to order this or wait till tomorrow and drop into Best Buy? Which is the better price?

The differentiators took a very different path. FedEx had had to build its infrastructures and systems on a proprietary and customized basis. It had come to believe that the information about the package was just as important to its customers as the package itself. More and more of its value dimensions placed the shipment in the background and highlighted time and reliability.

But without the Internet and the WWW, there was no way for FedEx to communicate that information without giving away a hundred thousand PCs to customers (something that would be unheard of today). It then had to build and maintain the software for customers to enter orders and track packages on PCs. Major customers that wanted to connect their billing and invoice systems to FedEx had to either invest in EDI or link their systems together through proprietary APIs. This is tech-talk, for they could do it, but only through tools available in given countries, provided by given vendors, and using given standards and systems.

Once the Internet took hold for business and consumers in everyday life, FedEx no longer needed all its proprietary infrastructure and could more simply use the web to enable customers to interface with the company's services and information.

Enter Amazon: Nifty, but How Will It Keep Growing?

In the beginning, Amazon looked far more like other dot-coms than a platform company such as FedEx. It opened its doors, so to speak, in July 1995, offering customers a selection of one million book titles. Within a month, it had filled orders from all fifty states and forty-five other countries. Within two months, it was selling $20,000 of books a week. It had the advantage of all the early dot-com movers in that it could offer compelling new dimensions of customer value, most obviously online shopping from home, a wide selection of titles—hundreds of times more than the number carried by a single book superstore—being open for orders 24/7, and with no sales tax outside the state of Washington.

It enjoyed compelling new dimensions of company value, too: no capital outlays for brick-and-mortar stores, instant global reach, and limited inventory costs. It exploited the obvious ecocomplex opportunities, carrying only two thousand titles in its warehouses and getting the rest from book distributors such as Ingram Books. Amazon then packed and shipped them to customers. Even two years into the business, Amazon was filling only 5 percent of its orders out of its own inventory.

By the end of 1998, Amazon had expanded far beyond its initial dimensions of value. It increased the titles offered from 1 million to 3.1 million. It created, and tried to patent, its 1-Click shopping for easy checkout. The web was enabling companies to offer new dimensions of value not possible in the physical world, which accounts for the early success of so many dot-coms and also their early demise as they commoditized.

But Amazon was taking it further by creating its own compelling dimensions of value that built on the use of the web, rather than on the web's technology per se. These included recommendations, reviews, and the associates programs—innovations that were not possible in the physical world and that the other dot-coms weren't thinking of or could not deliver.

Amazon added to the customer experience via:
- Multiple browsing options: ways to find what you want and for Amazon to point you to items you may not have thought of or known about.

- E-mail alerts and shipment notification: just about every interaction you make with Amazon triggers a message to keep you effortlessly informed.
- Personalized recommendations based on past purchases.
- New departments, such as gift lists, packaging, assistance in selection, and music and video stores. (After launching these two stores, it only took Amazon one quarter to become the leading online music store and six weeks to become the largest seller of online videos.)
- Customer reviews—more than eight hundred thousand within months of the start-up—allowing both positive and negative ratings to help customers evaluate options and build their trust in Amazon.
- The affiliates program that gave individuals, associations, and companies up to 15 percent commission for books sold on their sites; their sites interfaced to Amazon, which managed the orders and fulfillment. (It had signed up 30,000 sites by Feb 1998, 60,000 by June, and 140,000 by year-end.)
- More rapid delivery with expansion of titles carried in its distribution centers by increasing warehouse capacity from 50,000 square feet at the end of 1996 to 285,000 square feet in 1997 and the opening of an East Coast fulfillment center.
- Improved customer service by setting a goal to ship 95 percent of all in-stock orders the same day.

This is a long list, which is the point. There was no single Amazon breakthrough, just a series of integrated initiatives that set the Innovation Cube spinning and spinning. While the branding blueprint—this is who we are, and these are the dimensions of value we put together for you—was kept front and center, no face was or could have been ignored. The innovations draw on Technology, Corporate Assets (fulfillment facilities and processes), Finance, Ecocomplex Relationships (Associates Program and customer reviews), and Human Capital by putting them together into capabilities.

At this stage, there were still many skeptics, but an insightful *Businessweek* article pinpointed what Amazon was doing:

Rivals have since copied those tactics (referring to some of Amazon's dimensions of value), but Amazon continues to give customers the red-carpet treatment.

Certainly the number 1 bookseller (Barnes & Noble), which built its first store 125 years ago, is a savvy merchant, but it proved vulnerable when it came to the ways of the Web. For one thing it was late in arriving, and its store-trained executives took longer to learn the new rules of e-commerce than Amazon's Net-centric staff.

Even after Barnes & Noble went online, it was slower to take advantage of the Net's ability to customize its site to each shopper. That allowed Amazon to use its appealing customer experience as a branding tool far more powerful than conventional advertising.[172]

Eighteen months after Barnes & Noble went online in the first quarter of 1997, Amazon's sales were eleven times Barnes & Noble's, and its customer base was four times as large.

Adapting the Platform via the Technology Base

Growth continued. Amazon had built to a billion-dollar sales rate on just $30 million in inventory and $30 million in net plant and equipment (1998 annual report).

The financial component of its value narrative centered on working-capital efficiency. It carried fifteen days of inventory and got immediate cash for the sale of a book on a debit or credit card, and the distributors and publishers were paid forty-five to ninety days after Amazon purchased the book. This generated a $25 million float in 1998. The company passed along the cost savings to customers in the form of lower prices.

The next major iteration in the value architecture was bringing customers into the Amazon "store." The firm had tried out a variety of ways to provide a "vast" selection of items. These included inviting other sellers and third parties to display their products on the Amazon site; auctions ("but we didn't like the results"); and zShops, an online equivalent of a mall ("we still didn't like the results").

In January 2000, the executive team decided at a planning session to create one store, eliminating the separation between Amazon products and marketplace products (its zShops). The meeting started by trying to figure out a way for the marketplace sellers to have access to Amazon's product detail pages. But as Bezos recalled: "We realized that what was most important to the marketplace sellers was demand—access to prospective buyers. So, the idea of the "single store" was to give them a level of access equal to our own—listing their goods right alongside ours."[173]

As you might imagine, the single-store decision was controversial. If you were a seller, for instance, all your competitors could now market in the same store as you. Making all the relationships harmonious was a challenge. Bezos's explanation of how it was resolved is instructive: "Whenever we are facing one of those too-hard problems, where we get into an infinite loop, and can't decide what to do, we try to convert it into a straightforward problem by saying, 'Well what's better for the consumer?'...We don't make money when we sell things; we make money when we help customers make purchase decisions."[174]

What we are observing in action here is the work and tradeoffs across three faces of the Cube. The ecocomplex relationship managers think this is a great idea. The product inventory owners are against it. But at the end of the day, the customer is the final arbiter. If it works for the customer, it is good for the company. But the next problem is, how do you make it work? That is an issue of human capital capabilities.

Bezos is reported to have commented: "One of the keys to making this work is to try to get our economics to the point where we are agnostic about whether the customer buys from us or from a third party...To that end, we have tried to engineer fee structures for third-party transactions in such a way that they provide the correct incentives for managers that are responsible for their own P&Ls."[175]

The move to a single store provides a counterintuitive example of how an ecocomplex relationship platform evolves when your value architecture is defined from the customer perspective back to the company's resource base and operational capabilities. It's counterintuitive in that Amazon should naturally want to protect the sale of its own products; listing others' products would inevitably detract from its leverage on its own site.

It's intuitive once you switch focus and adopt the perspective of the customer. Amazon was aiming to be the place where customers could find, discover, and buy anything online. It thus needed to seamlessly integrate the offerings for the customer, whatever their provider of origin. The decision was not just about the ecocomplex relationships, but also about enhancing the branded customer experience.

An interesting outcome that the article goes on to point out is that: "In the wake of the changes in 2000, many in the organization began to think of Amazon as a platform for commerce rather than as a retailer." Bezos and his executive team were changing the value narrative, including the metrics, to assure that Amazon was building the right kind of customer and partner relationships it needed to drive value long term.

Amazon's leadership had made a very key decision to shape the culture, provide a better customer experience, and create a win-win relationship with partners. Now it needed to invest in the technology to make it possible to implement the plan. At the time, its technology blueprint was based on a single monolithic application that serviced a large back-end database.

Amazon was obviously interfacing to customers and partners through standardized interfaces, but the system architecture would not support the desired growth and offer the kind of options we have discussed. It was a bottleneck analogous to a line of applicants queuing up at, say, the state Department of Motor Vehicles to process a wide variety of applications. The central system gets overloaded and access to needed data taps into a massive single archive. Amazon needed modular processes, and it is very difficult to have modular processes if your technology is not modular

According to its chief technology officer: "For years the scaling efforts at Amazon were focused on making the back-end databases scale to hold more items, more customers, more orders, and to support multiple international sites. This went on until 2001 when it became clear that the front-end application couldn't scale anymore."[176]

Amazon then decided to re-architect its technology platform, based on modular application and data components with a standardized application interface of which data encapsulation was the key component. We mention encapsulation as a reminder that in IT development, jargon may hide immensely important business issues; essentially, this technique is what makes Amazon's personalization of the customer relationship possible. The CTO adds:

Operating such a diverse set of services at this scale is not something that many people have done before, especially not with the kind of [service and data] isolation that we wanted to achieve...It has been a major learning experience, but we have now reached a point where it has become one of our main strategic advantages. We can now build very complex applications out of primitive services that are by themselves relatively simple. We can scale our operation independently, maintain unparalleled system availability, and introduce new services quickly without the need for massive reconfiguration.[177]

The modular application/data structure, known as the e-commerce platform, enabled Amazon to implement its single-store vision and create various mix and match services for partners. In July 2002, the internal technology base became an external business. Amazon made its first announcement of Amazon Web Services (AWS) by extending its platform to partners and third-party developers.

Amazon's press release pointed out that developers could now build applications and tools "to incorporate many of the unique features of Amazon.com into their web sites—free of charge." With this announcement, the Associates Program had just been expanded to an open ecocomplex with development tool kits and access to Amazon content. In 2012, it extended these services to a one-stop cloud shopping service directly equivalent to its e-commerce offers to its affiliates and small businesses, including billing logistics, vendor evaluations, and free software. This AWS Marketplace makes cloud computing just another trip down the virtual aisles to fill a shopping cart.

In the early 2000s, Amazon described its business as its Virtuous Cycle. The greater the selection and convenience along with lower prices, the more the number of customers, which drove more traffic, which drove more sellers, which in turn drove more selection, which drove more customers. To afford the low prices Amazon had to lower costs, which in turn would lower prices.

Think of the capabilities required to make this happen: website design and management, fulfillment, seller coordination, distribution center design and operations, customer service, pricing, forecasting, inventory management, cost control, selection management, customer reviews, coordination with sellers and shippers, to name just a few. All of this was done by leveraging the resources structured into an opportunity platform.

Amazon's Current Opportunity Platform

Today Amazon's platform has morphed so radically that some might not recognize it, and yet in many ways, its blueprints are evolutionary, not revolutionary. Let's start with the Corporate Asset blueprint. It is estimated that Amazon owns and operates something north of sixty fulfillment centers and multiple large data centers. But remember that the fulfillment centers and data centers are both modular in structure (and the technology is composed of both modular software and hardware), and they both serve dual purposes.

The fulfillment and data centers support the customer experience and are also offered as services across Amazon's ecocomplex, directly bringing in revenue and also contributing to the effectiveness of partners. The Amazon Web Services range from computing on demand to storage to e-commerce support and networking. The processes are also all modular, so Amazon can configure whatever it needs to make a deal or expand its dimensions of value.

The Financial blueprint is still focused on investing for the long term, driving down costs on behalf of the customer, and cash flow.

The Technology platform is now one of the largest and best cloud services available. But it is still focused on delivering the greatest customer experience, although that customer list has been expanded to include sellers and developers. The product offerings are increasingly of a digital nature, from e-books to videos and music.

The Ecocomplex Relationship blueprint, which started out with its affiliates program for other websites selling books, now includes over two million sellers; hundreds of thousands of developers; content owners of music, movies, and books; and plenty of frenemies such as Netflix. But the basis for the relationships has not changed. It is still about win-win.

The Amazon Branded Customer Experience has continued on the same track it started on: continue every day to make it better, and at the same time continue to expand the customer dimensions of value. That includes error-free fulfillment, free shipping, expanded selection, e-books, digital content, and the Kindle. The list could easily fill the page. One would be hard pressed not to say that Amazon has not only lived up to its vision of being the most customer-centric company, but exceeded it.

Building the Innovation Culture

That leaves us with only one resource domain for Amazon we have not discussed, which is Human Capital. When Jeff Bezos was asked who was setting strategic direction at Amazon, he responded that a senior team meets every Tuesday and also for a couple of days once or twice a year to delve into strategy issues.

But he went on to say that strategy setting also happens "fractally" throughout the organization, where the person responsible for a piece of the business, such as Fulfillment by Amazon, makes sure strategic thinking also happens for that part of the business. These comments were made in an interview published in the *Harvard Business Review* in 2007, under the title "The Institutional Yes."[178] The interviewer, Thomas Stewart, is a noted business-book writer.

We close this chapter with three key practices at Amazon: the planting of seeds and letting them grow, the focus on things that won't change rather than those that will, and avoidance of failure of strategy through errors of commission rather than errors of omission. To Bezos, these are all part of Amazon's innovation culture.

On the planting of seeds, he commented in the interview: "First, we are willing to plant seeds and wait a long time for them to turn into trees. I'm very proud of this piece of our culture, because I think it is somewhat rare." He added that "when we plant a seed, it tends to take five to seven years before it has a meaningful impact on the economics of the company." This is clearly a company that thinks in terms of long-term opportunities, and it permeates through the organization.

On the second point, Bezos said: "When I'm talking with people outside the company, there's a question that comes up very commonly: 'What's going to change over the next five to ten years?' But I rarely get asked 'What's *not* going to change over the next five to ten years?' At Amazon we're always trying to figure that out, because you can really spin up flywheels around those things."

He gave the example that customers will always want selection, low prices, and fast delivery. Why would that change? How you build on that will change, of course, but the focus itself is at the very core of the value narrative.

On the third point, when asked about the nature of his biggest strategic mistake, he zeroed in on what companies *don't* do rather than what they *do* do: "I think most big errors are errors of omission rather than errors of commission. They are the ones that companies never get held to account for—the times they were in the position to notice something and act on it, had the skills and competencies or could have acquired them, yet failed to do so. It is the opposite of sticking to your knitting. It's when you shouldn't have stuck to your knitting but you did."

This last one speaks volumes about the Amazon culture and the kinds of seeds that get planted. It centers on ensuring an opportunity platform and creating different operational capabilities when the opportunity is there. It is a different culture, one most companies would like to have in today's rapidly changing business terrain. But without the other faces of the Innovation Cube, those opportunities would never get beyond a dim glimpse followed by hesitation and dismissal.

Will Amazon continue its growth? Who knows? It's hard to think of any company better positioned in terms of its value architecture to be in charge of its own destiny.

14 From Worst to Best: The VHA

Our final example of how an organization builds a value architecture that enables a flow of innovations comes from a mammoth public-sector agency: the US Veterans Health Administration. The VHA was, for decades, marked by conspicuous mismanagement, poor patient care, weak accountability, gross inefficiency, and financial waste. It is now one of the preeminent care providers in the world, ranked at or near the top of every major survey of hospital performance in terms of treatment quality and outcomes, safety, cost, technology, and services.

We use the well-documented story of its turnaround to show how lessons from ultrasuccesses that move forward to become superextenders apply to any organization. This one was about as weak as it could be without collapsing; it had no value path, just an aimless lurch down a budget trail.

Its transformation shows the same management principles put to work as the two firms we reviewed in our previous chapters, FedEx and Amazon. It indicates once again that there really is no single factor that determines the ability of an organization to innovate. Yes, leadership is vital, but it is only a part of making the value architecture effective. Yes, a collaborative culture is vital, too, but...the same is true for R&D and innovation budgets; change management programs; productivity improvement; business process management; and all the body of methods, tools, and facilitators of best practice.

The VHA story could be that of Tesco in making the leadership value narrative a lever for innovation, Amazon or Wal-Mart in the use of its enterprise information technology architecture as a core to its ability to coordinate its services, Li & Fung in removing the soft dollar waste along the supply chain, and FedEx in using detailed metrics to guide value creation across the faces of the Innovation Cube.

But had the transformation effort relied just on leadership development, or just on IT, supply chain reengineering, or KPI (Key Performance Indicator) metrics, or on a Balanced Scorecard, it would surely have been a well-intentioned, fizzled squib, not a brilliant firework that fills the sky with color and dazzle. We could list examples of often highly touted initiatives in each of these areas that flared for a while and then disappeared, but we'd like to keep the length of our book under nine hundred pages.

The US Veterans Health Administration medical service was described in the mid-1990s as dangerous, dirty, and scandalous, with "filthy conditions, shortages of everything, and treatment bordering

193

on barbarism."[179] The most appropriate adjective to put on any area of it was "dysfunctional." Culture, organization, service, operations, management, costs, administration, incentives, metrics—you name it, the VHA stunk. The culture largely resisted any efforts at innovation, often openly so.

Yet the leadership repositioned its value narrative, renovated its value engine, and created an expansive opportunity platform. The story captures how the many factors that create such transformation come from an aspect of leadership that tends to be downplayed: coordination. An underlying theme in the history of superextenders is a gradual shift across organizations from principles of control to those of coordination.

For a century, for instance, organizational structure was seen as a critical foundation for a firm, captured in the adage "structure follows strategy" that originated with the business historian Alfred Chandler in the late 1960s. His conclusion was based on an analysis of four of the firms that had most dominated their industry since the 1920s: DuPont, Sears, US Steel, and General Motors.

Today, in the era of adaptation and ecocomplexes as central to making change an opportunity, there is very little discussion of organizational design. What, for example, is Amazon's organizational structure or Google's? Cross-functional collaboration has displaced formal lines of reporting, functional units, and well-defined hierarchy as the cultural priority.

Coordination is the building of effective *collective* purpose through the management of interdependencies. It relies on capabilities in interlinking processes and on sourcing and synchronizing capabilities. Above all, it rests on harmonizing the different priorities and self-interests of the actors and stakeholders involved in the organization's ecocomplex.

Coordination is the glue for all the elements of the value architecture. Its opposite extreme, which certainly marked the VHA and most organizations, is fiefdoms and functions that impede collective purpose; fragmentation that turns interdependencies into conflicts, duplication and waste; a swamp of separate processes with heavy overhead and administrative burdens; "politics"; and value chains that limit business degrees of freedom.

In 1994, Kenneth Kizer, the newly appointed VHA undersecretary for health—in effect the CEO of the VHA—launched a complete restructuring and reorientation of the system. By 1998, when his appointment expired, his leadership team had moved the VHA from disaster to exemplar, making major transformations in health care that have been on the public agenda for decades but that other organizations have been unable to bring off.

The transformation was almost total. The VHA was about as dysfunctional as any agency could be and close to a disaster, with many calls for it to be broken up and its services outsourced. It was famed for occasionally losing patients who wandered off the premises and were later found dead.

In less than four years, it became a model of performance along any measure of service, cost, quality, or efficiency. Yet there were no new products or services, no new facilities (indeed, many existing ones have been closed), and no R&D breakthroughs. The initiatives all took place in a period of tight budget constraints, downsizing, and political stresses.

What changed was its shift to a sector-leading, quality-based value narrative built around coordination on behalf of the patient of all health-care activities and processes. This replaced the old traditional value chain of case-by-case functional and geographic operations built around the facilities and staff. But this coordination did not come easily. It rarely does.

Kizer's coordination efforts focused on the transformation of the firm's value engine. This required the development and execution of the necessary operational capabilities to deliver quality at a lower cost of service. Actions included:

- *A major change in management accountability*, incentives, and funding that helped build a unitary system out of fiefdoms and a failing mixture of overcentralization and overdecentralization.
- *Process reconfigurations* that relied on moving from individual professional centers of excellence to patient-centered coordination of these operational capabilities.
- *A technical architecture for coordination* of information gathering, access, and analysis to ensure enterprise resource optimization.
- *Opening up the organization to build relationships* for resource sharing and coordination of information and activities.
- *Objective and comparable collective metrics* of performance.

Obviously, the path to value creation is never a simple one or ever complete. It is easy to find problem areas of differences among individual VHA hospitals and concerns of legislators and veterans about priorities and needs. It is just as easy to find equivalent examples in, say, Apple's relationships with providers and apps developers and its problems with hardware and software reliability, or Wal-Mart's missteps in global expansion and adding branded fashion clothes to its stores.

The long-term and sustained robustness of the VHA transformation is captured by what is described as the most exhaustive survey of the impact of information technology on performance in four thousand US hospitals, published in the *American Journal of Medicine* in November 2009.[180] The report is scathing in its conclusions that "computerization hasn't saved a dime, nor has it improved administrative efficiency."[181]

A coauthor of the study explained that much of the cause is that "most software is designed around the accounting and billing needs of hospitals, not the clinical side." She adds that the VHA stands out as an exception, because its systems and processes allow physicians to focus instead on delivering care: "The VHA system now has our nation's highest quality and patient approval ratings."[182]

By 1994, when Kizer took over, the VA had become the largest health-care provider in the United States, with 1.1 million admissions a year to its 172 acute-care hospitals, 131 nursing facilities housing 72,000 elderly and disabled veterans, 350 outpatient clinics with 24 million patient visits a year, and 206 counseling facilities.

All of this was run with 210,000 employees on a $16.3 billion medical-care budget. Oh and by the way, it also managed 32 golf courses, 29 fire departments, and 1,740 historic sites. By any measure, this was a large, complex organization.

It had been run for decades via an ineffective combination of centralization of planning and management and decentralization of operations. The Washington bureaucracy was "so ossified and top-down" that even a purchase of a computer cable required central approval.[183] At the same time, hospital operations were highly autonomous, with physicians, psychologists, and other professional groups making their own decisions.

Funding for the hospitals was intensely political, with congressmen demanding that facilities in their own district automatically get more—and never, ever less—money, even though in 1994 a quarter of all VHA hospital beds were empty and facilities needed to be closed. Demographic shifts had meant that many veterans of World War II, Korea, and Vietnam had moved from the "snowbelt" of the urban North and Midwest to the South, leaving some hospitals and clinics underutilized and others overstrained.

Kizer's first move to shift the VHA to a patient-centered value complex was made quickly. He grouped the (then) 173 hospitals into 22 VISNs (Veterans Integrated Service Networks—pronounced "visions," a deliberate term of reference).

One aim of the reorganization was to open up the boundaries that had created largely independent units. While the VHA is still centrally administered and fully integrated, it is now far more an ecocomplex than a value chain; its relationships comprise more and more of its capabilities than do its historical asset-based resources.

In 2007, 130 of its reduced number of 153 hospitals were university-affiliated teaching hospitals, and about 70 percent of the physicians held university teaching appointments. As part of its mission, the VHA trains more than 100,000 health-care professionals annually across 40 disciplines through affiliations with more than 1,100 universities and colleges.

Veterans also seek care at other facilities. As a result, the VHA is working to share information with other organizations in an effort to improve patient care and, where possible, reduce costs. According to the *Wall Street Journal*, the VHA and the Defense Department exchange information on 3.4 million patients who are treated by both agencies.[184] A pilot program was launched in early 2010 with Kaiser Permanente to coordinate information on patients seen by all three providers.

By themselves, Kizer's initial reorganization, downsizing of facilities and staff, and cost cutting are the typical Band-Aids and holding actions for getting control of an underperforming organization, not means for positive transformation. He leveraged and complemented these initiatives by changing the management incentive and measurement systems; this was the very cornerstone on which every other initiative rested.

Before Kizer began this transformation, there were no formal metrics of quality or performance. In the year before his appointment, not a single one of the 477 VHA executives had received a grade in their annual review other than "fully successful" (in a system where, in a widely reported and notorious instance, three bodies of patients were found on the grounds of one hospital months, and in one instance fifteen years, after their deaths; they had wandered off, but no one reported their disappearances).

Kizer gave the directors new levels of authority and discretion. In return, they had to sign and be held accountable for "tough" individual performance agreements. The basis for allocating funds was changed from number of existing beds and hospital size to the number and nature of future expected and intended patient treatments.

The VERA (Veterans Equitable Resource Allocation) system tracks detailed metrics that are used to "put the money where the vets are," not where the buildings are. In the first round of the new system application, nine of the VISNs lost funds and thirteen gained. In a later year, one VISN actually returned unneeded funds, to the distress of a congressman, who "lambasted" the director and accused him of doing so just to earn a performance bonus.

Any large organization's budgeting system is its basic coordination mechanism: coordination of priorities, resources, and organizational effort. The VHA shifted planning from rationalization of the hospital asset base to bringing services to the customer. Its Health Care Demand Model has been refined and fine-tuned every year. It states that "the demand model has revolutionized the VHA's budget, planning, and policy-making *processes.*" (Our own emphasis is added here.) The model is centered on demand, not on allocation of supply.

To fund this, Kizer shifted the financial base for VHA operations, using a "30-20-10" principle: cut costs by 30 percent, increase the patient base by 20 percent, and rely on 10 percent of funds coming from reimbursement from third parties such as health-care insurance providers.

Getting such repayments has long been a neglected and very difficult task, hindered by deliberate blockages by the third parties and administrative muddle in the VHA; only half the money owed was being collected. This is a reminder that operational capabilities are all in the details; the VHA was sadly adrift in matching its processes to its value generation.

Kizer himself took the lead in establishing entirely new collaborative ecocomplexes, including coordination with the Department of Defense's medical service, in itself a $20 billion operation, to provide treatment to vets through each other's facilities and to make it easier for them to get access to information and services.

It was not at all easy to make this work. Kizer commented later that it demanded "huge negotiations" on a constant basis and that if he and his counterpart in the DOD had skipped a month of their meetings, the collaboration would have ended: "All this sharing seems straightforward. It is not...And every new idea has to work its way up two commands, each with its own clashing culture."[185]
A driving force for the cooperation was the growing cost of specialized care and the opportunity to negotiate joint volume discounts in purchases of drugs, a move that saved a reported $369 million in 2002. One example of the payoff from sharing facilities is in specialized care, for which the VHA sends patients to an Army medical center that it reimbursed for $5 million in 2002, a figure well below the cost of using private-sector services. As with Southwest Airlines, Dell at its peak, Bharti and Li & Fung, coordination as a cornerstone of the value architecture brings with it many opportunities to streamline costs on behalf of the customer.

VistA: Coordination Technology as Integrator

Kizer's transformation achieved a dream of the entire health-care system. This is the complete integration of the patient relationship and treatment history via a central and comprehensive electronic medical record. This was as much a cultural challenge as a technical one, since it intruded on the perceived prerogatives and authority of VHA doctors, pharmacists, and psychologists.

Information has now become an enterprise resource that, for instance, gives new roles in daily care to advanced practice nurses. The patient is no longer the doctor's but the VHA's. A veteran on vacation or one who has moved does not have to wait for the standard delays in transferring records; the information moves with the patient. In the hospital or clinic, the information is in effect *on* the patient in the form of the bar-coded bracelet that indicates his or her identity and is accessed by a wireless scanner.

Kizer set up an independent National Center for Patient Safety to gather information on errors and "near misses" (a specific categorization in system records) in VHA patient care. Studies show that hospital errors in the United States account for as many as ninety-eight thousand deaths a year, 4 percent of the national total. In too many instances, a surgeon does the right procedure but on the wrong patient! Medication errors are frequent. So, too, are failures of procedures—"protocols"—for diagnosis and treatment planning.[186]

There are few standards for treatment, information, and administration in hospitals. A widely publicized "simple" mistake—a miscoordination error—resulted in the death of a seventeen-year-old girl at one of the very best US hospitals because she was given a heart and lung transplant with the wrong blood type.[187] That cannot occur in those VHA hospitals that use its electronic medical record system (not all of them do as yet) except through criminal sabotage; the information ensures the coordination of surgeon, nurse, blood bank, anesthetist, pharmacist, and so on.

For every known error in hospitals, there are anywhere from twenty to six hundred near misses. These are failures in quality management, which may sound like a somewhat cold-blooded term for a human tragedy, but it is a recurring problem that can be remedied only through systematic process design, standards, and change in metrics.

Kizer saw the lack of reliable and objective data as a major impediment to creating value in health care. He identified as commonplace the overuse, underuse, and misuse of health-care resources and offered as explanation the lack of clear goals for quality improvement, the lack of reliable and complete data, and the lack of effective information systems.

His solution was to accelerate the extension of a decade of work in the VHA to build a comprehensive information platform, VistA. A bar-coded identifier on a bracelet is the base for *all* diagnosis, treatments, follow-on care, and patient communication. Doctors and nurses carry laptops that access the complete patient history via a wireless network by scanning the bracelet. Orders are entered electronically, so that when pharmacists, for example, fill a prescription, VistA both maintains a record and prints out the label and relevant information.

One anecdote illustrates the impact of the system on near misses. Before administering any treatment, nurses must scan the barcode. "One nurse tried to get the computer to accept her giving an IV, and when it wouldn't let her, she said, 'You see, I told you this thing is never going to work.' Then she looked down at the bag. She had mixed it up with another, and the computer had saved her from a career-ending mistake."[188]

VistA (Veterans Information Systems and Technology Architecture) was built on the existing Computerized Patient Record System (CPRS). What turned CPRS from a record-keeping system to a process- and information-coordination platform was a local innovation that Kizer saw in action in a 1998 visit to the VHA's medical center in Topeka, Kansas. *Fortune* reports that the center had built a prototype that used bar-coded scanners to match patients' drugs and doctors' orders. A long-time nurse had come up with the idea, after watching an Avis car-rental agent use a portable wireless scanner to check in her car and print out an invoice in seconds.[189]

Kizer used a patient safety conference to announce that the VHA would install scanner and bar-code technology in all of its hospitals and many of its clinics. By late 2000, 170 were using it. (The quality of care in those that are not using it is markedly and visibly lower.)

The impact of VistA on quality, process, and productivity has been far-reaching. VistA is the shared communication base among all VHA professionals, regardless of where the patient is or in which hospital. Patients can now access their entire medical records via the Internet or give permission to the family to do so.

This service helps them prepare claims for disability awards for which they must provide evidence to support the application. Authorized billing clerks, quality reviewers, and specialists also use it on a read-only basis. Access has been extended, with careful attention to privacy and security concerns, to the many veterans service organizations to which patients have granted power of attorney.

In 2002, VHA processed over a million requests for copies of veterans' health records needed by other agencies and parties. My HealthVet gives veterans direct access to, and also permits them to view and update, their own health information, a requirement under recent government legislation.

The system is based on industry standards, which over time means it can be the base for data repositories for health-care research and also for the automatic transfer of records. This is particularly valuable as individuals leave their service in the armed forces, where their records are held and maintained by the Department of Defense. Afterward, their patient care is provided by the VHA. The system makes the transition seamless.

VistA has expanded from a patient record-keeping system to a multipurpose enterprise infrastructure. When Merck announced that its arthritis drug Vioxx was responsible for many deaths around the world, VHA doctors knew within minutes which patients were being treated with Vioxx and authorized alternative medications.

In 2004, when there was a national shortage of flu vaccines, the VHA used VistA to prioritize patients. In a number of other situations, data analysis revealed the explanation for dangerous anomalies in individual patients or groups of patients. For example, when an outbreak of rare pneumonia occurred in a Kansas City hospital, analyzing the database of electronic records showed that this was caused by a bad batch of nasal spray. Action was taken immediately. Dozens of such examples are reported in the press.

The VHA's *Vision 2020* report, published in 2003, opens with a chapter that begins with a section on "VHA Leadership: The Next Generation," which is immediately followed by one on "Turning Information into Insight." It is how information is used that generates insight; here it is the basis for turning crises into routine problems to be responded to.[190]

Businessweek gave an example in early 2005. The article, whose subheading is "More physicians and hospitals are putting their medical records online," leads off with a story about a VHA physician who received a phone call at home one night from a nurse concerning an elderly man in intensive care who was displaying life-threatening symptoms.[191]

You can guess the rest. The doctor did not have to rush into the hospital but simply accessed the patient's history over the VHA intranet, including the X-rays that revealed the problem: a potentially fatal buildup of fluid in the lungs. The physician prescribed a diuretic—via the intranet, of course.

It is discouragingly striking that in 2005—nearly a decade after the VHA flow of innovation began—*Businessweek* came up with only one other hospital to provide a comprehensive example of the use of electronic medical records.[192] It claimed that only 15 percent of US hospitals and doctors used such systems at that time, but that they would be in place in 70–80 percent of hospitals by 2008.

In 2009 *Businessweek* noted that a report published in the *New England Journal of Medicine* on March 25, 2009, indicated no or negative progress, far from the predicted 70–80 percent.[193] The researchers surveyed 3,049 US hospitals and found that only 1.5 percent (no, that is not a misprint) had a comprehensive health record system and that only 10.9 percent had even a basic system, which was used in only one area of the hospital.

Given the proven success of the VHA system and the mass of statistics that show reductions in errors, savings in paperwork, and other benefits, why has it taken so long to reach the 1.5 percent figure? Why have the VHA's efforts to encourage other health-care systems to adopt and adapt VistA had little success despite its demonstrated value? Is the real issue technology? It surely cannot be cost, since VistA is a free resource and in the public domain (though the costs of configuring computer and communication systems for physicians are still a perceived barrier).

Is the solution leadership built around value narratives, incentives, metrics, technology standards, process change, resource management, and education and training? (The VHA reports that training turns out to be a far more complex challenge than anticipated.) We can think of no other plausible explanation.

Resistance to Coordination

The impacts of the VHA enterprise information coordination go well beyond localized and individual task improvements. It enabled Kizer to give new authority to licensed advanced practice nurses, a move strongly opposed by many physicians. This was successful in terms of productivity and quality of care, but not popular in the VHA fiefdoms.

One former VHA physician published a highly vitriolic attack in 1997 on the "interference" in the doctor–patient relationship and loss of physician authority. He accused Kizer of "brutally converting the VHA into as unimaginative and harsh an HMO (health management organization) as any in the private sector." He predicted its imminent demise. "The momentum to convert the VHA into the world's worst HMO is only accelerating."

Around the same time, "dozens" of VHA doctors met publicly to vent their frustration over changes they felt were "leaving them and their patients out in the cold...One of the trends that angers doctors most is giving increased responsibility to advanced-practice nurses." Kizer countered that this is a matter of "combining skills and talents," not replacing doctors. A doctor countered the counter. "Like most physicians, I wish Washington would leave us alone to practice medicine."[194]

From the perspective of ecocomplex coordination, the choice of phrasing is instructive and highlights a general resistance to coordination and a preference for decentralization. You could substitute in the quote "headquarters" or "finance" or "top management" for "Washington," and a whole range of functional or professional fields for "medicine"—"engineering," "selling," or "service," for instance. "Leave us alone" means let us have our own authority rather than be part of collective action and coordinated responsibility.

Another doctor at the meeting objected to business terms, such as "client" and "customer," being applied to patients. VHA psychologists similarly saw interference on the horizon. "The [Kizer] plan would deemphasize traditional discipline-based service and could eliminate the historical independence of psychologists...The breadth of psychological services [is] at stake."

Obviously, many in the VHA organization saw coordination as interference, and their arguments deserve consideration; they are passionate in their belief that intrusions on their autonomy mean a drop in health-care quality. Such views certainly cannot be ignored, and much of leadership is about whose view of the landscape will become the "reality" that defines planning and policy.

Previously, physicians operated autonomously, often choosing their own hours (many held positions in other institutions, such as university teaching hospitals). Surgeons were idle for much of the time. They had tenure. Kizer persuaded Congress to eliminate tenure, and a tenth of the staff were laid off and others offered relocation. That can hardly have convinced the internal skeptics and objectors.

Yet in general it is apparent that Kizer's view of the landscape has been accepted as reality by the physicians. This may be as a result of time, the success of the transformation, resignations, and layoffs. The changes took hold, and far from the patient-physician relationship being damaged, patient satisfaction has increased to industry-leading levels.

The Impacts and Fallouts

As the physicians' and psychologists' objections indicate, the transition from fiefdoms to coordinated architecture was not automatic and easy. Kizer ran into constant troubles in the political sphere, too. Like the medical professionals, many other parties had an investment in preserving the status quo.

Kizer's renomination as undersecretary was blocked in committee several times, and in the end he withdrew his name. One congressman "repeatedly took Kizer to task for considering closure of the nursing home and outpatient clinic at Fort Lyon, Colo., a location so remote that the VA facilities there must run their own sewer system and fire department."[195]

His successors have continued and extended just about all of Kizer's initiatives. They inherited his clear vision and his work to communicate and implement the model. In a system where the CEO is a political appointee, named for a four-year term by the US president and subject to confirmation by the Senate and Congress, this is somewhat surprising, especially since Kizer was in essence forced out of the VA.

Thomas Garthwaite, who took over from Kizer in 1999 (he had been his deputy since 1995), extended the quality and information focus: "It's been tough to buy healthcare services based on value, because we never measured quality very well...We knew what we were spending but not a whole lot about what we were getting."[196]

The measurable results have been striking and publicly recognized. The *New England Journal of Medicine* reported that on eleven measures used by Medicare (the $331 billion federal government health-care funding program) to assess the quality of "pay-for-fee" service, VHA was significantly better than private sector hospitals.[197] The National Committee for Quality Assurance found that it was number one in rank in every one of seven categories.[198] Patient satisfaction was well above the average for all hospital systems.

The number of beds has been cut in half, and from 1995 to 1998, bed-days per patient dropped by 62 percent, a major cost saving. Meanwhile, ambulatory visits grew by 43 percent.[199] Survival rates for critically ill patients are among the highest across US health care. The VHA's costs average two-thirds those of Medicare. Between 1999 and 2003, the number of patients treated grew by 71 percent, while funding increased by just 41 percent.

Near misses and errors are now routinely tracked, not hidden; there is no sanction or punishment for reporting them, only for not doing so. As a result, the data is available to assess and respond to problems; the reduction over a four-year period has been thirty-fold for errors and nine-hundred-fold for near misses. One study showed that medication errors in one VHA hospital had been cut by 70 percent as a result of VistA. Data, or rather the coordination of the use of data, now drives the system, in the sense that it is integral to policy, planning, performance assessment, and business process design.

This contrasts strongly with the UK National Health Service (NHS), which similarly relied on data as the driver of its proposed transformation of a failing system, but used it basically just as a scorecard that did not provide the same dynamic feedback the VHA has built. Data is a means to an end for the VHA, but for the NHS it became an end in itself.

The NHS integrated national computer system was initially budgeted at $20 billion, with later estimates that it would take $60 billion to complete. More consequentially, it was intentionally designed to increase central *control* rather than coordination: one review in late 2009 describes the NHS reform in words that sound exactly like those used about the old VHA: too centralized and too bureaucratic and in a condition of high-managed mediocrity. While expenditures have increased from $80 billion to $180 billion in ten years, almost every major measure of patient care has fallen.[200] The project was abandoned entirely in late 2011 at a write-off of about $20 billion.

The VHA data feedback loop centers on quality. (The NHS's reforms focus on cost.) All performance metrics are published quarterly, so that each VISN and hospital knows where it stands in relation to other comparable operations and to private-sector institutions. The new undersecretary comments that, "By having very objective measures of performance we were able to change behavior."[201] He has invested heavily in senior executive self-assessment reviews that are being extended to the regional managers.

The VistA system has been adopted in many countries, including Finland, Germany, Mexico, India, and Egypt, and is free of charge. The VHA set up a new organization to extend its use by health-care providers, but in late 2004 a leader in the field commented, "I have not seen a rush by hospitals and doctors to request the VistA technology." His article is titled "VA Technology: A Federal Threat to Private Sector Health Care IT?"[202]

One of the article author's main criticisms of VistA is that it is technologically obsolete and does not meet the very varied needs of the private-sector health-care community. It is not used by *any* US private-sector hospital system. The critique might have more force if there were any better implementations of electronic medical-record systems.

The article is, in any case, misleading. As the technical architecture of VistA has evolved around open standards, it has since been adopted by several thousand health-care facilities worldwide, linked to their existing systems, and customized for very different countries and languages.

Many of its modules are marketed and supported through the WorldVistA Software Alliance by such vendors as GE, SAIC, and Medsphere for research and decision-support applications; nursing, pediatrics, and other specialties not part of the VHA services; equipment maintenance tracking; and responding to patient complaints and compliments. A new module connects directly to other information and software services within the architecture.

While the information technology system is the support base for the wider organizational, process, and incentive shifts in the VHA, without this modular, flexible, and adaptive architecture, Kizer would not have been able to move the agency to become a modular, flexible, and adaptive organization. Equally, without a leadership program that fused information, incentives, and quality metrics focused on the patient, VistA would have been just another computer system. This last fact points both to the scale of Kizer's achievement and how unique it is.

The future of the VHA is unclear; the landscape is very cloudy. Wars in Iraq and Afghanistan have not only added a new population needing care, but the balance of treatments has shifted with far more requirements for mental-health care and counseling. The VA medical budget has been consistently increased to handle an additional million patients. The criticisms that the VHA is moving toward "assembly-line care" continue. That said, the VHA is no longer profiled as a representative example of how bad government is, but as a shining instance of what it can be made to be.

Given the leadership driver, all the many available tools of information technology, knowledge management, collaborative relationship development, organizational development, and change management are levers for innovation and value creation. Without this, they are sure to continue to produce exciting pilot successes, disappointing larger-scale rollouts, and the standard explanation that the culture is just too hard to change. The VHA story is a promising blueprint for any organization to build the coordination edge in sustaining innovation.

The founders of the most noted superextenders all have a profile that includes sensitivity to and command of coordination. Examples are Fred Smith, Sam Walton, Michael Dell, the Fung brothers, and

Jeff Bezos. (Steve Jobs fits the profile, though the almost total coordination of Apple came from his dictatorial mandates.)

The VHA case similarly shows a leader who doesn't fit the Clint Eastwood or Lone Ranger executive gunslinger/hero profile but is a true builder. To a large extent, the value architecture reflects the architect. That said, many fine leaders, especially in ultrafades, seem to get locked into their own school of design and may freeze the evolution of their companies, which end up being Bauhaus or Grecian Revival artifacts in an era of high-tech Structural Expressionism.

Here, then, is how value narrative, value engine, and opportunity platform fit together: leadership for coordination. Operational capabilities fit together to enable an innovation culture through resource management coordination as captured by the Innovation Cube.

But it all starts with taking a fresh view of value and being alert to how and where the forces of disturbance open up new choice spaces and new opportunities to create compelling new dimensions of value. Then organizations move from business models and value chains for an era of *givens* to thriving in a world of *ifs*.

15 Conclusion: Innovation Every Day

In this conclusion, we offer some tentative answers to the question "What can I do?" It's all very well to pitch the analysis and recommendations at the level of corporate abstraction and make it all sound so simple. If a firm has a strong value narrative, productive value engine, and adaptive opportunity platform, then everything about innovation does become simpler and the message is "Just do it." But what if it doesn't have this advantage? What do you do to help change that and find opportunities that are practical now?

We offer some recommendations for your own everyday contribution to innovation based on one key assumption: whereas in more placid times, it was often acceptable and even sensible to avoid being seen as an innovator, that is less and less the case. We are well past the days of pensions as the guaranteed reward for long service; negative connotations of innovation with trouble-maker, loose cannon, or risk-taker; and pressures to be a good corporate citizen and conform.

Indeed, as companies continue to cut jobs and in many instances relegate yesterday's core competence to tomorrow's early retirement, if you are not seen as contributing to innovation, then you have little to offer, and your experience is a growing cost if it doesn't add to the firm's capabilities.

So we argue that your firm is likely to be more and more ready than heretofore to listen to ideas for innovation and the culture more likely to mobilize to turn them into action. Realistically, "more" may not equate much beyond an incremental shift, and many firms will be marked by caution and conformity. But on the whole, businesses everywhere recognize that living on or in the past is not a viable option. That means that if you are not active in the innovation dialog, you are part of the problem of change, not the solution.

It's the solution that matters, and in a time of change the solution has to equate to innovation. Our recommendation is that you (1) consciously take a fresh view of value and value shifts in looking for opportunities, (2) frame business justification in terms of the elements of the value architecture where you can have most impact, and (3) focus the specific goals for any innovation on the Innovation Cube resource/capabilities linkage.

The Forces of Disturbance

One simple and useful message for your own innovation that we hope emerges from *The Value Path* is to "think about it." "It" is value, of course. Our logic is that all the evidence shows that the single factor that most determines a company's chances of consistently, not just occasionally, achieving superior performance is the extent to which it treats value as fluid, not fixed. Hence our choice of the term value "path." Value will shift. Can your firm shift with it as a well-run company or get ahead of the pack? That is what innovation is about.

Your organization may be as competent as any of its competitors and stand out on measures of best practice. Competently moving in the wrong direction can feel like progress until the path runs out. By picking out ultrasuccesses for our analysis, we factored out the incompetents in advance. This sharpens the lessons to be learned from the experience of the competent ones that nonetheless became ultrafades and those that built in a different way on their own record of competence to grow as superextenders.

The ultrafades largely erode because they don't refresh their thinking. They then too easily ignore or discount dynamic shifts in choice spaces and the resulting impacts on the Value Realities. They start to treat their value narratives as a truth or a heritage to be protected. They put resources into their value engines at the neglect of their opportunity platform. They do not keep a balance among the faces of the Innovation Cube.

So, look outward in your own thinking and always keep alert to the forces of disturbance that send signals about where to focus innovation. Quite often, these signals are more apparent to the people who work at the point of customer interaction—the sales force, store personnel, and customer service agents—than in head office or one of the functional areas of the organization, such as HR or finance.

Sometimes these signals are hidden to the very same people because they get overfocused on what they see and deal with directly on a daily basis. Someone must make scanning and interpreting the shifts in the choice spaces their personal style of thinking. Here are some pretty obvious points:

- Know that the forces will disturb your business terrain.
- Think in terms of customers of tomorrow, not just today.
- Ask who your competitor of tomorrow is.
- Apply the Value Realities as a test of any innovation opportunity or proposal.
- Think ecocomplex and win-win-relationships.
- Recognize that it will be harder and harder to differentiate through products and technology.
- Use the Innovation Cube as a useful starting point for making your own contribution to the opportunity platform.

Conclusion: Innovation Every Day

The forces *will* disturb your business terrain. Take that as an assumption, not a possibility. You can hope it will be otherwise, but the odds are not at all in your favor. Their imprints are already all over traditional manufacturing, music, newspapers, retailing, health care, Big Pharma, car manufacturing, consumer electronics, IT, and airlines. It's less apparent in many areas of nonconsumer sectors, such as mining, energy production, or construction, but just mutter words such as "trade agreements," "nanotechnology," or "materials science," and, of course, "China."

As for financial services, maybe all you need to do is add a few murmurs and a groan; the murmurs are about regulation, cost, mobile payments, and balance-sheet funding, and the groan is for the general level of customer value that the industry is now associated with, from service to cost to credit.

Can you name any industry where the three forces have worked in support of companies with weak brands, unexcited customers, and poor technology? When you see a choice space where the establishment is generally viewed as mediocre, you can be sure that entrepreneurs somewhere are looking for the opportunity.

So, look for one, too. If your firm has a strong opportunity platform, then the looking should be aggressive and aimed at making short, sharp shocks a source of strategic advantage. There is a rich literature describing the relative success of being the first mover in a major area of technological or market innovation, versus being a fast responder and learning from the pioneer's problems and experience. Google, Tesco, and Amazon use their platforms to be frequent and fast movers. Nokia and RIM are very much struggling at being fast responders.

If your company doesn't have a strong opportunity platform, you can help move it in the needed direction by ensuring that each specific innovation you propose or help implement is consistent with the resource blueprints of the Innovation Cube. For instance, every decision you influence that involves some aspect of technology should make sure it is modular, every hiring decision should enable an externally focused and collaborative culture, every financial decision should contribute to capital efficiency.

Think in terms of customers of tomorrow, not just today. What is it that they will value that is the same as today? This is Jeff Bezos's principle of focusing on what doesn't change. What will become a commodity dimension of value? That's the principle of being customer led in everything.

The most effective contribution you can make to innovation is to identify opportunities to add compelling new dimensions of value that will help build the relationships that attract and retain the customer of tomorrow.

Ask who is your competitor of tomorrow. There is a new ecocomplex coming soon to your business neighborhood that will mess it up for you and others. You can expect some foreclosures, and you don't want to be one of them. In general, firms maintain a pretty sharp lookout for their direct and known competitors, but many of the new ones don't announce themselves and don't draw attention by constructing facilities or launching hiring drives. They are just sort of there, often without ever seeming to have arrived.

Industry thinking is dangerous to your innovation. Customers increasingly don't care what industry you think you are in. The moment you accept the industry perspective, you orient your thinking around an inherited collection of truisms, assumptions, and reference points. These will generally pull you back into the mind-set of business models, value chains and core competencies, and away from the four Value Realities, value architecture, ecocomplexes, and opportunity platforms.

The Value Realities define the competitor of the future, and you obviously should look for appropriate opportunities to be the intruder on anyone's traditional industry presence.

Apply the Value Realities as a test of any innovation opportunity or proposal:

- Reality 1: The buyer determines value. So, what is the value dimension we add in this innovation?
- Reality 2: Value is always relative and shifting. Who is the competitor of tomorrow that can and will offer a new choice similar to or better than the one we plan?
- Reality 3: Companies leverage ecocomplexes. Is the competitor of tomorrow a company or an ecocomplex? Is our competitive opportunity based on in-house capabilities or relationship opportunities?
- Reality 4: Entrepreneurs will offer new dimensions of value. What are our people telling us about the questions customers are asking, the products and services they used to buy that somehow don't have the old appeal, and new online companies they are starting to talk about?

Think ecocomplex. That should go without saying. The effective organization of the future will increasingly be defined by its capabilities in coordinating relationships. How are you helping here? How would key suppliers and contractors describe working with you, your team, and your company? Get away from thinking in terms of "vendor" and "supplier" contracts where the goal is to squeeze the other party. Look for ways to mesh value-creation interests and opportunities. One question to keep in the back of your mind is the growth of Dell, Apple, and mobile-phone companies through their use of Taiwanese and Chinese companies. Did they outsource manufacturing and assembly to firms such as Foxconn and HTC as the base for their successful growth, or did the Asian players outsource sales and marketing to Dell and Apple as the foundation of their own growth?

Recognize that it will be harder and harder to differentiate through products and technology. If you are not contributing to helping your firm brand the customer experience, then you are not an innovator, though you may be an effective inventor. You are an effective innovator if, and only if, you add to the innovation culture through your awareness of and response to all the faces of the Innovation Cube.

The Innovation Cube is a useful starting point for bringing all these issues together at a practical level of everyday work. It defines the next best practice as evidenced by the superextender archetypes that have been the main focus of our sense making. Take the cube, look at each face. Reflect, identify needs and opportunities, and see if you can offer some innovative proposal. Rotate it again. As you do so, you are escaping the final Value Trap, the Business Model Trap, and shifting to thinking in terms of the opportunity platform, how the firm moves beyond the business model.

A business model defines the boundaries for value creation. That is obviously necessary; no company can be all things with all products to all customers in all markets. But it closes down many options. That is unnecessary and greatly increases the likelihood of your company at some point not so much falling into the Asset, Commodity, or Invention Traps as suddenly finding it's already in them without having noticed this was happening.

Business-model thinking narrows your scanning, alerts, and interpretation of the impacts of the forces of disturbance across the business terrain. It establishes what is "relevant" in planning and defines what exactly is meant by such terms as "our" market, customer, competitor, industry, and growth. Business models imply a given type of value chain. Chains are not exactly the most useful items to bind your arms and legs with when you start out on a journey into the unknown.

Throw them away. Travel light. Keep your eyes looking around you, not down at your feet. Be prepared to change course. And expect to be waylaid, diverted, or blocked in your progress.

That is the navigation guide for your firm's value path. Happy innovating!

Index

Endnotes

[1] "The Sony Story," Sony Corporation,

[2] Sony Corporation, "Consolidated Financial Results for the Third Quarter Ended December 31, 2011," news release, February 2, 2012, http://www.sony.net/SonyInfo/IR/financial/fr/11q3_sony.pdf.

[3] See, for instance, Robin Bloor, "Dell—Awesome Manufacturing—Says It All," Bloor website, March 12, 2003, http://www.bloorresearch.com/analysis/3563/dell-awesome-manufacturing-says-it-all.html.

[4] K. Talley, "Wal-Mart Names New Head Merchant, *Wall Street Journal,* January 28, 2011.

[5] D. ben-Aaron, "Nokia Uses More Partnerships to Achieve Its Targets," *Bloomberg,* November 11, 2010, http://www.bloomberg.com/news/2010-11-11/nokia-uses-more-partnerships-to-achieve-its-targets-update1-.html.

[6] Gartner Releases Phone Market Share Report for 2011, February 15, 2012 http://www.gsmarena.com/gartner_releases_phone_market_share_report_for_2 011-news-3832.php feb 15 2012

[7] D. Bass, "Microsoft's Kinect Has Unanticipated Uses," *San Francisco Chronicle,* March 11, 2012.

[8] M. Isaac, "Upcoming Kinect Development Kit Could Change In-Store Shopping, *Wired.com,* October 31, 2011, http://www.wired.com/gadgetlab/2011/10/xbox-kinect-sdk-microsoft.

[9] D. Bass, "Can Kinect Make Windows Cool Again?," *Bloomberg Business Week,* March 8, 2012, http://www.businessweek.com/articles/2012-03-08/can-kinect-make-windows-cool-again.

[10] 16 M. Wolf Politico's Washington Coup, *Vanity Fair,* August 2009 http://www.vanityfair.com/politics/features/2009/08/wolff200908

[11] J. Cutler, *The Washingtonienne* (New York: Hyperion Books, 2005).

[12] M. Schrage, "For Innovation Success, Do Not Follow Where the Money Goes," *Financial Times,* November 8, 2005, http://www.ft.com/cms/s/0/b10da862-4ffb-11da-8b72-0000779e2340.html#axzz1qI3vv7Ox.

[13] A. Troianovski, "Sprint Adjusts Bonus," *The Wall Street Journal,* February 14, 2012.

[14] K. Rushton, "Apple' Offers to Settle Ebook Price Fixing Row in Europe but Will Fight Case in the US," *Telegraph,* April 20, 2012, 'http://www.telegraph.co.uk/finance/newsbysector/mediatechnologyandtelecoms/electronics/9217264/Apple-offers-to-settle-ebook-price-fixing-row-in-Europe-but-will-fight-case-in-the-US.html.

[15] Publisher's Innovation Conference website, last accessed February 9, 2012, http://www.publishinginnovation.com/2012/conference-programme/.

[16] "Google's Heliostat Control System," *wordlessTech* (blog), June 11, 2011, http://wordlesstech.com/2011/06/11/googles-heliostat-control-system/.

[17] M. Wagner, "Is Google TV Doomed?," *ComputerWorld Blogs,* October 8, 2010, http://blogs.computerworld.com/17125/google tv doomed.

[18] M. Martino, "Pfizer's Dolsten: Less R&D Spending Is Better," *FierceBiotech,* April 1, 2011, http://www.fiercebiotech.com/story/pfizer-rd-chief-less-rd-spending-better/2011-04-01.

[19] *Rolling Stone,* June 29, 2007. According to links to the article, it is no longer on *Rolling Stone*'s website.

20 D. Goldman, "HP Kills Touchpad, Looks to Exit PC Business," *CNNMoney*, August 18, 2011, http://money.cnn.com/2011/08/18/technology/hp_pc_spinoff/index.htm.

21 M. Collins, "The Innovation Gap," *Manufacturing.net*, February 3, 2009, http://www.manufacturing.net/articles/2009/02/the-innovation-gap.

22 R. Hemming, "The Next Viagra," *Investors Chronicle*, July 11, 2008, http://www.investorschronicle.co.uk/2011/12/06/the-next-viagra-ot1fkqVJGhx2kroKZZDf9M/article.html.

23 "Pharmaceutical R&D and the Evolving Market for Prescription Drugs," *Economic and Budget Issue Brief*, Congressional Budget Office, October 26, 2009.

24 J. Rockoff, "Lilly Taps Contractors to Revive Pipeline," *Wall Street Journal*, January 5, 2010, http://online.wsj.com/article/SB2000142405274870424750457460450392201908 2.html.

25 E. Zeman, "Does It Matter How Many Kins Microsoft Sold?," *InformationWeek*, July 8, 2010, http://www.informationweek.com/news/mobility/smart_phones/showArticle.jhtm l?articleID=225702679.

26 Microsoft News Center, October 11, 2011, http://www.microsoft.com/en-us/news/features/2011/oct11/10-31KinectEffect.aspx.

27 K. Ziegler, "Nokia CEO Stephen Elop Rallies Troops in Brutally Honest 'Burning Platform' Memo?" (update: "It's Real!"), *engadget.com,* February 8, 2011, http://www.engadget.com/2011/02/08/nokia-ceo-stephen-elop-rallies-troops-in-brutally-honest-burnin/.

28 S. Lyall, "No Apologies from the Boss of a No-frills Airline," *New York Times*, July 31, 2009, http://www.nytimes.com/2009/08/01/world/europe/01oleary.html?pagewanted= all.

29 P. Vallely, "Michael O'Leary: Plane Crazy," *Independent*, October 7, 2006, http://www.independent.co.uk/news/people/profiles/michael-oleary-plane-crazy-419044.html.

30 "'O'Leary interview (English original): The Next Big Thing—Eliminating Check-in Baggage," *Spiegel Online*, May 28, 2004, http://www.spiegel.de/wirtschaft/0,1518,301722,00.html.

31 A. Clark, "The Guardian Profile: Michael O'Leary," *Guardian*, June 24 2005, http://www.guardian.co.uk/environment/2005/jun/24/theairlineindustry.travelne ws.

32 Lyall, "No Apologies from the Boss of a No-frills Airline."

33 D. Teather, "'I Hate Ryanair' Website Has Its Wings Clipped...for a While," *Guardian.co.uk,* October 12, 2010, http://www.guardian.co.uk/business/2010/oct/12/i-hate-ryanair-website-closed.

34 E. Oswald, "Vizio Aims to Disrupt the Crowded Budget PC Market, but Can It?," *BetaNews,* January 2012, http://betanews.com/2012/01/07/vizio-aims-to-disrupt-the-crowded-budget-pc-market-but-can-it/.

35 G. Mies, "Nokia Lumia 900: Windows Phone Gets the Hardware It Deserves," *PCWorld*, January 10, 2012, http://www.pcworld.com/article/247786/nokia_lumia_900_windows_phone_gets _the_hardware_it_deserves.html.

36 Financial figures and market data for Bharti Airtel taken from their investor website unless otherwise noted:

http://www.airtel.in/wps/wcm/connect/About%20Bharti%20Airtel/bharti+airtel/investor+relations/.

[37] "Business Model Reinvention," chief executive officer speech by Manoj Kohli, http://www-935.ibm.com/services/us/gbs/bus/pdf/kohli.pdf.

[38] "Realty and Telecom Most Corruption-prone Sectors in India, Says KPMG," *ESG Insider*, March 15, 2011, http://www.esginsider.com/?p=281.

[39] "World Development Indicators," World Bank, http://mpra.ub.uni-muenchen.de/18099/1/Indian_Telco_FDI.pdf.

[40] T. Khanna, K. Palepu, and I. Vargas, "Bharti Tele-Ventures," *Harvard School Press* no. 704-426 (2004).

[41] K. Basu, "India's Per Capita Income Seen at $10,000," *Financial Express*, June 23, 2011, http://www.financialexpress.com/news/India----s-per-capita-income-seen-at--10-000/809887/.

[42] A. Sharma and E. Bellman, "Bharti, MTN Disconnect Deal Worth $24 Billion," *Wall Street Journal,* October 1, 2009.

[43] Chief executive officer speech by Manoj Kohli.

[44] C. Prahalad and M. Krisman, "Bharti Airtel(B)," *William Davidson Institute at the University of Michigan*, case 1-428-864, May 23, 2011.

[45] "IFFCO and Airtel Join Hands to Usher in the Second Green Revolution," iffco.nic.in, May 2, 2008, http://www.iffco.nic.in/applications/iffcowebr5.nsf/0/89b6f7f9c1950e3465257442003ae142?OpenDocument.

[46] "Actual Tele-density Is 41 Not 66 Percent: Study," *Silicon/India News*, May 3, 2011, http://www.siliconindia.com/shownews/Actual_teledensity_is_41_not_66_percent_Study-nid-83038-cid-3.html.

[47] A. Troianovski, "How the iPhone Zapped Carriers," *Wall Street Journal*, December 21, 2011.

[48] These figures are taken from published company financial reports.

[49] Verizon-Wireless-Ahead-Of-Schedule-For-LTE-Build-Capex-Trend-Down-For-2012, *RCRWireless*, October 24, 2011 http://www.rcrwireless.com/article/20111024/carriers/verizon-wireless-ahead-of-schedule-for-lte-build-capex-trend-down-for-2012/

[50] Troianovski, "How the iPhone Zapped Carriers," 1.

[51] C. O'Sullivan, "Japan's Mobile Operator Battle: NTT Docomo Profits Slide while Softbank Continues to Shine," *GoMoNews*, July 30, 2011, http://www.gomonews.com/japans-mobile-operator-battle-ntt-docomo-profits-slide-while-softbank-continues-to-shine/.

[52] Historical financial data for Tesco in this chapter is mainly taken from the company's published statements and press releases. The UK press is the source for recent competitive data, some of which are estimates and reflect the growing volatility of the retailing scene since 2010.

[53] CBS Interactive Business Resource Library, June 17, 1999, http://findarticles.com/p/articles/mi_m0DQA/is_1999_June_17/ai_55041044.

[54] "Our Strategy," Carrefour website, March 12, 2009, http://www.carrefour.com/cdc/group/our-strategy/.

[55] Tesco corporate website, http://www.tescoplc.com/about-tesco/our-values.

[56] D. Welch, "Wal-Mart Expands Its Web Presence to Keep Up with Amazon.com," *San Francisco Chronicle*, April 1, 2012, http://www.sfgate.com/cgi-bin/article.cgi?f=/c/a/2012/04/01/BU181NSQ07.DTL.

57 "Carrefour to Sell Online Shop," FoodandDrinkEurope.com, February 6, 2004, http://www.foodanddrinkeurope.com/Retail/Carrefour-to-sell-online-shop-report.

58 "Carrefour Halves Dividend, Halts Key Revamp Plan," Reuters.com, March 8, 2012, http://www.reuters.com/article/2012/03/08/carrefour-idUSL5E8E685W20120308.

59 Walmart, "Walmart Reinforces Its Commitment to Deliver Low Prices. Every Day. On Everything," news release, April 11, 2011, http://www.walmartstores.com/pressroom/news/10573.aspx.

60 "Asda's Market Share Falls Again," *Telegraph*, April 26, 20012, http://www.telegraph.co.uk/finance/newsbysector/retailandconsumer/7765306/Asdas-market-share-falls-again.html.

61 H. Wallop, "Why the Tesco Flag Had Slipped to Half-mast," *Telegraph,* April 14, 2012, http://uk.finance.yahoo.com/news/why-tesco-flag-slipped-half-203608770.html.

62 K. Capell, "Tesco: Wal-Mart's Worst Nightmare," *Bloomberg Businessweek*, December 29, 2008, http://www.businessweek.com/globalbiz/content/dec2008/gb20081229_497909.htm.

63 Ibid.

64 "C. Rohwedder, "No. 1 Retailer in Britain Uses 'Clubcard' to Thwart Wal-Mart," *Wall Street Journal*, June 6, 2006, http://online.wsj.com/article/SB114955981460172218.html.

65 "Tesco 'to Tailor Deals Based on Income,'" Money.uk.msn, January 23, 2012, http://money.uk.msn.com/save-money/tesco-to-tailor-deals-based-on-income.

66 All quotes in this paragraph are from H. Liptrot, "Tesco: Supermarket Superpower," *BBC News,* June 3, 2005, http://news.bbc.co.uk/2/hi/business/4605115.stm.

67 Tescocompare.com, http://www.tescocompare.com/gasandelectricity.shtml.

68 "Tesco Bank," *Wikipedia*, http://en.wikipedia.org/wiki/Tesco_Bank.

69 L. King, "Tesco Bags 15 Percent Online Growth," *ComputerWorld UK*, April 19, 2011, http://www.computerworlduk.com/news/it-business/3275265/tesco-bags-15-online-growth/.

70 "How Tesco Shops for Value from IT," *ComputerWeekly.com*, April 17, 2007, http://www.computerweekly.com/news/2240081333/How-Tesco-shops-for-value-from-IT.

71 Tesco, "Tesco 'One-in-Front' Campaign Wins Prestigious Retail Week Award Using IRISYS Queue Busting Camera Technology," news release, March 2, 2007, http://news.thomasnet.com/companystory/Tesco-One-in-Front-Campaign-Wins-Prestigious-Retail-Week-Award-Using-IRISYS-Queue-Busting-Camera-Technology-511226.

72 "Tesco's IT Standardisation Paves Way for Global Expansion," *ComputerWeekly.com*, May 1, 2007, http://www.computerweekly.com/news/1280096441/Tescos-IT-standardisation-paves-way-for-global-expansion.

73 "Supermarket Sweep: Philip Clarke Tries to Fix Tesco's Business in Britain," *Economist*, April 21, 2012, http://www.economist.com/node/21553049.

74 "Tesco Pushes Back Break-even Date for Fresh & Easy," *Progressive Grocer*, April 18, 2012, http://www.progressivegrocer.com/top-stories/headlines/industry-intelligence/id35219/tesco-pushes-back-break-even-date-for-fresh-easy/.

75 "ASDA Group Ltd.," *eNotes*, http://www.enotes.com/topic/Asda.

[76] "Aldi: A Low-cost Retail Giant's Distinctive Business Practices," case code BSTR 252, IBS Center for Management Research, 2007, http://www.icmrindia.org/casestudies/catalogue/Business%20Strategy/Aldi-Low-Cost%20Retail%20Giant%20Distinctive%20Business%20Practices%20Case%20Studies.htm.

[77] C. Blackhurst, "MT Interview—Alan Leighton," Management Today, August 25, 2005, http://www.managementtoday.co.uk/news/492390/MT-Interview---Allan-Leighton/?DCMP=ILC-SEARCH.

[78] E. Schein, DEC Is Dead, Long Live DEC: The Lasting Legacy of Digital Equipment (San Francisco: Berrett-Koehler, 2004).

[79] S. Levy, In the Plex: How Google Thinks, Works, and Shapes Our Lives. (New York: Simon and Schuster, 2011), 18.

[80] "Top 100 Websites," PC Magazine, February 9, 1999, http://web.archive.org/web/19991001132301/http://www8.zdnet.com/pcmag/special/web100/search2.html.

[81] "Ten Things We Know to Be True," Google website, http://www.google.com/about/company/philosophy/.

[82] Levy, In the Plex, 75.

[83] S. Karp, "Google AdWords: A Brief , May 27, 2008. AdWordshttp://publishing2.com/2008/05/27/google-adwords-a-brief-history-of-online-advertising-innovation/

[84] Google Forum, February 24, 2009, http://productforums.google.com/forum/#!category-topic/adwords/chit-chat/xJsdpT-TNXM.

[85] J. Crook, "As Bing Bleeds Billions, Microsoft Applies Tourniquet," Techcrunch.com, September 22, 2011, http://techcrunch.com/2011/09/22/as-bing-bleeds-billions-microsoft-applies-tourniquet/.

[86] Ibid.

[87] S. Raice, "Is Facebook Ready for the Big Time?," Wall Street Journal, January 14, 2012, http://online.wsj.com/article/SB10001424052970204542404577157113178985408.html.

[88] Levy, In the Plex, 238.

[89] Gartner, "Gartner Says Sales of Mobile Devices Grew 5.6 Percent in Third Quarter of 2011; Smartphone Sales Increased 42 Percent," news release, November 15, 2011, http://www.gartner.com/it/page.jsp?id=1848514.

[90] A. Sorkin, "Is Google Turning into a Mobile Phone Company? No, It Says," New York Times, August 15, 2011, http://dealbook.nytimes.com/2011/08/15/google-turning-into-a-mobile-phone-company-no-it-says/.

[91] E. Chonfeld, "Larry Page: Mobile Revenues at $2.5 Billion Run-rate, 190 Million Android Devices," TechCrunch.com, October 13, 2011, http://techcrunch.com/2011/10/13/page-google-plus-40-million-mobile-2-5-billion/.

[92] E. Raymond, "Microsoft CEO Takes Launch Break with the Sun-Times," Linux Journal, June 1, 2001, http://en.wikiquote.org/wiki/Steve_Ballmer.

[93] R. Metz, B. Ortutay, and J. Robertson, "Jobs Questioned Authority All His Life, Book Says," Associated Press, October 20, 2011, http://finance.yahoo.com/news/Jobs-questioned-authority-all-apf-1873950574.html?x=0.

[94] Kurt Hummel, Glee, season 3, episode 10.

95 All financial and company figures for Li & Fung are taken from its website unless otherwise noted: http://www.lifung.com/eng/global/home.php.

96 F. Norris, "U.S. Apparel Prices on the Rise, Particularly for Women's Clothes," *New York Times*, February 24, 2008.

97 All financial figures for Inditex (Zara) are taken from its investor relationship website unless otherwise noted: http://www.inditex.com/en/shareholders_and_investors/investor_relations/share. All financial figures for Gap are taken from its investor relations website unless otherwise noted: http://www.gapinc.com/content/gapinc/html/investors.html.

98 "Zara Profits Slide but Still Beat Forecast Figures," ThisIsMoney.co.uk, September 16, 2009, http://www.thisismoney.co.uk/money/article-1213836/Zara-profits-slide-beat-forecast-figures.html.

99 G. Gereffi and O. Memedovic, *The Global Apparel Value Chain: What Prospects for Upgrading by Developing Countries* (Vienna: The United Nations Industrial Development Organization, 2003), http://www.soc.duke.edu/~ggere/web/UNIDO-Global%20Apparel_2003.pdf.

100 Gereffi, *The Global Apparel Value Chain,* 6.

101 "Burlington Industries, Inc.," Funding Universe, http://www.fundinguniverse.com/company-histories/Burlington-Industries-Inc-Company-History.html.

102 G. Gereffi, "Global Sourcing in the U.S. Apparel Industry," *Journal of Technology and Apparel* 2, no. 1 (2001).

103 Gereffi, *The Global Apparel Value Chain,* 7.

104 Gereffi, "Global Sourcing in the U.S. Apparel Industry," 2.

105 J. Magretta, "Fast, Global, and Entrepreneurial: Supply Chain Management, Hong Kong Style," *Harvard Business Review,* product number 2020, September 1998.

106 B. Einhorn, "Li & Fung: A Factory Sourcer Shines," *Bloomberg Business Week*, May 14, 2009.

107 Li & Fung website.

108 "'The Democratization of Fashion': William Fung and Vera Wang on the Implications of Going Global," *Knowledge@Wharton*, April 13, 2011, http://knowledge.wharton.upenn.edu/article.cfm?articleid=2752.

109 J. Booth, "Li & Fung Takes Its Middleman Role to Extremes," *Asia Wall Street Journal*, December 14, 2001, http://www.lifung.com/eng/newsroom/lifung_news/news011212.htm.

110 V. Fung, W. Fung, and Y. Wind, *Competing in a Flat World: Building Enterprises for a Borderless World*. New Jersey: Pearson Prentice Hall, 2007).

111 Magretta, "Fast Global, and Entrepreneurial," 8.

112 Li & Fung website.

113 V. Fung, *Competing in a Flat World,* 92–93.

114 V. Fung, *Competing in a Flat World,* 90.

115 J. Wells, and E. Raabe, "Gap Inc.," *Harvard Business School*, case 9-706-402, July 20, 2006.

116 D. Dennis (Susan Caminiti reporter associate), "How the Gap Keeps Ahead of the Pack," *Fortune*, February 12, 1990.

117 R. Mitchell, "The Gap," *Bloomberg Businessweek*, March 9, 1992, http://www.businessweek.com/archives/1992/b325554.arc.htm.

118 C. Emert, "Old Navy Posts Dramatic Growth," *San Francisco Chronicle*, October 21, 1999, http://www.sfgate.com/cgi-bin/article.cgi?f=/c/a/1999/10/20/BU30093.DTL&ao=all.

[119] S. Ferrara, "What to Know When Investing in Retail Stocks," *Value Line*, August 31, 2011, http://www.valueline.com/Tools/Educational_Articles/Stocks/What_to_Know_When_Investing_in_Retail_Stocks.aspx.

[120] "Old Navy," Funding Universe, http://www.fundinguniverse.com/company-histories/old-navy-inc-company-history.html.

[121] V. Manning-Schaffel, "Can Gap Mend Its Brand?," *Brandchannel.com*, April 1, 2002, http://www.brandchannel.com/features_effect.asp?pf_id=86.

[122] J. Popovec, "Hanging by a Thread," *Retail Traffic*, May 1, 2007, http://retailtrafficmag.com/mag/retail_hanging_thread/.

[123] D. Mattioli and K. Hudson, "Gap to Slash Its Store Count," *Wall Street Journal*, October 14, 2011.

[124] L. Kaufman, "Scrambling to Regain Its Cool," *New York Times*, February 24, 2002, http://www.nytimes.com/2002/02/24/business/scrambling-to-regain-its-cool.html?pagewanted=all&src=pm.

[125] L. Lee, "Paul Pressler's Fall from the Gap," *Bloomberg Businessweek*, February 26, 2007, http://www.businessweek.com/magazine/content/07_09/b4023067.htm.

[126] Ibid.

[127] A. McAfee, V. Dessain, and A. Sjoman, "Zara: IT for Fast Fashion," *Harvard Business School*, case no. 9-604-081, September 6, 2007.

[128] "Fashion for the Masses: Global Stretch," *Economist*, March 10, 2011, http://www.economist.com/node/18333093.

[129] McAfee, "Zara: IT for Fast Fashion," 7.

[130] K. Capell, M. Kamenev, and N. Smainather, "Fashion Conquistador," *Bloomberg Businessweek*, September 4, 2006, http://www.businessweek.com/magazine/content/06_36/b3999063.htm.

[131] Nuruzzaman and A. Haque, "Lead Time Management in the Garment Sector of Bangladesh: An Avenue for Survival and Growth," *European Journal of Scientific Research* 33, no. 4 (2009).

[132] P. Chemawat and J. Nueno, "Zara: Fast-fashion," *Harvard Business School*, case no. 9-703-497, December 21, 2006.

[133] J. Gallaugher, "Zara Case: Fast Fashion for Savvy Systems," Gallaugher.com, September 13, 2008, http://www.gallaugher.com/Zara%20Case.pdf.

[134] D. Hardman, S. Haper, and A. Notaney, *Keeping Inventory—and Profits—Off the Discount Rack: Merchandise Strategies to Improve Apparel Margins* (Chicago: Booz & Company, 2007), http://www.booz.com/media/uploads/Keeping_Inventory-andProfits-Off_the_Discount_Rack.pdf.

[135] Chemawat, "Zara: Fast-fashion," 13–14.

[136] K. Ferdows, M. Lewis, and J. Machuca, "Rapid-fire Fulfillment," *Harvard Business Review*, November 2004.

[137] A. Palladino and J. Garcia, *Zara and Benetton: Comparison of Two Business Models*, June 28, 2010, http://upcommons.upc.edu/pfc/bitstream/2099.1/9620/1/67041.pdf.

[138] J. Santos, B. Spector, and L. Van Der Heyden, "Toward a Theory of Business Model Innovation within Incumbent Firms," *INSEAD & Northwestern University*, March 20, 2009, http://org.business.utah.edu/opsconf/pages/vanderHeyden_Paper.pdf.

[139] Chemawat, "Zara: Fast-fashion," 7.

[140] "Fashion for the Masses: Global Stretch," *Economist*, March 10, 2011, http://www.economist.com/node/18333093.

[141] P. Doeringer and S. Crean, "Can Fast Fashion Save the U.S. Apparel Industry?," research paper published by Federal Reserve Bank of Boston, January 28, 2005, http://www.bos.frb.org/economic/nesg/papers/Doeringer.pdf .

[142] P. Longman, *Best Care Anywhere: Why VA Health Care Would Work Better for Everyone*, 3rd ed. (San Francisco: Berrett-Koehler Publishers, 2012).

[143] L. Gerstner, *Who Says Elephants Can't Dance?* (New York: Harper Collins, 2002).

[144] W. M. Cox and R. Alm, "About the Author of Creative Destruction," *Library Economics and Liberty*, http://www.econlib.org/library/Enc/CreativeDestruction.html.

[145] "Fred Smith on the Birth of FedEx," *Bloomberg Businessweek*, September 20, 2004, http://www.businessweek.com/magazine/content/04_38/b3900032_mz072.htm.

[146] M. Porter, *Competitive Advantage: Creating and Sustaining Superior Performance* (New York: Free Press, 1985), 1–2, 446.

[147] Ibid., 474.

[148] A. Lashinsky, *Inside Apple: How America's Most Admired—and Secretive— Company Really Works* (New York: Grand Central/Business Plus, 2012).

[149] "Fred Smith on the Birth of FedEx," *Bloomberg Businessweek*.

[150] C. Lovelock, "Federal Express (B)," *Harvard Business School*, case 9-579-040, June 1, 1982.

[151] "Emery Air Freight Corporation," Encyclopedia.com, http://www.encyclopedia.com/doc/1G2-2841000137.html (original source: *International Directory of Company Histories* [1992]).

[152] "Fred Smith on the Birth of FedEx," *Bloomberg Businessweek*.

[153] C. Kjelgaard, "Federal Express, the Memphis Connection," *Flightglobal*, 1981, http://www.flightglobal.com/pdfarchive/view/1981/1981%20-%200946.html (original source: *Flight International*, 4, April 1981).

[154] R. Frock, *Changing How the World Does Business: FedEx's Incredible Journey to Success—The Inside Story* (San Francisco: Berrett-Koehler Publishers, 2006),144.

[155] C. Dalton, "On Time, All the Time: An Interview with FedEx Corporation's Alan B. Graf Jr.," Indiana University Kelly School of Business, *Business Horizon* 48 275-283, 2005.

[156] C. Lovelock, "Federal Express Quality Improvement Program," *IMD International*, IMD 286, 1990.

[157] "Fred Smith on the Birth of FedEx," *Bloomberg Businessweek*.

[158] Lovelock, "Federal Express Quality Improvement Program," 6.

[159] A. Farhoomand, "FedEx Corp: Structural Transformation through e-Business," Center for Asian Cases, HKU098, January 1, 2000.

[160] L. Grant, "Why Fed-Ex Is Flying High," *Fortune*, November 10, 1997, http://money.cnn.com/magazines/fortune/fortune_archive/1997/11/10/233785/index.htm.

[161] Unless otherwise noted, the next three pages were largely pulled from M. Basch, *Customer Culture: How FedEx and Other Great Companies Put the Customer First Every Day* (New Jersey: Financial Times Prentice Hall, 2002).

[162] "Delivering the Goods at FedEx," *Bloomberg Businessweek*, June 13, 2005, http://www.businessweek.com/magazine/content/05_24/ b3937073_mz017.htm.

[163] D. Taylor and L. Sanford, *Let Go to Grow: Escaping the Commodity Trap* (New Jersey: Prentice Hall, 2005), 174.

164 J. Bezos, Letter to Shareholders 2010, *Amazon.com*, April 27, 2011, http://phx.corporate-ir.net/phoenix.zhtml?c=97664&p=irol-reportsAnnual.
165 J. Bezos, Letter to Shareholders, *Amazon.com*, March 5, 1999, http://media.corporate-ir.net/media_files/irol/97/97664/reports/Shareholderletter99.pdf.
166 J. Jannarone, "Retailers Struggle in Amazon's Jungle," *Wall Street Journal*, February 22, 2011, http://online.wsj.com/article/SB10001424052748 70447660457615812 3883200998.html.
167 Ibid.
168 J. LaHart, "Amazon Faces Taxing Times," *Wall Street Journal*, March 22, 2012, http://online.wsj.com/article/SB100014240527023038129045772976620241645732.html.
169 L. Patton, "Amazon Gained Brand Value at Best Buy's Loss, Interbrand Says," *Bloomberg,* February 21, 2012, http://www.bloomberg.com/news/2012-02-21/amazon-gained-brand-value-at-best-buy-s-loss-interbrand-says.html.
170 tanman, "Order Fulfillment—Over Promise, Under-delivered Seems to Be the Theme," comment on Best Buy Unboxed Discussion Board, December 1, 2010, http://forums.bestbuy.com/t5/BestBuy-Com/Order-fulfillment-Over-promised-under-delivered-seems-to-be-the/td-p/191503.
171 C. Garling, "Study Says Most IT Guys Are Ignorant," *Wired Enterprise*, March 12, 2012, http://www.wired.com/wiredenterprise/?p=14128.
172 R. Hof, E. Neuborne, and H. Green, "Amazon.com: The Wild World of e-Commerce, *Bloomberg Businessweek*, December 14, 1998, http://www.businessweek.com/1998/50/b3608001.htm.
173 T. Cummings and C. Worley, *Organization Development and Change,* 9th ed. (Mason, Ohio: South-Western Cengage Learning, 2008), 332.
174 J. Kirby and T. Stewart, "The Institutional Yes: An Interview with Jeff Bezos," *Harvard Business Review*, October 2007.
175 S. Leschley, M. Roberts, and W. Sahlman, "Amazon.com-2002," *Harvard Business School,* case 9-803-098, February, 13, 2002.
176 "A Conversation with Werner Vogels," *ACMQueue*, May 1, 2006, http://queue.acm.org/detail.cfm?id=1142065.
177 Ibid.
178 Kirby and Stewart, "The Institutional Yes."
179 Longman, *Best Care Anywhere.*
180 D. Himmelstein, A. Wright, and S. Woolhandler, "Hospital Computing and the Costs and Quality of Care: A National Study," *American Journal of Medicine* 123, no. 1 (2010): 40–46.
181 "Projections of Savings from Health IT Are Baseless, Harvard Researchers Say," Physicians for a National Health Program website, November 20, 2009, http://www.pnhp.org/news/ 2009/november/projections-of-savings-from-health-it-are-baseless-harvard-researchers-say.
182 Ibid.
183 Longman, *Best Care Anywhere,*
184 J. Zhang, "The Digital Pioneer: Veterans Hospitals Have Already Fought This Battle—and Offer Plenty of Lessons on How It Can Be Done," *Wall Street Journal*, October 27, 2009,. http://online.wsj.com/article/ SB10001424052970204488304574428750133812262.html.
185 S. Freedberg Jr. "Pentagon–VA Partnership Could Save Money, Improve Military Health Care," *Government Executive,* February 18, 2003,

http://gatekeeper1.govexec.com/defense/2003/02/pentagon-va-partnership-could-save-money-improve-military-health-care/13471/print/.

[186] A. Mokda, et al., "Actual Causes of Death in the United States," *JAMA, American Medical Association* 291, no. 10 (2004), http://proxy.baremetal.com/csdp.org/research/1238.pdf.

[187] C. Koop, "Anatomy of a Mistake," *60 Minutes*, February 11, 2009, http://www.cbsnews.com/2100-18560_162-544162.html.

[188] P. Longman, "The Best Care Anywhere," *Washington Monthly*, January/February, 2005, http://www.washingtonmonthly.com/features/2005/001.longman.html..

[189] D. Stires, "Technology Has Transformed the VA," *Fortune*, May 11, 2006, http://money.cnn.com/magazines/fortune/fortune_archive/2006/05/15/8376846/.

[190] Department of Veterans Affairs, Veterans Health Administration, *VHA Vision 2020*. (Washington, DC: VHA, 2003).

[191] "Between You, the Doctor, and the PC," *Bloomberg Businessweek*, January 31, 2005, http://www.businessweek.com/magazine/content/05_05/b3918155_mz070.htm.

[192] T. Mullaney, "A Growth Tonic for Digital Health Records," *Bloomberg Businessweek*, October 12, 2005, http://www.businessweek.com/technology/content/oct2005/tc2005104_7576_tc024.htm.

[193] S. Reinberg, "Few Hospitals Embracing Electronic Health Record Systems," *Bloomberg Businessweek*, March 25, 2009, http://www.businessweek.com/lifestyle/content/healthday/625431.html.

[194] L. Daniels, "VA's Uncertain Future: Changes 'Dilute' Care, Doctors' Group Says," *Federal Times*, November 17, 1997, http://clinicalfreedom.org/ VA01.HTM.

[195] A. Laurent, "The Tyranny of Anecdotes," *Government Executive*, March 1, 2000, http://www.govexec.com/magazine/2000/03/the-tyranny-of-anecdotes/6308/.

[196] B. Cain, "Profile: A Veteran in Rehab," *Medsphere*, June 1, 2002, http://www.medsphere.com/news/health-it-news/253-profile-a-veteran-in-rehab June 01, 2002.

[197] A. Jha, MD; J. Perlin, MD, PhD; K. Kizer, MD, MPH; and A. Dudley, MD, MBA, "Effect of the Transformation of the Veterans Affairs Health Care System on the Quality of Care," *New England Journal of Medicine*, May 29, 2003, http://www.nejm.org/doi/full/10.1056/NEJMsa021899#t=article.

[198] P. Longman, "The Best Care Anywhere," *Washington Monthly*, January/February, 2005, http://www.washingtonmonthly.com/features/2005/001.longman.html.

[199] R. Mayo, "Veteran's Health Administration: The Best Value in Healthcare," HS 6000, December 15, 2006, http://www.himss.org/foundation/docs/rachelmayo.pdf.

[200] R. Harker, "NHS Funding and Expenditure," *House of Commons*, September 14, 2011, http://www.nhshistory.com/parlymoneypapter.pdf.

[201] R. Rundle, "Who Leads the Online Race?," *Wall Street Journal*, June 10, 2002, https://medsphere.org/blogs/inthenews/2002/06.

[202] B. Fried, "VA Technology: A Federal Threat to Private Sector Health Care IT?," *iHealthBeat,* October 7, 2004, http://www.ihealthbeat.org/perspectives/2004/va-technology-a-federal-threat-to-private-sector-health-care-it.aspx?p=1.

Made in the USA
Charleston, SC
30 June 2012